Para mi amigo ~~Fernando~~

con todo el aprecio de

su autor en señal

de nuestra amistad

afectiva e intelectual

Mario

Middleburg   26 de julio, 1988

MARIO J. VALDÉS is Director of the Centre for Comparative Literature and Professor of Comparative Literature and Spanish at the University of Toronto. He is co-author of *An Unamuno Source Book* and co-editor of *Interpretation of Narrative*.

Professor Valdés presents a theory of literary criticism based on phenomenological philosophy – primarily the work of Husserl, Ingarden, Merleau-Ponty, and Ricœur. His basic argument is that literary texts are inexhaustible sources of imaginative creativity for their readers, and, further, that this openness does not inhibit serious commentary but rather enhances the critic's possibilities of exchange, dialogue, and intellectual enrichment. He argues for a system of classification of narrative texts according to phenomenological principles in which form is considered as a heuristic device established for the purpose of understanding the nature of literary expression. The only critical approach he holds to be untenable is that which lays claim to a definitive interpretation of a text, for such an approach would mean the death of the literary text as a creative source.

Valdés' presentation progresses from a statement of premises, through the construction of a critical approach, to a concluding historical generalization about literature. To introduce the richness of the Hispanic literatures and to elaborate an historical overview of one literary tradition, he has chosen to examine texts from Hispanic literatures exclusively, notably those of Unamuno and Cervantes.

MARIO J. VALDÉS

Shadows in the Cave: A Phenomenological Approach to Literary Criticism Based on Hispanic Texts

UNIVERSITY OF TORONTO PRESS
Toronto Buffalo London

© University of Toronto Press 1982
Toronto Buffalo London
Printed in Canada

ISBN 0-8020-5568-0

University of Toronto Romance Series 44

Canadian Cataloguing in Publication Data

Valdés, Mario J., 1934–
    Shadows in the cave
    Bibliography: p.
    Includes index.
    ISBN 0-8020-5568-0
    1. Criticism. 2. Spanish literature – History
    and criticism. I. Title.
    PN81.V34   801'.95   C82-094111-5

This book has been published with the help of a grant from the Canadian
Federation for the Humanities, using funds provided by the Social Sciences and
Humanities Research Council of Canada, and a grant from the Publications
Fund of the University of Toronto Press.

To María Elena and Paul

¿Cómo tu vida, mi alma, se renueva?
¡Sombra en la cueva!

Miguel de Unamuno, *Romancero del destierro*

Contents

Preface

This book was written over a twelve-year period. The final version is a distant relative of the first draft written in Basle in 1967, but over the years the project has remained true to the original aim of linking a philosophy of expression to literary criticism. In 1967 I embarked on what was clearly a long-range project in an attempt to narrow the gap which I felt existed between philosophical consideration of language and the practice of literary criticism.

My graduate training was primarily bound with traditional historical enquiry as it had developed from the nineteenth century in Romance philology. These years were also, however, the time of the excitement of *New Criticism* in North American universities and the aggressive challenge of structural linguistics. My professors demanded the strict application of historicist principles, but nothing less than a full encounter with the literary text on its own terms would satisfy me. I hasten to add that in this respect I was typical of my generation of North American graduate students. My doctoral dissertation, which was rewritten for publication – *Death in the Literature of Unamuno* (1964) – reflected this working compromise between history and analysis of texts.

Early in 1967 I completed the draft for my next book on Unamuno, *An Unamuno Source Book* (1973), and in the process began to study phenomenological philosophy with intensity. I moved slowly in my general enquiry into the philosophy of language through Husserl and Heidegger. The first draft of this book was strongly influenced by Heidegger as I attempted to work out basic philosophical premises of experience in literary criticism. There were a number of serious shortcomings in that first attempt which I was determined to resolve by teaching and responding to the issues with my graduate students. In 1969 while on leave I revised the entire manuscript for the second time. The project was still far from complete but I had managed to identify the major inconsistencies in my approach. The theoretical impasse I had reached was overcome in 1970 when I was privileged to work with Hans-Georg Gadamer, who was visiting professor that year at Toronto. In the same year, I joined the Programme in Comparative Literature and began teaching literary theory. The next major breakthrough came in 1972 when again I was the recipient of the generous mentorship of a distinguished philosopher.

Paul Ricœur was a visiting professor in Comparative Literature that year and taught the seminar which would eventually be published as *La Métaphore vive* (*The Rule of Metaphor*). Late in 1972 I began to publish the chapters of the book in various journals, reworking each along the way and adding descriptive materials. I was still uncertain of the strength of the argument as a whole and felt that I could gain insight and perspective by discussing the various chapters on their own strength.

The last revisions were made in 1978–9, when I published the remaining unpublished materials on criticism and on literary history. Following is the list of journals where the chapters have appeared as articles. I thank the various editors and my students in Comparative Literature, who have given me the opportunity to clarify my ideas on literature. The failings which remain in this book are my limitations. I am publishing the book at this time in order to encourage debate and certainly not to dismiss, reject, or deny any critical position.

I dedicate this book to María Elena de Valdés and Paul Ricœur, who have made it possible.

'Toward a Structure of Criticism' *New Literary History* (Winter 1972) 263–78

'Documents and Fiction in Julio Cortázar's *Rayuela*' *Reflexión* 2, II (enero-diciembre 1973) 83–6

'Le Texte narratif' *Etudes Littéraires* 8, 2–3 (1975) 201–40

'Unamuno's Hermeneutics of Reading' *Journal of Spanish Studies Twentieth Century* 4, 2 (1976) 243–57

'The Real and Realism in the Novels of Benito Pérez Galdós' *Hispanófila* 61 (1977) 23–7

'History and Myth in *La muerte de Artemio Cruz* and *Cien años de soledad*' *Reflexión* 2, 3–4 (1976) 243–57

'The Reader's Cervantes in *Don Quixote*' *International Fiction Review* 4
    (1977) 46–55
'Functional View of Literary Criticism,' in *What Is Criticism*, ed. Paul
    Hernadi (University of Indiana Press 1981)
'Heuristic Models of Inquiry' *New Literary History* XII (1981) 253–67

MJV

SHADOWS IN THE CAVE

1

Unamuno: the point of departure

This book seeks to examine in depth a relatively undeveloped aspect of Unamuno's thought, but one that is consistent with the whole of Unamuno's writings as I understand them. In Unamuno's philosophy metaphysics precedes anthropology and aesthetics and establishes the dialectic logic for the three. The radical nature of this logic and its extraordinary anticipation of phenomenological existentialism gave all of Unamuno's writings an aura of the Delphic oracle, whose cryptic injunctions are to be pondered by the thoughtful person and dismissed as paradox by the philistine. This was the prevailing view of Unamuno during his lifetime and it has not been fully dissipated today, as even a cursory examination of Unamuno criticism will attest.

Over the years Unamuno wrote a large number of short essays on diverse topics of general interest, in many of which he demonstrated how his philosophy was applied to experience. From 1917 to 1923 he wrote extensively on current events, most of which are of little consequence to anyone today except insofar as they exemplify his social criticism. If we keep in mind that in these years his metaphysics had already produced an anthropology, and that aesthetics was in its early stages, it is not surprising to find profound insights into a theory of interpretation of society.

The focus of this chapter is Unamuno's theory of interpretation. I have taken a minor essay to illustrate Unamuno's phenomenological perspective for two reasons: I argue that this is the theoretical basis for all his writing, major or minor, that it permeated everything he wrote, and that by examining a minor work we will not be distracted into commentary on the philosophy as a whole. Unamuno's philosophy needs no defence from any quarter and I do not propose to give one here. My task is to show a necessary development of a hermeneutic within the wider philosophical

problematic and to take these insights to their limits, which are implied
but not developed in the text which I shall use.

Unamuno published a short article entitled 'Cosas de libros' in *La
Nación* of Buenos Aires on 17 October 1918 (*Obras completas* [Madrid:
Escelicer 1968] IV, 437–40), one among some two hundred short articles
he published that year. The first of the nineteen short paragraphs of the
article reads as follows:

¡Gracias a Dios que se ha acabado el curso y que puede uno encerrarse unos días en
casa, tenderse sobre la cama rodeado de libros, folletos, revistas y diarios, y
empezar a viajar por las tierras y los tiempos, y a enterarse de lo que han hecho y
hacen otros, de lo que ha hecho y hace uno mismo! Porque no le deis vueltas: nadie
sabe ni aun lo que con sus propios ojos vió hasta que no lo oye o lee expresado por
otro, o por él mismo, en lenguaje humano. Al viajero le sirven sus diarios de viaje
para poder enterarse luego de lo que en él aprendió. Darse cuenta de algo es
haberlo, de una manera o de otra, expresado.

Thank God classes have ended and one can hide at home, and lie down
surrounded by books, journals, newspapers and other publications and begin
travelling through lands and ages and learn what others have done and are doing
and learn what one has been doing! There is no doubt in my mind that nobody
knows anything, not even what is seen with one's own eyes, until one can read it or
has heard it expressed in human language by someone else or in one's own words.
The traveller's diary will give the traveller the knowledge of what he learned on
the journey. To know something is, in some way or another to have expressed it.[1]

This introductory paragraph places the author in the tradition of
Humboldt's philosophy of language. The very structure of awareness, we
are told, is linguistic. To be aware of anything is to verbalize. Experience
thus becomes accessible as meaningful through the organizing patterns of
language and thus, we must conclude, thinking and language are
ineluctably entwined.

Unamuno goes on to dramatize the commonplace situation of the
tourist who takes a number of photographs in order to remember and
reconstruct the places where he has been. The point is that the
photograph as visual communication is basically different from linguistic
communication, oral and written. Unamuno proposes the picture as a
memory device which can be used to heighten the remembrance of the
experience depicted. On the other hand, expression is the prime ordering
of reality in the mind of the speaker. Both Gabriel Miró and Antonio
Machado were deeply impressed by this concept of Unamuno.[2]

The fourth paragraph reads as follows:

Es una vulgaridad eso de hablar de gentes que sólo conocen ciertas cosas por los libros. Las que por ellos sé, no las sé peor que aquellas otras de que he tenido eso que se llama experiencia directa e inmediata, y aunque de éstas puedo decir que si las conozco bien es gracias a los libros o a lo que haga sus veces. De mis propias ideas, si tengo noción algo clara, es gracias a haberlas puesto por escrito y a que las puedo leer. Expresar algo es enterarse de ello, ni nadie puede saber si sabe algo hasta que no lo ha expresado.

It is a cliché to speak of people who know certain things only through books. The things I have learned from them are not less known to me than the things of which I have had an immediate and direct experience. Of these I can say I know them well because of books or their equivalent. If I have a somewhat clear notion of my own ideas it is because I have put them down in writing and therefore I can read them. To express something is to understand it; nobody can be sure of knowing anything until he has expressed it.

We are now well into the heart of Unamuno's theory of knowledge. In brief: I know the world through my experience and I am aware of experience because I organize and form it and I can organize the world because I express myself. Consequently, language becomes the great mediator between man and the external matter that surrounds him, and it is only through the organizing function of language that external matter is knowable.

The fifth paragraph is a key one:

El lenguaje, la expresión, es el padre del conocimiento humano reflexivo. El Dr. Ward sostiene, con otros, que cada uno tiene su mundo y que no hay modo de saber si nuestros sendos mundos coinciden y concuerdan entre sí o no. Las presentaciones de un hombre no pueden llegar a ser las de otro. Cada espíritu es exclusivo dueño y retenedor de sus propias verdades y de sus propios errores. Para cada cual su propio mundo, para cada yo su propio no-yo. No hay elemento común a las varias experiencias ... Lo que hay es un lenguaje común y basta.

Language, expression, is the father of human reflexive knowledge. Dr. Ward, along with others, maintains that everybody has his own world and that there is no way of knowing whether or not our worlds coincide and agree. What stands as actual for a particular man may not be so for another. Every spirit is an exclusive owner and possessor of his own truths and his own errors. For each man there is a world; for each self there is a not-self. There is no common element for the various

6 Shadows in the cave

different ways of experiencing ... What there is is a common language and that is
enough.

Unamuno is here commenting on the philosophy of mind of the
Cambridge philosopher James Ward (1843–1925).[3] Unamuno had an
unusual facility for seeking out kindred spirits in the most diverse
quarters. The choice of James Ward as support for his argument is
excellent. Unamuno does not give us the bibliographical information on
his source; however, James Ward's many articles on philosophical
problems were later collected and published in two books: *Psychological
Principles* by the author himself and *Essays in Philosophy* by his colleagues
after his death. The former volume contains some ideas which are very
sympathetic to Unamuno. For example, in chapter 12, 'Intellection,'
Ward writes on the acquisition of language: 'But thinking – as a
permanent activity at least – it may be fairly said, owes its origin to the
acquisition of speech. It must here be noted that the higher development
of the individual is only possible through intercourse with other individuals, that is to say, through society. Without language we should be
mutually exclusive and impenetrable, comparable almost to so many
physical atoms; with language each several mind may transcend its own
limits and share the minds of others' (p 286).

In a subtle manner Unamuno's commentary on Ward and his
insistence on the central role of language closely anticipates the Wittgenstein of the *Philosophical Investigations*.

Unamuno further adds commentary by Henry Jones on Ward's
position in order to make his main point that the only link between
separate minds is language.[4] Losing no time, Unamuno involves his
reader in the sense of the argument: 'Somos hijos todos del lenguaje, de la
expresión' (We are all creatures of language, of expression) and in the
next paragraph goes on to express a philosophical position which I have
already cited as being closely in harmony with James Ward's principles of
psychology. By coincidence, Ward's final position on this matter, quoted
above, was published at the same time as Unamuno's article, but there is
no proof that Unamuno ever read it. Without a doubt Unamuno would
have been most interested in Ward's theory as finally stated in 1918.
Although other parts of *Psychological Principles* were previously published,
the chapter in question was published for the first time in this book in
December 1918.

The seventh paragraph presents Unamuno's version of the nominal-
istic thesis he shared with Ward and a few others of his generation in
Europe and America.

Lo que hay de común entre dos o más hombres, lo que se pueden comunicar no es sino el lenguaje, la expresión. El lenguaje es el fundamento de la sociedad y de la sociabilidad. ¿Qué importa que tú o yo veamos un chopo o una oveja o un carro de distinta manera si le llamamos chopo y oveja y carro? Dicen que la mayor parte de las discusiones lo son de palabras. ¡Naturalmente! En lo único en que se discrepa de veras es en las definiciones.

What is shared in common by two or more men, what they can communicate, is nothing but language, expression. Language is the foundation of society and sociability. What does it matter if you and I see a poplar, a sheep, a cart in a different way if we call them poplar, sheep, and cart? It is usually said that most arguments are about words. Obviously! Definitions are the only thing we disagree upon.

Unamuno has now begun to present the radical duality which he consistently ascribed to language. Language is to be understood as a mediating force which makes human existence possible. But this mediator has two levels: the first is that which we can best term the organizing power, through which the individual encounters reality and therefore the central basis of self-identification; the second level is the transcendent power through which the individual communicates with his fellow man. The tension between the two is the logical result of contact and encounter between men. It follows that man inherits the medium and is taught how to use it, but the inevitable result of the usage is the growth of self-consciousness, that is, the first level of language as a capacity to know. Thus, as the individual exercises his capacity for knowing, he is inevitably going to clash with others who are doing the same. This is not a problem of the physical encounter of each man as a living organism; the problem is entirely with the individual appropriation of the encounter, which is different in each case. The common ground between the two persons who confront the tree is not in the tree itself, but in the way in which they account for the tree, which is the linguistically dominated appropriation of the thing. When it becomes desirable for the tree-viewers to share their views they will fail to communicate if they attempt to base their agreement on the object; however, they will succeed if they base their search on their expression of the object.

Unamuno insists again and again that the common matrix of perception as being is expression. The living present, by which I mean self-identity, the possibility of repetition, the exploitation of secondary attributes, the very essence of the physical being in front of the object status are all contained in the concept of awareness, a concept that cannot be broken down into a subject and an object and which comes to be because the individual appropriates reality through expression.

The eighth paragraph has the now familiar allusion to Genesis. Unamuno symbolizes man's appropriation of reality through the organizing power of language in terms of the myth of creation. Adam's naming of things and animals is seen as emblematic of man's verbal creation of his universe.

Unamuno must make one last expansion to his thesis on language so that it can encompass 'paralanguage':

Cuando los hombres no hablan, no discrepan ni disputan, pero tampoco se entienden, ni en rigor son hombres. Sociedad no es más que lenguaje común. Aunque sea de gestos, aunque sea de dibujos. De la mayor parte de las cosas que vemos no nos damos cuenta hasta no haber visto dibujos de ellas. Los maravillosos dibujos prehistóricos de renos, de bisontes, de cabras, que se ven en cavernas, nos prueban que ya entonces había sociedad humana, es decir, conocimiento humano. Cuando uno de aquellos hombres cavernarios dibujó un bisonte, se enteró él mismo y se enteraron los demás de que había bisontes. Hasta entonces, aunque acaso hubiesen comido de su carne, no sabían que los hubiera.

When men keep quiet, they don't disagree or argue but neither do they understand each other nor as a matter of fact are they men. Society is nothing other than a common language, even if the language is one of gestures or drawings. We do not become aware of most things we see until we have seen drawings of those things. The marvellous prehistoric cave paintings of reindeer, bison, and goats prove the existence of a human society, that is to say human knowledge. When one of the cave dwellers drew a bison, he knew and all the others knew that bisons existed. Until then, even if they had eaten the meat of bison they did not know bison existed.

It should now be apparent that the dual levels of language discussed in response to the eighth paragraph are essential concepts for even an elementary understanding of Unamuno's philosophy of language. The essence of awareness in man is the semiotic presupposition of the sign as sign at the level of organization and appropriation by the self. The semiotic presupposition must be understood in relation to the second level of language, which is meaning, that is, the attempt to express, to use the signs. Unamuno's thesis is that the semiotic level is achieved through the semantic level of expression. Unamuno has to his credit that he treats the two levels of language from the perspective of a theoretical enquiry. He is, therefore, alluding to the birth of language in prehistoric man as a dialectic of sign and expression which eventually gave man the symbolic media of art and speech and made possible the abstract appropriation of matter.

In the tenth paragraph Unamuno begins a series of illustrative notes which touch upon the acquisition of language in children, educational theory, natural science, and history. In this rapid survey he does little more than suggest the consistent applicability of the theory he has been developing. Since I am not seeking to examine these insights in this chapter but rather to underscore the theoretical enquiry itself, I need not comment in detail.

De eso que llaman ahora los pedagogos lecciones de cosas, dicen muchos que no son más que lecciones de nombres. Y así es. Pero es que el nombre es la cosa misma. Un niño sin lenguaje alguno, oral o gráfico, de sonido o de figura, no sabe en qué mundo vive y ni si vive.

What professors now call learning from things, many say is nothing more than the learning of names. And so it is. For the name is the thing itself. A child with no language, graphic or spoken, of figures or of sounds, does not know the world in which he lives, nor does he know of his own existence.

Unamuno is not a proponent of some aspect of classical nominalism which would deny the material reality of the world. Unamuno insists on a radical nominalism; he holds that the world is knowable only because it has been organized by the knower through his use of the acquired language.

Hay quien se pregunta qué sería de un niño a quien desde pequeñito se le dejase solo proveyéndole de alimento y abrigo. No cabe hacer la prueba, pero si se hiciera, veríase que acababa por morirse de hambre pronto. Y no por otra cosa sino por falta de lenguaje de alguna clase. Las cosas, como no hablan ni escriben, no le enseñarían nada. Porque eso del Libro de la Naturaleza no es más que una frase y si la Naturaleza es libro, es gracias al Hombre, que le ha puesto las letras. Sin lenguaje, la naturaleza es un libro en blanco. Nadie aprendería nada de su propia experiencia si no tuviese a la vista el diccionario de la experiencia ajena, el lenguaje. Nadie distinguiría los síntomas de la Naturaleza sino gracias a los nombres que les hemos puesto.

Someone might ask what would happen to a child, who from an early age was abandoned but given food and clothes. The experiment cannot be done, but if it were done, we would see that he would soon die of hunger. And not because of anything else but for lack of some kind of language. Things, since they do not speak nor write, would not teach him anything. The so-called Book of Nature is nothing but a sentence and if Nature is a book it is because man has put letters to it. Without language, nature is a blank book. Nobody would learn anything from his own experience if the dictionary of everybody else's experience, language, were not at hand. Nobody would be able to distinguish symptoms in Nature if it were not for the names we have given them.

The wolf-children of France and India provide Unamuno with valuable support for this theory of language. The children who have survived in a wild state have done so through the instinctive succour of other animals.

The next paragraph focuses on the extreme limitation which sense impressions impose and the abstract-symbolic nature of experience.

Hace unos meses estuve en el frente italiano, y de allí me traje libros, memorias, diarios, folletos, apuntes, mapas, dibujos, fotografías, y gracias a todo esto conozco algo de aquel frente que vi y de lo que puede ser un frente en la guerra actual. Y el que está en uno de esos frentes sólo se da cuenta de él cuando lo ha visto así, a través de la traducción idiomática. Uno se percata de que su visión de la guerra, su comprensión de ella, apenas se ensancha ni se aclara después de haber contemplado su escenario y oído acaso tronar el cañón.

A few months ago I went to the Italian front and brought back books, memoirs, diaries, pamphlets, sketches, drawings, maps, photographs, and thanks to all of this I know something about the front that I saw and of what a front in the present war might be like. Those at the front only become aware of the front when they have seen it through a linguistic translation. One realizes that one's vision of the war, one's understanding of it, is only slightly expanded when one has been to the scene of war and listened perhaps to the blast of the cannon.

The last four paragraphs (16–19) serve as a conclusion to the theoretical enquiry and need a closer examination.

¿Teóricos y prácticos? ¡Bah simplezas! Cuando un hombre que ha hecho algo no os sepa explicar qué ha hecho, con uno u otro lenguaje, no os fiéis de él para que lo vuelva a hacer. Lo que sí puede ocurrir es que alguno, luego de haber hecho algo, so lo exprese a sí mismo, lo aprenda. Y si no se lo expresa, si no lo reduce a lenguaje, no lo volverá a hacer bien. Eso de que uno sepa algo y no expresarlo es un error. Lo que hay es que hay más expresión que la del lenguaje articulado y que el puro hacer algo no es siempre expresarlo. Pero todo hacer reflexivo supone una expresión.

Theoretical and practical people? Nonsense! When a man who has made something is not capable of explaining what he has made by means of one language or another, one cannot have confidence that he will be able to do the same thing over again. What can happen is that someone after having done something can learn how to do it again by articulating the process to himself. And if he does not express it to himself, if he does not reduce the multiplicity of experience to language, he will not be able to do it again with any degree of accuracy. The claim that one is able to do something, but not to express it, clearly is false. Expression is not only articulated language, and simply doing something is not always expression, but all reflective action presupposes expression.

The first of Unamuno's general propositions on interpretation is here stated: that the ground of awareness in man is the use of language. In other words, in order to be aware of something, we must express its being. A subtle point is made when he insists that although activity can be a form of expression, it can also be a habitual response and therefore non-expressive. We are therefore faced with the problem of defining what Unamuno means by *expression*. The term and the concept which underly it are not confined to this essay and are in fact a fundamental part of Unamuno's philosophy. In brief, the self *is* when it is engaged in a dialectic struggle against its negation (el yo y su no-yo); the activity I have characterized by the term 'struggle' is a constant reaffirmation of self. This reaffirmation is a conscious effort by the self to continue being. Therefore all activity by the self which asserts and reaffirms the self is expression. The conclusion we reach with this line of reasoning is that the division between theory and practice is an arbitrary concept, for in fact theory is not available except through the practice of thinking. Of course, theory as the expression of the practice of the theoretician is always faulty because the expression has not accounted fully for the necessary differences between the self and others. As Wittgenstein put it: 'Like everything metaphysical the harmony between thought and reality is to be found in the grammar of the language.'[5]

The second of Unamuno's propositions on interpretation is in the seventeenth paragraph:

¡Cosas de libros, sí! Así son todas las cosas humanas. Y los hombres mismos son hombres porque son de libros y cuando lo son. El fetiche de un salvaje, el tosco dibujo que graba en su cabaña, el adorno con que se atavía, son libros. Es decir, son memoria colectiva; donde no hay libro, no hay ni albores siquiera de racionalidad.

This is the stuff of books? Yes! And so are all human concerns. And even men themselves are men because of books, when they are such. The fetish of primitive man, the crude drawing on his hut, the adornment he wore, are also books, that is to say, they are all part of a collective memory; where there are no books, there is not even the onset of rationality.

Once we have equated human awareness with expression (paragraph 16) we are prepared for the second proposition: because the link between men is their common language, it follows that the collective memory of a group is based on their inherited mode of expression – linguistic as well as non-linguistic. Things, therefore, are never things by themselves; they are always the interpreted and appropriated objects of the human consciousness. The qualities ascribed to things partially result from the knower's needs and partially from the inherited values of the world view latent in the language through which we conceive them. Thus, for example, we might think of wooden stairs as firewood if we were in desperate need of warmth, but, on the other hand, the custom of piercing the ears of an infant girl could be found perfectly acceptable in one culture but unacceptable in another. An even more radical culturally determined interpretation would be the response to non-pasteurized ripe cheese.

The eighteenth paragraph is a specific application of the theory of interpretation.

Ahora que he quedado libre de mis tareas oficiales, ahora que puedo encerrarme en mi casa, entre mis libros y mis papeles y las notas que de mi experiencia reciente he tomado, ahora es cuando podré darme cuenta de la vida colectiva de que he participado, el juego de acciones y pasiones de que he sido testigo y acaso actor: ahora es cuando podré expresaros algo de la historia que estamos viviendo, de esta historia preñada de enseñanzas y de vida.

Now that I am free of my official duties, now that I can hide at home with my books and my papers and the notes I have taken of my recent experiences, now is when I will be able to become aware of the collective life in which I have participated, the play of deeds and passions of which I have been witness and maybe even an actor: now is when I will be able to communicate to you something about the history we are living, of this history full of teachings and of life.

Unamuno, the writer, has had experiences as part of a social collectivity, but he, like all others, is constrained to the idiosyncrasies of the immediate time and place in which he finds himself. Thus, we can say that there is a physical barrier of time and place which prevents the individual from knowing more than his immediate empirical response to stimuli. However, since man is both freed and bound by language he can at once break his physical barriers and encompass through abstraction the greater view of his collectivity. But we must not forget that his perspective is not objectively constituted, for his view is collectively and privately biased. These are not temporary conditions but rather the inherent characteristics of awareness. The third proposition is therefore that the highest goal of the interpreter is not an objective detachment, but on the contrary a radical self-awareness of one's subjective perspective.

The last paragraph conveys the broadest dimension of Unamuno's hermeneutics:

Y en tanto en torno mío las gentes no se quieren enterar de lo que pasa, de lo que les pasa, de lo que está pasando en el mundo. Parece que no hay otro problema que el de las subsistencias, pero el de las subsistencias materiales, que todo el efecto de la guerra se reduce a encarecer la alimentación. ¡Va a ser terrible el despertar!

While all around me people do not want to know what is happening, what is happening to them, what happens in the world. There seems to be no other problem than subsistence, material subsistence; the total effect of the war is nothing but the rise of the cost of living. It will be terrible to wake up!

Unamuno's last proposition for a theory of interpretation is stated as general social criticism which was, of course, the ostensible aim of the essay. In terms of a theory of interpretation Unamuno is stating that our world view is the elementary background against which we interpret the activities in which we engage directly and indirectly. Our world view can be largely an inherited web of clichés with little or no reflection or it can be a perspective of whose dimensions and limitations we are aware. Consequently, the fourth proposition of interpretation is that of radical awareness of the position of the interpreter and the world view from which he organizes and knows reality.

The reflective reader may have noted the marked resemblance which Unamuno's philosophy still has to Hegel. The Hegelian *Weltgeist* is in flux continually, but unlike Unamuno's reality the world spirit progresses continually toward liberty. Hegel's philosophy is eminently historical as the world spirit unfolds its potentialities through the stages and struggles of Stoicism, Romanticism, moral world view, religion as a vision, and on toward complete self-knowledge and freedom. The essential difference is that to Hegel the absolute spirit was the historical destiny of a process, but to Unamuno self-knowledge and freedom were the attainable goals of a lifetime and were in fact translated into a way of life. Undoubtedly Unamuno has added an existential anthropology to the metaphysical system received from Hegel. Unamuno's theory of interpretation aims at the individual achievement of liberty to the extent that the self escapes the prison of unreflexive routine and the mere repetition of the past. The achievement of interpretation is measurable in terms of the communication attained by the self with its pre-rational self. This relationship is a continuous dialectic which must constantly reinterpret reality as the present encounter in the world. The four propositions of interpretation are: awareness of self and world is possible because of language; the collective memory of man is gained through the language-dominated world view; the aim of interpretation is not objective detached observation, but rather the self-awareness of one's subjective perspective; and the social aim of interpretation is to gain the freedom which awareness of one's intersubjective world view can bring to the interpreter. This is as far as Unamuno's thought can take us in the elaboration of a theory of interpretation. I have suggested that Unamuno provides a starting point, but I must also insist on the originality and significance of his writing. He is in the company of Giambattista Vico and Wilhelm von Humboldt, radical thinkers whose legacy is an inexhaustible source of discovery for those who care to take their challenge and go further in the enquiry into reference and meaning. The argument which follows in this book is my response.

2

Phenomenological premises
for literary criticism

The life of the mind does not consist of understanding alone, nor can it progress unless it has some instinctive contact, however deeply buried, with the basic questions of man's capacity to create a work of art. Divorced from all consideration of basic principles, criticism, like philosophy, tends to become trite and precious. Generic criticism, which is imbued with the instinctive sense of the realization of art, is what I shall discuss in this chapter, for it also makes up the life of the mind as a vital part of the intellectual community.

An aesthetic principle, as I interpret it, is an historical perspective of artistic creation having an established and distinctive aim to fulfil. Aesthetic principles are necessary heuristic devices which must be erected as intellectual scaffolding in order to discuss the multiplicity of literary creation without falling victim to any forms of reductionism. The objective of this chapter is to establish a frame of reference for the ensuing study of the narrative. The next three chapters will examine the possibilities of meaningful commentary on the narrative, and this examination shall function within this heuristic framework. We shall move out of the frame of reference once we have clearly established the dialectic of expression and experience. At the risk of repeating the obvious, I must remind the reader that in this theory, structure is completely subordinated to function and that the discussion of function shall lead us back ultimately into the reintegration of expression and experience in the intersubjective participation of readers across time and space.

I propose the following set of premises:

1 I assume that the reality of literature is the reading experience, wherein there is a private encounter (of varying degrees) with the text,

and that this confrontation has meaning only insofar as it is assimilated into the thought process of the reader.

2 I shall argue that there are no objective points of support beyond language and thought. Meaning exists only within the thought process and the linguistic mediators that embody it. Objective reference is a necessary illusion.

3 My third premise is, consequently, that the only basis for agreement between various readers on what it is that they have experienced lies in their being able to agree on the bases whereby they interpret the reading experience.

4 Since there are no fixed points of objectivity it follows that the only stability possible is in the agreement of procedure itself. This tacit agreement offers us the possibility of communication.

5 The signs we read in the text are the common ground for all readers. However, it is the place that the signs hold in the individual reader's memory of experience and not the actual earth from which their meaning is derived. This dependence on memory is usually given as an objective reference to the actual earth. In fact, the reference in reading is always a reference to the memory of world and not to the earth itself. Thus, the outer point of objective reference is in all cases an illusion. It follows that agreement between readers can be based on a description of the signs.[1]

6 Interpretation, which in each case is the illumination of the reading experience, can be studied as the oscillation between two points: the signs and the purported outer reference which is in fact the reader's memory of experience.

7 Criticism, whatever the explicit claim of the critic may be, is a commentary on one's experience for the benefit of others who have had the same kind of experience, that is, a reading of the same text.

8 History of criticism, the commentary on texts, forms a cumulative body of reflection which merges into the whole of our cultural inheritance. This cultural whole is the necessary background of pre-understanding without which language could not function.

9 The three levels of operation identified for the literary text are all interrelated. Thus the text is at once operational: (a) as a formal cause, (b) as historical reflection, and (c) as a reading experience.

10 My last premise is the most far-reaching, for it goes beyond the issues of literary criticism to the consideration of literature in the social world. The criticism we write today is at the intersection between the history of past criticism we draw from and the future development of criticism we help to shape. We draw from the past in order to add to the

future. Literary criticism without its history becomes self-indulgent subjectivism.

I am not rejecting formalism and proposing a rival theory. Quite the contrary; I accept formalism, but only as a relational analysis of the linguistic artifact. In my view our comments about literature are always the product of the experience of the reader. The function of formal description of literary language is to establish the inner point from which I and all others may calculate the distance which we have created in our formulation of the text.

In brief, I think of interpretation as double dialectic. First, there is the encounter with the text and its immediate meaning; second, there is the more expansive dialectic relationship of the two world views – the textual viewpoint and the reader's – meeting in varying degrees of concord and opposition. If my understanding of interpretation is correct, it follows that literary criticism is an attempt to reconstruct the experience of the text by appealing to whatever criteria the critic can call upon in order to justify himself as a reader's reader. The mode of criticism which I shall argue in favour of is above all an open acknowledgment of the dialectic nature of the reading experience.

A methodology that is equal to the critical act as I describe it is a major task to which I shall address myself in the course of this book. Suffice it here to point out the general directions this is to take. The first dialectic is accessible through the description and analysis of language in its textual context. The second dialectic is achieved primarily through an awareness and examination of the intersubjective structures by which readers respond to the text.

My first point, therefore, is that all claims to objective description and analysis, even in the case of discourse analysis, are untenable because it cannot be shown that there is any ground whatsoever for establishing meaning beyond the awareness of the reader.

My second point is that there is a need for a basis which will grant independent support for our understanding of the text. The independent basis for meaning is, however, only an illusion of separateness and independence; it is in fact a necessary projection away from the self of the reader by the reader.

My third point is an argument for agreement between readers. I accept various interpretations of the same text and set them up side by side as evidence of alternative readings. The fact that separate and alternative interpretations of a text are knowable to us already indicates that communication is possible even if it is only to disagree about what has happened to us in reading the same text. Each interpreter can find a partial basis for agreement with his fellow interpreters if he and they first agree on the rules to be used in the description of the linguistic elements of the text which they have read. These rules or conventions are the necessary prerequisites for communication, but they are not objective facts.

This leads to my fourth point, which is perhaps the most radical of all. When one reader-interpreter addresses another, his message is based on a convention from which he will expand and explain his relationship with the text. Thus, there is no logical basis for distinguishing one interpretation as correct. Each is accepted on its own terms and is justified by its own internal standards as long as the interpreter keeps in mind that his version of the text is knowable to another only because of the implicit and tacit agreement of a shared convention of expression.

I think it would be well to distinguish between my reader-centred theory and orthodox formalism. The formalist approach is based on the search for validity through a comprehensive description of discourse. Any statement which is not clearly based on linguistic evidence is dismissed as psychologism. On the contrary, I am committed to a position that accepts all statements about the text as significant to the reader who is making them. Some of these statements will have claims which are not acceptable to others. When this is the case the reader-interpreter may be asked to explain. The only possibility of convincing those who do not share the specific views of the reader-interpreter lies in his being able to guide them to an analogous experience.

Consequently, the principal issue in interpretation is not whether one view is correct and another is in error, but, quite distant from this preoccupation, the real issue is whether an interpretation of a text can be shared with others. If we do not accept the traditional external criteria for validity in terms of objective truth, author's intentions, or Aristotelian first principles, it follows that we are fully concerned with the relative accessibility of one's experience for others.

By way of summary to the propositions I have introduced and will attempt to unfold in the ensuing pages, let me define my theoretical position. I view all questions of literary interpretation as having only one possibility of being more than the critic's personal therapy; that is, only one possibility of fulfilling the basic function of providing knowledge about a text to another reader, and that possibility lies in the critic's willingness to engage himself in his commentary with the language of the text. Since I reject all claims to an independent, objective basis on which the critic can justify his logical inference, it follows that the only possible basis for a critic's claim to validity lies in the coherence, consistency, and appropriateness of his interpretation. The critic's commentary may or may not be of consequence to other readers, but it is for the readers to judge and in order to do so they must have access to his process of discovery. Thus some critical statements appear to be self-evident because they parallel those of other readers, while other critical statements appear to be questionable and if process of thought is not made available other readers will simply dismiss the critic's views as arbitrary. The critic who aims to convince must address himself to the relevant facts about language in the text and demonstrate his relationship. I maintain that appeals to any authority outside the text are, in the full sense of the word, futile.

The critic cannot claim that the observations on language are in any way objective in themselves. His observations, if carefully documented, are at best intersubjective because he is dealing with the collective reality of man. Thus, the critic is making connections between things which are real to him, but may not be apparent to anyone else. Only the linguistic usage from which the connections have begun is available to other readers. The critic must consequently take care to make his connecting process evident to other readers if he wishes to be understood, and at the same time keep his own sense of totality in view. If, for example, the critic chooses to proceed in his analysis by way of paraphrasing the text he can maintain the linguistic orientation of his remarks but he is forced out of paraphrase when he attempts to express his sense of the text as a whole. The initial problem of criticism therefore lies in the critic's ability to convey to someone else his relation to the text in such a way that he may be able to see the textual segment's place in the whole work. All of this is much closer to the artist's expressing his sense of the real than that of the scientist's making a generalization.

The critic writes about a literary text with a specific appeal to the textual language and he also concerns himself with the sense of the whole work. There is a common ground to these two activities. In both, the critic is involved with relations which reach out from the particular (line, verse, or novel, poem, etc.) in innumerable directions, and these relations are what are unique to his reading and what he seeks to express.

The critic's experience of a text has been a double dialectic of meaning and generalization. This experience is fully realized only as the critic attempts to express it for the consumption of others. He cannot claim that he has discovered the latent significance of the work, or has responded to an objectively verifiable program in the text. He has in fact expanded his own experience by engaging himself with the text, and this engagement may be of interest to another reader if the critic provides a map of his intellectual landscape.

The premises of this book disallow the concept of objective truth in literary criticism. Yet in spite of these premises or perhaps on a deeper level because of them I shall argue in favour of the systematic study of literature as a necessary foundation for literary criticism. In this theory I shall establish heuristic models as a systematic frame of reference for critical enquiry. Further, I hold to the dual referentiality of reading literature and by extension suggest a critical dialectic for literary criticism. The path from experiencing the text to our expressing this experience is the major focal point of this book. The models which will be established are heuristic devices which are temporary, since structure must give way to function. The ultimate aim is therefore to describe the reintegration of the dual referentiality in the literary interpretation. This is a return to an integrated experience, but it is now the shared experience of a number of readers rather than the initial reading experience of the critic.

A phenomenological theory of literature approaches the literary text as the facilitating basis for performances by the reader which are variations on a theme. A fundamental corollary of this principle is that the intentionality of the text itself is variational. This idea takes into account an implicit inventiveness in the text which must be put into play if it is to be actualized. Thus considered, the essential activity of the writer and of the reader is playing the game of realization.

A note on phenomenology is essential at this point in order to identify my philosophical sources. Although I draw openly from a variety of books and philosophical positions, ranging from Husserl to Nelson Goodman, there are three books which serve as the foundation of my writing, and these are: *Der sinnhafte Aufbau der sozialen Welt* (*The Phenomenology of the Social World*) by Alfred Schutz; *Le Visible et l'invisible* (*The Visible and the Invisible*) by Maurice Merleau-Ponty; and *La Métaphore vive* (*The Rule of Metaphor*) by Paul Ricœur.

The phenomenology of language which I have understood from these philosophers relates language to the modes of grasping reality. Language for any speaker or writer always precedes his expression, therefore it is always prior to discourse; indeed it is only because of this prior existence of language that discourse can say anything to anyone. Language thus is not only the mediator (as Humboldt and Unamuno would put it) between man and the world, but it is also paradoxically tied to rules of operation (for the sake of communication) and also just as deeply rooted in the shared experience of world in which the speakers are cast. The task of expression is the struggle to move from the speaker's intention of saying something (which is rooted in his experience) to the articulated usage of rule-governed sounds to say something meaningful. This struggle can be seen as a dialectical relationship and the struggle can be understood as the process of communication itself.

These general observations on the inventiveness of realizing variations of the text are not contrary to the Aristotelian dictum that poetry (texts considered as literature) is ultimately more true than history, for it is only by exploring the possibilities of the mind's free play that discovery and creativity can be examined.

3

The narrative text

Literary criticism derived from philosophical hermeneutics starts with the recognition that the text is analytically accessible as distinct from the psychological recesses of the author's intentions. The data brought forth by the analysis of the text is not the hidden meaning, rather it is the requirement for reading addressed to the reader. The interpretation which follows analysis accordingly is a kind of obedience to this injunction which comes from the text. A text stands independently of its author because in it control has passed from the writer to the reader.[1] In the specialized case of fiction the reader's control of the text is usually mitigated by the narrator. Thus it follows that control in fiction is to a large extent dependent on the reader's ability to cope with the narrative voice or voices. The principal objective of this chapter is to examine the characteristics of a fictional text as a source of the reading experience. I have divided the argument into two parts: first, the expressive capacities of the fictional text and, second, the function which these capacities serve in the reading experience.

My starting point is that the work of fiction stands as a reality only insofar as the expressive capacities of the narrator are known to the reader. Further, let us understand the term 'text' to represent a specific system of morphemic parts which function together as a unit. I do not mean to invoke imagery of personification for texts. Any concept of textual unity which is based on organic unity is attractive but unfortunately misleading, for although we can apprehend a tree at once and not in parts, we cannot so conceive a novel. We are forced by the nature of the text to encounter it in a stream of mental and physical activity. In place of analogies of organic unity, I believe it is more useful to consider the literary text as a referential system which functions as a unit in the dialectic of its creation, which is the reading. The most accurate analogy, if one is needed, is the experience of a dialogue.[2]

To a very large extent language is not only an instrument we control but also a highly qualified medium which controls us. The same language which gives us freedom over time and space restricts us to its particular sensibilities and blind spots. Generations of the past therefore have a marked influence on our means of understanding and in a commensurate way our use of language today will shape thinking of future generations. Consequently any written text is controlled to some extent by the language which is used, and in the case of literature there is the further weight of the traditional conventions of genre and poetics. Literary creation is a participatory effort and cannot under any circumstances be considered as a private rendering of insight. The participatory creation is at once linguistic, historical, and ontological. The language is the basis of the experience, the historical intentionality of text adds the second dimension, and, finally, the reading experience itself – as the text addresses and is questioned in turn – makes up the ontological dimension. We can metaphorically view the reader as the centre of the creative experience, situated within his own historicity, surrounded by the mirrors of language, in dialogue with the text. Fiction differs from other written texts in the greater openness which it allows the imagination of the reader, but fiction will be denied if the reader is not able to listen and speak to the narrator.

The elementary observation of what form of address is used by the narrator gives way to the more significant question about the intended recipient. To whom does the narrator speak? Does it matter? I believe it does because different modes of narrating elicit different responses in the reader. There are two basic directions for the narration to take: reflexively, inwardly to the narrator himself, or outwardly to another. A first person narrative voice can go either way for an indefinite length of narration; a second person narrative voice can also go both ways but is somewhat more restricted in the duration of self-address. A third person narrative voice can express self-reflection as well as depicting to another but must do so indirectly and almost like a concerned shadow on the fringes of the main spotlight.

When the narrative voice addresses itself, the reader almost becomes a witness to the testimony of the narrative self. On the other hand, when the narrative voice addresses another, the reader's participation – in the rendering of the narrative reality – is furthered markedly. Hence, as the narrative voice speaks so the reader responds.[3] In a complex narrative text the voices are more often varied and changing throughout the reading and whether the reader is aware of it or not, his attitudes are also changing. He is constantly being drawn into the fictional reality or being excluded. As these shifts in position occur, a number of more subtle forces are also at play on the sensibilities of the reader, some of which will be lost on the more limited who fail to recognize a change in direction and only respond unwittingly. These forces can be summarized as the narrator's scope of vision, hereafter referred to as privilege; the reliability of the narrator's visibility in the narrative world, hereafter, dramatization. Together these capacities of the narrative voice make up the text's speaking to the reader.

The measure by which we consider the narrator's scope is always our own. The scale extends from an omniscient world view to the isolation of Beckett's voices but the norm is always human. The extremes of the scale are operative in the reading experience only because of the generous licence granted by the reader. On the other hand, the middle registers of the scale of privilege manipulate the modes of perception and knowing. The narrator sees a windmill, for example; one of the characters sees a windmill but another character sees a giant. What does the reader see? If the reader has given the narrator an extraordinary degree of privilege then of course he will see windmills. If, however, the reader has restricted the narrator because he has stated consistently that he was not a witness to the action but is only retelling the story as he has been able to piece it together from documents, the mode of perception of characters and narrator approach the norm of our own. Common sense may thereby dictate that the likelihood of seeing giants in the late sixteenth century traversing through the Spanish countryside is scant indeed. However, the significant aspect is that the individual mode of perception has been given due to the restriction of the narrator's privilege. Thus we may argue that the perceiver's field of vision may not only respond to the physical stimuli before it, but also to the perceiver's needs. The thirsty man does not see a glass of water in the same way as a swimmer. Of the three – the narrator and the two characters – only one had need to see a giant, and this need changed the windmill to a giant.

The degree of privilege granted by the reader to the narrator ought to be no more nor less than that explicitly demanded by the text. 'Ought' implies prescription of how the text should be read. The only valid prescription in reading literature is that dictated by the textual relationship of interdependence which in terms of the novel can be called interior distance. If we assume, for the moment, that the readers of a given novel are competent in their assigned task of realization of the text, we can find complete agreement on the question of the narrative voice's privilege or lack of it.

The fundamental issue of all communication is truth or the reliability of the message. The problem is at once philosophical and practical. In the reading of fiction it has become standard critical procedure to question the reliability of the fictional voice, especially in modern works. What has been overlooked – understandably because of the current widespread use of ironic narration – is that the question of truth underlies the reading experience of all texts. One can argue, perhaps, that in the case of nineteenth-century fiction, the reader has been lulled into a complete suspension of his native scepticism because of the extraordinary assertion of authority made by the narrative voices of this period. This argument, however, fails to consider that in every reading of fiction the granting of authority must be won anew, and that a text that does not establish the basis for authority cannot make use of it. Consequently, in nineteenth-century fiction the continued assertion of omniscience and the total dependence on the narrative voice are the bases for the all-pervasive truth claim. Nevertheless the limitation of authority must be established and respected by the narrative voice if the value structure is to stand within the narrative world. Thus in *Middlemarch*, for example, the limits are recognized when the narrative voice says: 'If we had a keen vision and feeling of all ordinary human life, it would be like hearing the grass grow and the squirrel's heart beat, and we should die of that roar which lies on the other side of silence.'

The most problematic of all the narrator's capacities is the clear establishment of authority or the lack of it. The inferiority of many novels and the low reputation of the genre with respect to lyric poetry stems from a basic misunderstanding on this point. We need go no further in search of an example than *Don Quixote*. The text clearly established (a) that the narrator is presenting a document another has written, (b) that after a few chapters he cannot go on because he lacks further documents, (c) that his continuation is taken from an Arabic historian whose trustworthiness cannot be vouched for, and (d) that the continuation is a translation by an unknown Mosarabic scribe. All of this apparatus is far too lengthy and involved to be merely another basis for parody of the chivalric novels. The subtlety of the novel depends on the equality of the characters with the narrator on the matter of authority. It is not that the narrator is unreliable but merely that he has no superior claim to truth.

The narrative voice constantly moves along a spectrum of self-identification as he speaks of the novelistic world. He may be situated in the extreme position of first person participant or he may be at the other pole as hidden source of revelation, or at any point in between the extremes. It is highly significant for the understanding of fiction to be clear on the position and changes which may occur in dramatization. The degree of narrative voice involvement and presence in the narration are the means by which the novelistic value structure is established. The involvement of the narrator, for example, is at once a liberation and a limitation. The personality of the perceiver is released from its role as distant source and has the possibility of establishing a complex set of relations with inner and outer representations, with past and present as well as 'I-thou' encounters. On the other hand, there is also a severe limitation cast upon all judgments which transcends the knowledge, intelligence, and insight of the individual.

Thus far in this chapter I have outlined a series of distinctions of the speaking voice of fictional texts. That these attributes of the narrative voice must be fully exposed to the reader is a basic premise of literary study as I see it. I do not believe in the virtue of innocence. The competent reader is the master of the text and its properties and it is only because of this mastery that he is entitled to speak to others about his reading experience. A naïve reading experience may have been a moving and perhaps profound experience in the confines of the individual reader, but it has nothing or very little in common with the experiences of other readers of the same text, since there was but limited knowledge of the casual relationship initiated by the narrative voice in the text.

As one reads, the potential attributes we have been looking at are transformed into the functional aspects of the central performance, which is the narration.[4] The specific expression which every literary text becomes reveals a set of assumptions of interdependence which I identify as the intentionality of the text. I shall postpone for the next chapter the discussion of the author's intentions as distinguished from textual intentionality. The reason for the priority of studying textual intentionality before considering the author should emerge as one of the basic conclusions of this book; however, let it suffice here to say that all questions relating to the text are readily verifiable in the text while questions relating to the author are of a more speculative nature. Consequently, if we are to proceed from the more reliable base to the lesser, we must understand textual intentionality before attempting anything in the author's *Lebenswelt*.

The study of textual intentionality is divided into three phases: the immediate response to the language, the intermediate realization of interdependence, and finally the cumulative total effect. To put it in the traditional terminology of literary study, this is a consideration of the style, structure, and theme in the reading experience of the implicit reader. With 'implicit reader' let us understand the reader of competence who wants and is able to master the text in order to realize better the significance of what he has experienced.

I would like to begin by describing what happens when the competent reader encounters a fictional text.[5] When we read, 'No one saw him disembark,' we recognize that these words express both an event – a voice has spoken – and an expression – a series of recognizable words have been spoken which express a relationship. There are further distinctions which are more or less implicit in these words. There is, for example, an immediate identification of 'him' as the person spoken of, but we also assume that he is part of a general class, man. In a more embellished example we also could have distinguished between the way in which the statement was made and what the force of the statement itself was. In our example we can say our speaker speaks with great economy. Compare, for example, 'None of us saw the gaunt man disembark,' with the terse, 'No one saw him disembark.'

The statement itself has a significant impact on the reader because of the implicit paradox it contains. If no one saw him, how is it known? This effect is due to a more significant distinction in our analysis. The words we have read have – at the level of understanding – a specific polarity. On the one hand this combination of words has basic sense; it is not nonsense but rather communicable meaning. Or to put it in more analytical terms, this phrase is made up of a variety of morphemic parts which together function to make a communicable message. Words as part of a language have an established meaning which we can paraphrase or translate if need be. We are also aware that the words have a reference. They refer to something beyond themselves and this reference is not fixed. Not only is the reference not fixed but it has two separate orientations. The words can refer to an extralinguistic reality beyond the immediate expression and can also reflexively refer to the speaker himself. Thus the words, 'No one saw him disembark,' have sense insofar as they express the basic meaning which we can paraphrase as, 'A man is performing a specific activity of getting out of a boat sometime in the past, unseen by anyone.' These words also refer to the human activity of using boats and getting out of them and, further, they also refer to the speaker, whose presence is negated by his very statement. There is therefore a problem of interpretation in this simple five-word sentence.

The paradox contained in these words is a problem of the referential aspects. The meaning itself is clear. We recognize that 'no one' in English is exclusive of all. We further understand that 'no one' eliminates 'seeing' and that the activity not seen is 'disembarking.' Now, turning to the references of the meaning we are led to postulate (a) disembarking, (b) seeing, and (c) telling, as activities referred to in the sense-meaning. (a) and (b) are activities of a referential world and (c) is an activity of the speaker himself, that is, self-reference. Consequently, we must conclude that in order to have 'telling' about an 'unseen disembarking' we would have to make a choice among various assumptions about the reference. We could read the words as referring to (1) 'disembarking,' which is not a visible activity, or (2) a speaker who is not excluded by 'no one,' or (3) a speaker who has information which enables him to tell what was unseen. If the present example had taken place as normal discourse between two speakers the third assumption would be the most plausible and, most likely, it would take the form of a query to the speaker; 'If no one saw him, how do you know?' Of course, the commonplace response would be, 'He told me.' In literature, however, in contrast to normal language, we cannot rule out the other two possibilities. We may of course take the commonsense route in reading but it may well be that one of the other two possibilities is called for by the subsequent text. The point I am making is that literary language constantly opens up into complexities of reference and that these ambiguities are understood (not resolved) only by the interdependence of the words that follow. For example, say that the problematic, 'No one saw him disembark,' is followed by, 'In the unanimous night, no one saw the bamboo canoe sinking into the sacred mud, but within a few days no one was unaware that the silent man came from the South and that his home was one of the infinite villages upstream, on the violent mountainside, where the Zend tongue is not contaminated with Greek and where leprosy is infrequent.' We find that the referential dimensions least likely in normal discourse are in the literary language of Borges the basis of understanding since the words have reference to an ideal world of 'unanimous night' and 'infinite villages,' and the self-reference is to an omniscient narrative voice.

The fictional language has been thus far considered from the level of meaning as well as that of reference (self-reference and extralinguistic reference), but it remains to be seen how language operates on the reader.

Literature has a direct impact on the reader's sensibility, which is flung open by the expansion of references such as we have been discussing. This impact or effect on the reader is largely a matter of the reader's predisposition to references. I do not wish to minimize the reader's role in creativity. However, since I will devote an entire chapter to that aspect, perhaps for purposes of clarity I can concentrate here on the functions of literary language as potential effect or as textual intentionality.

There are four functions which I discern in literary language: (1) to establish correspondences between parallel realities (the reader's and the fictional); (2) to erode the reader's resistance to explicit references and thus convince; (3) to displace the reader's reality with an ideal substitute; and (4) to create a unique correspondence in the act of reading. It will be recognized that these functions are closely related to temporal dimensions of the genre as well as to the fuller question of the dimensions of interpretation.

We are now concerned with the action of literary language in general and with the examination of the action of specific written words on the reader. This is possible only by first establishing the patterns of significance: textual self-reference and textual reference to extralinguistic a priori concepts. Consequently, we reach the stage where we can ask about the uses of literary language (not the response, which is another problem) and I conclude that there are four functions to literary language. I believe that it is essential to maintain the distinction between subjective response and intrasubjective function. Thus, although it is perfectly clear that when reader A states that the words gave him a distinct feeling of joy and reader B maintains that the same words only caused him to reflect on the transitory nature of life, we are engaged in a discussion of response and not of function. The function of literary language can rapidly and correctly be gauged by reflection on the phenomenal relationship which the language establishes with the reader's own reality. Thus it may well be that the words which caused joy in one reader but meditative reflection in another could have been clearly identified as having established correspondences between the parallel realities of reader and text. The point of my argument is this: it serves no one to know that reader A felt joy while reader B experienced reflection, but it is of consequence to know that the words established the possibilities of identification within the narrative world because of a parallel basis.

The first function we have identified – correspondences between parallel realities – is the primary assumption upon which all realism operates. It is an inducement to the reader to accept the narrative reality as a functional extension of his own. Thus the words are constantly establishing correspondences and moving between the parallels. Consider the following statement in terms of reference and function: 'She was sitting on the veranda waiting for her husband to come in for luncheon.' There is no self-reference and the extralinguistic reference is explicit in its assumption of person, objects, custom, and social convention. The resulting function is to establish an organized set of correspondences between the unfolding literary world and the world of the reader.

Another illustration will provide us with contrast: 'Everything about the Arms was excessively modern, and everything was compressed – except the garages.' The extralinguistic references in this example point to a recognizable conglomeration of buildings and garages, but there is a further reference to a judgment which is being impressed on us. When we turn to function, it is the value judgment of the world that overtakes the correspondences which we recognize. Consequently the direction and action of the language is one of convincing the reader to share more than the correspondences; he is to share explicit value judgments on the world of the novel. In this case, it means to pass the same judgment on our own world.

We have already given a good example of the third function – 'No one saw him disembark in the unanimous night' – wherein the referential aspects of the language displace the reader's world. The fourth referential function of literary (figurative) language is the creation of unique correspondences. For example, 'Time and the bell have buried the day,' operates on a basis not merely of referential correspondences but rather on the new correspondence of death and burial of the day as the effect of time and the keeping of time (the bell).

Consequently we can speak of four functions to the focal effect of linguistic reference: to establish a correspondence of references, to have the reader accept value judgments in the references, to displace the reader's references with a constructed image or concept, and finally for the reader to create a new correspondence.

The full impact of literary language is given within the intimacy of the personal reading experience. The initial meaningful message is transformed into experience as an expression of the reader's personality as well as the re-creation of the objectified external references. What we have been attempting to define is the function of literary language within the reading experience. An intersubjective framework of the effect of reading has been the result of this enquiry, for it has become evident that the more we ask, 'What does it do?' the closer we get to a generalization about readers and reading.

The hypothesis of the four functions of literary language is the result of inductive reasoning which has been tested by the experience of many readers. Its usefulness as an intersubjective structure will be argued in the remainder of this chapter and will be referred to throughout this book. Its validity will ultimately be established or rejected through the criticism of the wider public to whom I am addressing these remarks.

We now come to an aspect of textual intentionality which has been developed mainly in this century and mostly by European theoreticians.[6] The importance of the narrative's structure in the search for knowledge cannot be minimized. Anyone attempting to study the novel in the absence of a clear and articulated view of structure is prone to lose his way in a labyrinth of fragmentation. However, it is also important to remember that the study of the novel's structure is but a way station on the road to humanistic literary knowledge. One must be reminded that the goal of literary study is not the text in itself, but rather the text as the common basis for readers to realize the reading experience. Indeed we may even venture to say that the novelistic structure cannot be studied without taking into consideration that the actualization of the novel lies entirely in the activity of the knowing subject – the reader. Therefore the study of structure must point toward the fuller consideration of the novel as experience in the reader's *Lebenswelt*.

By novelistic structure let us understand the general and formal rules of interdependence within the novelistic world. There are four different kinds of rules which must be identified before we can elaborate the system or structure by which they operate. The four classes are the rules which govern the narrative voice or voices, the rules of temporality, the rules of qualitative and quantitative dimensions of space and, finally, the rules which govern participation in the novelistic world. All novels have sets of rules for each of these classes, but each novel has the potentiality of a unique system of organization at the level of realization.

We can think of the relationship between the four classes of structural rules as a system of interdependence which serves us to understand the novelistic world as a whole. The novelistic text is a continuous stream of concepts emanating from the narrative voice about the narrative world. This internal stream is in flux, with one or all of its component classes changing. Let us consider the stream in a schema of growing complexity. First let us say that the narrative voice is fixed. We are quickly assured that he has certain attitudes and capacities and these do not change. Let us further say that in the same example time is just as clearly established to be a chronological balance of experience and summary. Let us add fixed characters to this formula and we have only to contend with a growth and development of novelistic space. Thousands upon thousands of novels have been written in this manner, and the fact that the structural system is a simple one in no way implies a deficiency. I am not here concerned with criteria of evaluation. It would certainly be absurd to make complexity of structure a basis for value judgment. In the abstract formula I have described above we have the internal stream of valuative expression concentrated on the presentation of world. We can thus refer to a novel with this kind of a system as a novel of spatial structure. The problems in structural analysis come with various components in flux. Continuing with the same model let us change the fixed characters to fictional characters whose personalities are developing and growing in intellectual and sensitive awareness as the novel progresses.

It now becomes imperative for our study to determine where the organizational axis for the structure lies, with the character or in the narrative world. The text is a stream of expression adding one link after another, overlaying image, concept, and symbol upon each other in a succession which becomes a complex system for the development of a structure of space or a structure of character. These two prototypes of structure are therefore complex or unitary depending on the variability of the four classes of rules we have enumerated.

I have postponed discussion of a third structural system for last because it is often the object of confusion. In this structure all four classes are fixed; there is no elaboration of narrative voice, nor of time, space, or character. We are confronted with events or action in sequence. This structure of action is the basis of the Romance, the adventure story, the detective story, and other forms of popular literature.

The structure of action, consequently, can be recognized as a prototype organization for story-telling first in oral tradition and subsequently in written expression. Its strength lies in the unambiguous clarity with which it depicts events and their consequences. Indeed every possible subtlety of speculative thought is sacrificed to the all-pervasive force of direct action. Event follows event in a pattern of causality that allows only an inevitable stream of events to take place. The sense of fate is closely bound to this narrative structure.

Three structural prototypes have been discussed. Each organizes the narrative around a structural priority: character, world, or events. All of this has been presented convincingly by Wolfgang Kayser and others, but beyond the descriptions of the structural prototypes lies the question of how the sets of rules operate upon each other or, to put it differently, the question of how interdependence of the formal rules makes up the structure.

The rules of narrative voice are the means of control for the stream of narration at the source. Consequently, as a class, the particular character-istics of the narrative voice – point of view, privilege, authority, and dramatization – constitute a functional governance over the accumulat-ing unity which is narrative world.[7] On the other side of the stream we have the rules of internal order which make up the spatio-temporal limits of the narrative world. Temporality exists as a narrative dimension for the world and for the character. We can thus speak of the time of experience for character or voice within a chronological system, of a time of experience of chronology, of the narrative time-span in total and, ultimately, of the implicit or explicit reference to historical time.

Similarly, space is a narrative dimension, one of potential movement which becomes realized as action for the character. The general rules of space in the novel determine the organization of physical scene, the narrative setting viewed through the narrator's value prism, the narrative setting viewed through the character's subjective eye, and also the implicit or explicit use of historical setting. The two classes of temporality and space operate together to bind the narrative world's objects into a value-structured whole whose dimensions are the limits of potential movement and action. We have thus far considered the two terminals of the narrative stream from source to world and the links of interdependence which operate between them. We have yet to focus on the heart of the narrative, which is participation not only in the narrative world but also in the narrative stream itself. The fictional characters or voices are participants in the reality of the narrative world and they are also participants in the stream of narration although they are only occasionally aware of this ontological participation. The rules in this case are the relative freedom to speak, the capacity to know, develop, and experience reality, the relative independence from the narrator, and, finally, the character's reflection of the social structure of the narrative world.

The fullness and richness of the narrative is not well served by structuralist schemes, no matter how ingenious, for they have no means of considering the ways in which the structure is aimed at the implicit reader and only realized through the real reader. Therefore in going beyond structure we must build a series of bridges between the components of structure on the one hand and the function which they serve for the implicit reader on the other. The sum total of this strategy of writing for the implicit reader is what I have been calling the intentionality of the text and the status of implicit reading is what I have named the fictional context. If we redefine the four aspects of narrative structure as four classes of structural rules, each of which serves a specific function for the implicit reader, we can lay the foundation for the phenomenological study of the novel. An outline of structural rules and their corresponding intentional function will help to clarify my position:

Class I: expression
   A general rules of narrative voice
      1 point of view
      2 privilege
      3 authority
      4 dramatization
   B intentional function of narrative voice:
   governance over narrative life-world

Class II: temporality
   A general rules of narrative time
      1 narrative experience as chronological order
      2 narrative experience suspended from narrative chronology
      3 the narrative sequence as time
      4 extratextual sequences as time
   B intentional function of narrative time:
   establishment of a basic formal complement for the narrative world order

Class III: phenomenal world
   A pulse of reference to extratextual physical dimensions
      1 perceived matter within a system of physical causation
      2 perception as expression of the narrative voice's value structure
      3 perception as expression of the character's value structure
      4 perception as expression of the reader's value structure
   B intentional function of perceived matter:
   establishment of a basic complement for the narrative world order

Class IV: participation
   A rules of realization of experience
      1 direct experience by the character
      2 capacities of the characters
      3 relative autonomy of the characters
      4 the character as a socio-economic organism
   B intentional function of participation:
   transformation of movement and awareness into action and thought in the narrative world.

We have gone as far as possible in our consideration of the text as an intentional creation passing from writer to reader. We must now turn to the examination of these two terminals in their respective *Lebenswelt.*

4

The author

The novelistic text has been in the central position of this enquiry thus far. We must now seek to enlarge the scope of enquiry by considering the relationship of the text to both the author and the reader. If we can accept that author, text, and reader are in a continuous process of transmission, we can readily agree that the process can be approached from either the perspective of the author or that of the reader. In the case of the author there is a creative dialectic as the writer engages himself in the objectivization of his own experience. In the case of the reader there is a re-creative dialectic as the text is made to yield its referential field and the reader is pressed to respond.

There are a number of ways open for consideration of the author in relation to his work. The study of the author as craftsman reaches into the earliest phases of the literary creation and can reveal the patterns of writing which define the implicit reader who is present in suppositions of a particular author. Another approach to the study of the author is to concentrate on the capacity of imaginative insight and particularly on the transformation of experience into expression. There are other approaches but in these two we encounter the basic problems which are common to all imaginative writers as linguistic artists: craft and insight.[1]

If we examine the notes, drafts, and manuscripts of an author, a tentative reconstruction can be made of the creative process of writing. But we must be quite clear in recognizing the motives for such a study and, more importantly, what significance such evidence has for the understanding of the reading experience.

Since the process of creative writing is here the subject of study and not the realization of the work through the reader, it follows that the results of this enquiry are valid only in application to the biographical consideration of the author and by extension of analogy to the creative process in general. The basic ambiguity of imaginative expression will not yield before such an approach. In all creative expression there is an element of spontaneity which thrusts together previously unrelated elements into a single whole, and it is this undeniable spontaneity that imposes very rigid limitations on historical reconstruction. In brief, the study of the process of creative writing of a specific author can only revolve around the writing itself but cannot enter into the significance of the work. There are therefore two fundamental ways in which an author works at literary creation. One is a detached form of thinking about the materials he is using and the other is an inner form of insight into the potentialities of being which become only through the activity by the author.

The creative writer consequently thinks in two languages: one, the conventional language of his speech community, and the other, the interior language of imaginative becoming which is analogous to the language of fantasy and of dreams. The activity of creative writing is a dialectic encounter between the two languages. The author's efforts, which are often extreme, consist fundamentally of transforming the speech of the imaginative language into the conventional language.[2]

The author as craftsman works on the conventional language and through his effort attempts to make the expression faithful to the language of creation. In the narrative specifically, the words of the narrator create the world in which he is present as source in all events. Because the words are the specific words uttered by the narrator, however, they also reveal him and his vision. The craftsmanship of the author alters the quality and quantity of this dual significance, but can never change the essential duality of narration as expression and self-reference.

Let me take a specific example in order to illustrate what I am saying. In studying the manuscript of Miguel de Unamuno's *San Manuel bueno, mártir* I discovered that there were a number of lengthy additions between the first and the final draft.[3] Examination of the additions exposed a pattern of symbolic expansion. The symbolic elements in the first draft were developed into fully recognizable symbols of mother creatrix, redemption, and so on. Unamuno the craftsman, by rewriting, in this case by adding to the text, altered the novelistic expression. He made the implicit symbolism explicit. The essential point I am making is that the duality existed before and after the additions. The words expressed a specific state of affairs among men and women and also revealed a powerful mythical vision in the imaginative language of the author. In this case the duality was more open after the rewriting but it was not a result of the changes.

We can now answer the question posed at the beginning of this chapter about the significance of authorial craftsmanship. The information about an author's writing process has importance only within the creative dialectic of the languages of expression and of imagination.

We should now consider the inner language of the creative imagination in spite of the obvious complexity of the topic. Although it is not possible to develop the full study of literary insight, I am compelled to provide sufficient background for an understanding of the creative dialectic I am sketching.

At the basis of creative insight lies a dialogue between the author and his world which becomes a 'you,' the other through which the 'I' can emerge. There is freedom in the response given to the other, but there is also a necessity of direction imposed by the other. The author speaks in this dialogue of the imagination but he is also spoken to by his world; therefore he is changing experience through his participation, but the world which is becoming is also imposing changes upon the author. The 'I' of the author is inconceivable without the other of his world and the reciprocity of the dialogue is the language of imagination.

The objectifying and reflective awareness of the dialogue between self and world is common to all artists, but in the case of the author it can remain hidden behind the medium of expression. Whereas the sculptor or the painter uses materials, the writer works with language, thus having the added risk of submerging the creative dialogue beneath a layer of conventionality.

We all share language and we also share the world, yet few of us can share the world through written language. This is essentially the task of the author and the main topic of this chapter.

If we are to achieve some clarity on these complex relations, we must begin with acknowledged foundations. What is given for the author or any man is usually designated by the term 'life-world.' However, behind this term we have a plurality of living organisms directed by very different and sometimes conflicting aims. The living organism feeds on other lesser organisms, so all construction implies a certain destruction. Now then, if we conceive of life as this kind of struggle between life and death we can better understand that the author's dialogue involves life in a positive sense, for dialogue is the positive counterforce to violence and destruction. In this sense we can assert that the world-creating dialogue of an author has its creative power because of an acceptance of the other by the 'I.' Because the author enters by choice into the relationship of constituting a vision he has to accept the other as a voice to which he must listen as well as speak. In other words, the creative dialogue takes place only after the author considers the other worthy of exchange. On the level of expression there may be a language of indignation and rage as the result of the author's writing. But on the primary level of insight there must be an 'I-you' relationship as the imagination constitutes the world. The negation of the dialogue is not disagreement with the created world for this is one among many forms of constituting the world. The negation of dialogue is silence.

Let us continue our enquiry into the nature of the primary level of constituting the world through the dialogue. The 'I-you' relationship is one of stress, change, and conflict, but it remains open as long as the author is willing to encounter his world. The 'you' concept is not the projected world view of the author; it must be the authentic 'other' who shares the world with the author. By openly choosing to enter the world and to encounter the other, the author has entered into the dialogue.

A unique transformation ensues as the author begins to write, for he is attempting to express, to bring to the surface of conventional language what lies within the inner language of the creative dialogue. The author now seeks to find words which will be faithful to the inner language and will also reproduce some of its significance for the implicit reader. The difficulties of expressing the imaginatively constituted world are due to this double aim of writing: to be faithful to the inner dialogue and to reach the reader with its significance.

The transformation of author's experience to expression can be illustrated with the specific problems of the novelist. A few basic notions of literary perspective must be reintroduced at this point. A novelist cannot imagine a world of pure abstraction. The complete specifications of a world would take more than any man or group of men could write or read. Further, since thought and language are ineluctably entwined, his very thoughts, however chaotic, are conditioned by language and memory of language use. Finally, it would be impossible to express, and for the reader, to imagine, a world that was original.

The task of the novelist is to produce an imaginary world by stating only a relatively small number of terms which are meaningful to the reader and serve as basic signs for the imagination. The reader immediately supplements and expands the textual clues and experiences of an imaginative world by reference to his memory of the actual world. Nothing short of a complete muddle will result if we lose sight of these basic notions, which can be summarized as: (a) the author does not control the construction of the imaginative world since he can only provide the initial clues; (b) the reader creates the imaginative world by reference to his memory of the actual world, not to the actual world itself; and (c) the imaginative world suggested and provoked by the novelist's words is best described as a modification of our memory of the actual world.

By careful study of an author's manuscripts we may arrive at some tentative conclusions about his use of language. With far less certainty we can attempt to reconstruct the author's creative dialogue in his world. This inductive speculation into the creative process is a valuable asset for literary interpretation and literary history if it is directly and convincingly tied to the intentionality of the author's texts. To attempt to make the author the basis for verification of meaning contradicts the dictum of proceeding from the better known to the lesser known in an enquiry.[4] The author's position is not an a priori given, but rather a very tentatively reconstructed position; therefore the author's relations to his world can never be appealed to as the basis for determining the validity of an interpretation.

There is another purpose for the study of the author which we have not yet considered: the historical understanding of the social group in which the individual author was formed.

Literary history shares with all historical enquiry the radical paradox of constituting a rational perspective from the present cast upon the irrational milieu of life in the past. As a specialized branch of history, literary history mediates between epochs and the individual lives which have left their mark through creative writing. Consequently, the reconstruction of the epoch is dependent upon the reconstruction of the literary author and the forms he has used. There are a number of catalogues and surveys of writers grouped together into approximate affinities and traditions, but the essential source has remained the reconstituted author related to his writing. A history of literary authors can fulfil its objective of reconstruction only if it is complemented with a history of literary form.

The study of literary history is therefore an ancillary facet of literary study; it cannot be substituted for direct study of texts, for to do so would necessarily grant to a given perspective the place of the literary work itself. We can today readily assess the folly of much pedagogical dogma when we recognize that in the twentieth century the student is being trained to see the seventeenth century, for example, *Don Quixote*, through the perspectives of nineteenth-century scholarship.

The work of literature has only one historical destiny for a twentieth-century reader and that is the present perspective. The author exists only as the implicit author throughout the creative encounter of reading the text. The implicit author can become the historical author, that is to say, the historically reconstituted individual who lived and wrote in the past, only through a direct rational enquiry into the man and his milieu. These remarks are not intended to deny or reduce the importance and significance of history for literary study. Indeed, literary tradition is and has been a most powerful formative influence on writers of any period.[5]

Whether we are reading a classic work of literature or the writing of a contemporary and relatively unknown author, the work realizes its potentiality quite independently of the real author. However, there is an awareness of the implicit author which emerges during the reading encounter. Writers vary greatly in the degree of openness with which they reflect upon themselves, but they all cast a shadow which is discernible.

In general there are two distinct ways in which the implicit author enters the reader's literary experience. First, there is the external evidence of biographical information; this may take the elaborate form of an established reputation which is derived from critical commentaries on the man and his work, or it may be reduced to a simple biographical note on the dust-jacket of the book. Without a doubt this is the most common way in which the implicit author appears. The second, although less frequent way, is through internal evidence provided in the text itself. These indicators may be explicit autobiographical references to the author behind the narrator but they may also be more oblique references to his milieu. Whatever the case the internal indicators all function to point to the author, who has been engaged in the creative task of writing.

What, we may ask, is the role of the implicit author in the literary experience? That there is a role is undeniable, because the fact of existence of the implicit author by external or internal means makes this concept a viable part of the experience. Let us take the case of external evidence first since this is the most common. Whatever we know or think we know about the purported author of the text we are reading has already partially determined our attitudes toward the text. Thus if we read where and when the author was born, what his intellectual credentials are, what others (critics) have written about his work, and even what his general views on life are, we become predisposed in a direct way to the text. Our expectations are built up and our curiosity is aroused as we begin to project into the text before reading it. The anticipation of the text can be based on a multiplicity of external indicators of which the purported author is one, albeit a most important one.

In the case of internal evidence about the implicit author our reaction is quite different. This view of the implied author comes when we are already immersed in the experience of the text and the references to the shadowy author force us out of the literary world into the author's historicity. The internal indicators project us out of the work but never allow us to rest in history, for the author's milieu is completely subordinated to the fictional milieu, for example, Gide's *Les Faux-monnayeurs*. These indicators touch upon the distant *Lebenswelt* of the experiences which have been lived by the author, but this fleeting glimpse vanishes because the indicators obtain their internal meaning from the fictional context and not from the historical position of the author.

I have indicated that the implicit author functions in two contrary ways. The external evidence of the implied author projects into an anticipation of the text while the internal evidence has us cast a glance backwards toward the remote historicity of the implied author. Both projections, forward or backward, indicate the central background of the text as an experience. The implied author can therefore be identified functionally as part of the text's background of nonactualized potentialities for the reading experience. The richness of this background is not diminished by what is actualized because as an implicit horizon it is always only partially revealed.[6]

When the background of implicit consciousness takes shape in the reading experience there is the distinct possibility that it can become the context of the work itself. For example, when we consider a novel narrated in the first person and with explicit autobiographical indicators written by a known author, we are confronted with a dialectic situation between the narrator and the implicit author. It is a dialectic of revelation and secrecy, of openness and the hidden. The narrator owes his visibility and his very identity to the concealment of the implied author. To what extent is this dialectic present in all narratives? The answer to this question must be incomplete owing to the incomplete status of my study at this point, but I can at least outline the fuller answer. Just as the real author establishes a dialogue with his world which is subsequently transformed through conventional language, so also does the implicit author function within the implicit background of the text. It would therefore be quite arbitrary to assign to the implied author the whole of the implicit horizon against which the narrative takes actuality. The implied author is the centre but not the whole, since the whole is a relationship.

The principal focus of the novelistic reading experience is on the narrator and what he has to say. As discussed earlier, this is an emergent world conditioned by the effect of the narrator's viewpoint on the reader's imaginative capacities. Let us, for the sake of clarity, separate this imaginative visual field into foreground and background. The foreground consists of the narrator or narrative voice and the narrative world. The background is made up by the implicit author and his implicit world. The relationship between the implicit author and his world has the same directional pattern as the relationship which we have considered between the narrator and the narrative world. In both cases the centre of consciousness is in the voice/author and the potential field of mental and physical movement is in the respective worlds. The pressing question for us to consider is how the background (implicit author − implicit world) operates in relation to the foreground (narrator − narrative world).

In order better to organize the problem I propose to use an analogy from the physical sciences. The world as the physicist knows it is not composed of the objects we experience, but rather is made up of molecular and atomic activities which cannot be appreciated in a sensory way at all. These 'real' forces are conceived of only through the effects produced on the physicist's instruments. One such force is a form of energy called light which affects the eyes. It is largely the result of light upon the eyes that produces perception and the whole of human constructs we know as objects and which make up our reality. There is no perception without there being a specific point of view which segregates certain portions of the visual field, organizes it, and synthesizes it as an object. Not only does the visual point of view accomplish this construction every time there is perception, but it also grants a lasting identity to the construct and situates it in relation to other construct-objects. Finally, we must also note that the perceiver confers a temporal continuity to the multiplicity of objects which fill his world. Now then, the foreground of the field of vision is the constructed object, and the background the array of parts of visual field which are not seen because they do not adhere to the object formation. Therefore we see only the foreground while the background remains invisible. Because the background is invisible it is all too easy to dismiss it, but by eliminating it we oversimplify physical reality and must also give up understanding it since the physical forces are operative whether we see them or not. This brief and superficial trip into physical relationships provides us with a valuable concept which is analogous to the relationship of foreground and background in the novel which I seek to isolate.[7]

In the novel, as in life, to see an object is to have a point of view, to be oriented toward it; to perceive is to have a position that is an attitude. When the narrative voice speaks of an object he is exercising this directional attitude in fixing the object in the narration. But we must now add to the discussion the consideration of the real albeit invisible background. Behind the narrative voice stands an implicit author who has discarded everything else which could have possibly appeared in this context in favour of the precise object the narrator presents. Similarly behind the object itself stand the numerous could-have-been objects. The solidarity of the narrative world is made up of this continuous process of background becoming foreground and foreground receding into back- ground. One is unattainable without the other. The narrator is constantly presenting the narrative world, which is to say actualizing the passage from background to foreground and vice versa. But behind the narrator stands the implicit author. What is his ongoing relationship to his narrator? This is truly the question we have been preparing. The implicit author can emerge from the background and into the foreground as the puppeteer who is pulling the strings of a choice of objects or he can submerge himself deeply into the background, allowing his narrator the stage. This relationship is by no means fixed or constant, for every word has the potentiality of opening the veil of the literary convention.

The narrative world does not just rise out of a system of references to objects and involvements for action, nor does it just take shape as world view. If the narrative world were nothing more than a fragmentary conglomerate of things for a story to happen, the novel would indeed be nothing more than a minor form of entertainment. The narrative world does not take shape out of nothingness, for it is the actualization of totality. The objects of the narrative world are condensations of reality. So it is also with the narrative voice. The narrative voice is not a personality pulled out of a void; it is the actualization of an aspect of the implicit author's personality.

By way of conclusion to this chapter I would like to comment on Merleau-Ponty's insight into the author-narrator relationship.

The word is no longer there in order to indicate a perceptual evidence; rather it is there to introduce us into the spectacle of the world which makes itself in it. The role of the narrator, as has been said since Proust, illustrates this state of affairs well: on the one hand, the narrator is amid the events; on the other hand, he keeps a certain distance from what happens. The word of the things and the word of himself are superimposed in his language. And we, the readers, we assist in the spontaneous encounter of these two sorts of word in the symbolic system which is the work. Thus we have the right to see what happens both within the author and around him at the same time (p 335).

These lecture notes from Merleau-Ponty's last lecture before his death in 1961 convey essentially the hypothesis I have been developing during this last decade. Therefore the recent publication of the notes by Alexandre Métraux, 'Vision and Being in the Last Lectures of Maurice Merleau-Ponty,' has provided me with support.[8] What Merleau-Ponty calls the writer's password is akin to my concept of the language of creative dialogue finding its expression in conventional language. Further along Merleau-Ponty distinguishes the two directions of the narrator's language, which is very close to the idea I have held that the narrator's referential directions are aimed at the things of the narrative world as well as establishing his own distance from that world. My central proposition of the narrative as a spontaneous encounter and celebration in which we attend and participate comes forth emphatically in these notes. Finally, my last proposition of background and foreground, which places the implicit author and his world in a process of revelation and manifestation through the reading experience, was originated by Merleau-Ponty.

5

The reader

I maintain throughout this book that the reality of literature is to be found in the reading experience. When a reader takes up a text he is the realization of an anticipated or implied reader who the writer had in mind as he put language to paper. We shall consider the important distinctions between real readers and implicit readers in the last part of this book: for our purposes in the present context we shall only be concerned with the person who reads and thus gives the text reality. My main point is that the text becomes an aesthetic object in the activity of reading. There is a fundamental unity to this act which I have called the reading experience.

Some general observations are in order at the outset. The textual meaning is an actualization of the intentionality of the text itself, for if the text itself lacked meaning, the reading would not be an actualization; it would be creation. There is, therefore, an intentional act of reading which actualizes what is intentional in the text. Now then, the actualization of the textual meaning cannot be construed as a simple 'finding' or illumination of a fixed conceptual order. Actualization is not a passive recognition of a message which is to be comprehended to a greater or lesser degree depending on the receptive ability of the reader. The reader's actualization of the text, the primary level of the reading experience, is far more complex; it consists of seeing, communication, assimilation, and conceptualization. Therefore, there is a process which produces meaning based on the intentionality of the text. A secondary level of the reading experience takes place almost simultaneously with the primary level, and this is what I call the referential level. The actualized meaning refers beyond itself to either an extralinguistic referent or to the speaker himself. There is finally a third level where the meanings of the reading experience can themselves by objectified and thus through reflection be made the objects for further thought. The first two levels just described are common to all readers of all texts. The third is the domain of the enquiring reader. The process of the reading experience becomes in the case of literature a radical enrichment of the reader's reality. This is a question taken up at length in the next chapter.

The primary and secondary levels of the reading experience function as part of the reader's subjectivity. It is within the reader's particular subjective mind that the actualization moves in an ongoing dialectic of meaning and reference.[1] For the average reader encountering a text in a language he can read without hesitation, the primary level is hardly apparent. He passes instantly from linguistic meaningfulness into the referential association. This does not mean, however, that there has not been an initial dialectic between the reader's linguistic capability and the inherent characteristics of the language which control the verbal dimensions of expressibility. It merely shows that a reader who is completely at home in the written language of the text can be unaware of the media of language itself. He can take it for granted unless there is some aspect which disturbs his anticipatory flow of language. Thus when the reader encounters the words: 'She opened the window, looked out, and fell into reverie,' the verb *fell* breaks the anticipatory train for just a moment. Perhaps the now linguistically conscious reader could even be moved to think that 'was lost in thought' would be better than 'fell into reverie.' The point is that the dialectic of language and reader which operates on the primary level of the reading experience has emerged to interrupt the flow of meaning.

The normal process of reading is a constant interweaving of the anticipated words and thoughts with a retrospection to what has come before and is now the context for what is emerging.[2] It is within this process that the referential dialectic takes place. The reader of the novel is constantly actualizing a multiplicity of references to the world taken from his own experience, and he is also aware of the fact that there is a narrator who is the initial source of the narration. Thus there are two directions in which the secondary dialectic of reference unfolds; the reference to the reader's *Lebenswelt* and the reference to the narrative relationship proper. The reading experience of the novel extends over a relatively long period; thus, an added dimension of temporality must be considered. The narrative world with its voices and participants unfolds as an imaginative experience of greater concentration and duration than any other experience except life itself; consequently, it is to be expected that the reader will come to find himself in two worlds at once. This dialectic between the narrative world and the reader's world is the acute potentiality of the imaginative reading experience which distinguishes it markedly from other forms of reading.

The reader of the novel is producing an imaginative construct which is actualized only if he has the capacity to grasp the linguistic significance of language and at the same time to relate its references to his living experience. Consequently any theory of the novel which is to deal with the reality of the novel must take into account the text and with equal deliberation the experience which is the response to the text. We can openly acknowledge the difficulty of describing this subjective process of actualization which we call the reading experience. We can, however, draw attention to the various cognitive processes which participate in this complex activity.

As we read the novel the words begin to create a situation of 'seeing-again.' The accumulation of references is inducing us to grasp an order of objects which assumes, to varying degrees, a similarity to our prior experience. The prior experience is our subjective reality. This is in a very basic sense a *re-cognition* which takes place when there is an explicit presentation to our subjective structures of awareness. This presentation ranges widely from simple images to irrational sensations as well as complex thoughts. Of course the re-cognition of the narrative world differs in order of magnitude from one object to another. This fundamental level of the imagination is perhaps the deepest in man since it appears to be the very cradle of literary expression. Thus the repeated telling of the ancient tales such as the Norse sagas, or the singing of epic verse, or the annual performance of *Don Juan* in the Hispanic world, or the singing of the folk ballad, all come together as a form of re-cognition of the community's past and therefore its identity. So it is at the very core of reading the novel: we begin with a basic re-cognition of the narrator as speaker on the one hand and his story as an operational medium of movement on the other. This structure, on which I shall elaborate, can initially be expressed in the figure below.

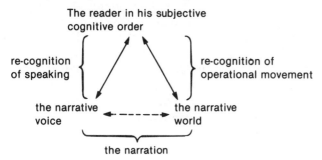

The re-cognition of ourselves and what is analogous to us, as centres of human awareness, is the ground for the experience of the novel. Beyond re-cognition there is a more powerful subjective force which I shall call *association*. This is, properly speaking, a function of memory which enables us to link parts of our intimate history with the awareness of the narrative events. These intimate feelings vary greatly in intensity from one reader to another but in all readers they provide us with the capacity to imagine the experience of the other person. In its most elementary form the novel is the story of the other person. Even those aspects of memory which are most private and not speakable, such as deep-seated fear and anxiety, can be drawn into the reading experience if the text happens to present the proper referential signs. The reader is integrating his personal past – both public and private – to the present of the narrative *presentation*. The potential power of association within the reading experience is almost unlimited; it can in the best cases make the other person an intimate reality for the self who is the reader.

There is yet another distinct possibility for the reader which derives directly from the level of association; this is the expansion of the experience beyond the limitations of self and object into an awareness of what is the common ground of human existence. The philosophical term *intersubjectivity* best expresses this common bond of consciousness. When the reader is engaged with the particulars of his intimate history and with the emerging personalities and events in the novel, he is on a level of identification which is the necessary consequence of the encounter, but it is a severe limitation of the reading experience to an affective awareness. The capacity to generalize is a basic disposition in most readers; this faculty is realized in the reading experience, the reflection of which involves self-awareness of the reader as reader and participant. It almost goes without saying that the degree of radical awareness available to the individual reader varies widely, but the capacity is present in most of us.[3] I shall consider *intersubjectivity* as a given facet of the reading experience, but shall return to consider it as a goal to be attained in the next chapter.

If I utilize my previous illustration of the reading experience I can now give a resumé of this discussion. (See figure on next page.) The triangle expresses the base of reader re-cognition of the narrative voice as speaker and the narrative world as a human medium. The intermediate stage adds the responses of affective association between the reader's intimate history and the emergent narrative. The last stage represents the full awareness of the reader as a part of a generalization of the common ground of 'self-in-world' reality.

Concept of intersubjectivity

reader's generalization of his reading experience through an awakened awareness of himself in his world	final stage
stage of affective association comprising the union of subjectivity and expression	intermediate stage
stage of re-cognition	

reader in his <u>Lebenswelt</u>   primary
stage

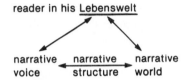

narrative   narrative   narrative
voice   structure   world

How is it possible to speak or write about a personal experience which is grounded in the subjectivity of each reader?[4] We can objectify the personal reading experience because we are considering a subjective phenomenon which is the result of two dialectical exchanges beyond the limitations of the self. The reader, as noted from the outset, is responding first to language from within a language community as a member and second to an organized text. Both of these relationships are dialectical and both have an explicit structure which can be studied. Yet both language and the literary text are only realized as human mediums of subjectivity. It follows that both language and the text are structures of intersubjectivity. Consequently, although it may be argued that subjectivity is closed to direct analysis and can only be approached through the shadow it casts, this is not the case with intersubjectivity of literary reading, which stands as the relationships developed between the reader and his reading.

If we begin with the dual concepts that the text has an intentional structure which can be fully described and that the reader has a reading experience which is uniquely his own, we can turn our full attention to the ways in which the intentionality of the text affects the reader. We shall see that the apparent contradiction is only superficial.[5] Of course, it also means that we shall have to reformulate the whole problem of validity of readings. Since we have accepted each reading experience as unique there can be no basis for saying that one reading is better than any other. However, if we have a clear understanding of the intersubjective relationship between reader and text and a competent analysis of the text, we can trace the reading experience from unique subjective experience back to initial encounter and actualization. I shall return to this important question in the next chapter, but let it suffice here to state that the aim of a discussion of readers and their respective readings cannot be held to be the attainment of a uniform legitimate interpretation, but rather a mutual enrichment of the respective readings.

The reader, I have insisted, encounters textual references of two different orientations in his dialectic of actualization. Certain references constantly move the reader beyond the text to the extratextual reality of objects while other references propel the reader into an awareness of the narrative speaker. These two orientations to which the reader responds in his reading make up the basic intersubjective structure of the novelistic reading experience.

If we examine a sample of very simple narrative discourse we can establish an outline for the intersubjective structure of reading: [6] 'She opened the window, looked out, and was lost in thought. The day had begun with the pristine clarity that makes even the routine minded clerk think of the infinite. Might not one agree with the philosopher that all men by nature desire to know!' We can separate the referential direction of these sentences in the following way. The first sentence ('She opened the window, looked out, and was lost in thought') is the narrative voice's presentation of the relational operations of the narrative world. The reference moves from the narration to the extra-discourse reality of the reader. This orientation is what I have termed the external reference. Returning to our sample discourse we can readily recognize that the second sentence ('The day had begun with that pristine clarity that makes even the routine minded clerk think of the infinite.') is quite different in direction. It begins as description of visibility in the narrative world but the narrative voice then expresses a condition of the narrative world that presents the condition as well as the personality of the speaker, who holds the opinion that clerks are usually dull. We have had both a condition of the narrative world – pristine clarity – and self-reference of the narrative voice by expressing a generalization about clerks. The two basic orientations are in motion now as the reader is being addressed with references to the world and self-references of the speaker. The third sentence ('Might not one agree with the philosopher that all men by nature desire to know!') is again different from the other two, for in this case the narrative voice is addressing himself to another who can only be the reader; thus with this sentence only the orientation of self-reference is actualized. The reading experience in this very limited sample has brought into play the whole of the intersubjective structure.

We can now begin to discuss the more complex patterns in which the intersubjectivity performs. The reader is the recipient of two directions of discourse. Both are the actualization of an internal relationship which moves out to its fulfilment in the reading experience. The internal relationship is the unfolding of the textual intentionality as the narrative voice presents the narrative world. The external relationships are the two directions discussed above. Therefore our intersubjective triangle now can be expressed in terms of relationships between centres of consciousness in the reading experience.

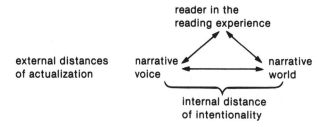

Chapter 3 examined in detail the internal distance between the narrative voice and the narrative world. We can now concentrate on the means by which the external distances of actualization are related to the internal distance of intentionality. It should be noted that in chapter 7 an argument will be made in favour of bringing analysis and interpretation into a unified critical model. The external distances are the separate actualizations of the narrative voice and of the presentation within the text, which come together in the unity of the reading experience. Thus the consideration of these relationships as separate rather than in the unity of the reader's experience is the result of our examination of the intersubjective structure rather than the subjective realization, which as I have said before is individual and unique.

Let us consider how the external distance between the reader and the narrative voice functions. The reader is situated within his *Lebenswelt* and it is only in this subjective context that he actualizes the references made by the text. Consequently, when the reader recognizes, associates with, and generalizes upon the narrative voice's self-reference he is granting to textual expression a quality usually reserved to a speaker in dialogue. Without a doubt the variation of self-reference from one text to another or even within the same text is great indeed, but my point is that it is always a factor of importance in the novel. No matter how impersonal and distant a voice may appear, self-reference is built into the language itself. Of even more consequence, the presentation itself can have a reflexive effect of revealing the personality of the viewpoint that perceived or conceived the perspective itself.

We must think of this relationship between the reader and the narrative voice as a dynamic encounter which is in process from beginning to end, developing the most subtle aspects of intentionality within the reading experience. The participation of the reader is not a mere passive reception. This impoverished view of reading has no relation to the reading of literature wherein the reader must actualize the expression into a construct of the imagination. The reader provides the entire subjective fabric which realizes the textual intentionality. Thus even in cases where the narrative voice provides detailed information on his personal opinions, these opinions imply a living personality which can only be provided by the reader's imagination.

The second external distance which we have identified moves between the reader and the narrative world as a focal point of operational movement and thought. The narrative world gradually assumes capacities of its own with a potentiality of autonomy from the narrator with the emergence of the independent voices of the fictional characters. In the narrative world we have not only objects and movement but also thought – all of which is, to a greater or lesser extent, under the control of the narrative voice. Consequently a diminishing in the authority of the narrative voice will have great consequences in the narrative world, for it is only through the authority of the speaker that the narrative world purports to be true. The reader responds to a vast array of extratextual references from the narrative world. All of the material objects, states of mind, and action within the narrative world are referentially directed to the reader's subjective world experience. Each descriptive word is meaningful only as a part of the subjective context of the reader and his capacity to actualize it on his own basis.

The external distances between the reader and the novelistic text are constantly changing, enlarging, and sometimes reversing themselves as the emergent phenomena of the reading actualize into the full reading experience. The background concept discussed in the previous chapter must be considered as the innermost development of the reading experience. It is in this aspect of the imaginative realization of the novel where narrative voice is linked with implicit author and where narrative world is defined and discovered against the background of the implicit world.

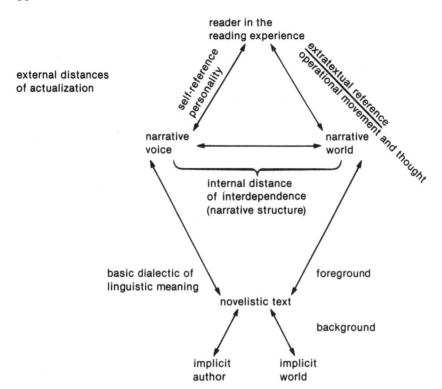

external distances
of actualization

reader in the
reading experience

self-reference
personality

extratextual reference
operational movement and thought

narrative
voice

narrative
world

internal distance
of interdependence
(narrative structure)

basic dialectic of
linguistic meaning

foreground

novelistic text

background

implicit
author

implicit
world

We can now expand the original illustration into a complete depiction of the intersubjective structure of the reading experience.

There still remains consideration of the question of the reader's capacity to recognize and respond to the textual references.

Without a doubt there is an implicit reader present in back of every novelist's effort to improve his writing. To concentrate on the revelation of the implicit reader, however, is to chase the will-o'-the-wisp of the author's intimate intentions. In my commentary on author I have distinguished carefully between personal intentions and textual intentionality. This is a distinction we must again call to mind in discussing the implicit reader. It is not the implicit reader which the writer had in mind that matters for the discussion, but rather the implicit reader which emerges from the intentionality of the text. It follows therefore that the measure of the implicit reader will be found in the text and not in psychological speculation about the writer.

Let me begin this discussion with a simple but basic notion about the reader. I propose that the real reader is the implicit reader of textual intentionality as long as he can read and actualize the text. A separation begins to make its mark when the real reader encounters textual passages which he cannot actualize, that is, re-cognize, associate, and generalize. When these blocks occur there are several possibilities for the reader. He can give up on the text as being beyond his capacity to understand; he can try to understand and fail but continue reading in spite of the handicap; or he can try to master the passage and succeed in attaining a working hypothesis to be proven by the ensuing context. Only the third possibility defines the implicit reader of textual intentionality. The greater the demands on the reader the more select the implicit reader becomes. The problem of the reader's capacity to actualize the text encompasses the essence of the theory of literature upon which this discussion is based and the hermeneutical process which I have also been discussing. At one end of the spectrum we have a text whose implicit reader is only definable as the most intimate 'other' whom the creative self addresses and in whom he creates. And at the other end the implicit reader is identifiable with linguistic competence and nothing more.

I can now make the second proposition of this enquiry. The gap – whenever there is one – between the real reader and the implicit reader must be closed if there is to be an enrichment of the reader.[7] If the gap remains open we have met with a genuine failure, an abortive creation, since in my view the reality of the novel, of the work of literature, resides in the actualization by the reader.[8] There are a great number of distinct factors which enter into the breakdown of imaginative communication, but in general we can approach the problem through the structure of intersubjectivity which I have developed.

The failure of actualization can thus be traced to an inability to grasp the referential aspect of the two relationships discussed as 'reader-narrative voice' and 'reader-narrative world.' When the reader cannot recognize, and therefore act upon, the narrative voice's self-reference or the extratextual references of the narrative world, an impasse has been reached. In the case of the novel this is usually not a matter of an opaque style, but rather an inability to grasp the internal distance of the novel, the internal structure of interdependence. If the present theory of the novel is valid, it follows that the external distances between the reader and the textual intentionality are dependent to a very large extent on a mastery of narrative structure. Therefore, on considering the specific case of the novel we can say that the implicit reader is one who has mastered the structure of the novel, and since the structure of the novel is analytically demonstrable, a failure in understanding the structure lies squarely with incompetence of the reader's imaginative faculty. There are, of course, hermetic symbols and images but there are no hermetic narrative structures. The structure of the novel, by definition, is the elaboration of the means of textual interdependence. I can best illustrate the reader's complex and often hidden intersubjective experience by this reader's commentary on two contemporary Hispanic American texts.

PRELIMINARY COMMENTARY: READER'S APPROPRIATION

In Mexico until very recently – by this I mean the post-revolutionary period – Mexicans found themselves psychological aliens in their own country because the mythical dimension, which survived the conquest in the basic religion of the people, could not be co-ordinated with the historical flow of events as these were ordered by a rational historical method. History and historiography have their domain and I do not imply a challenge to it. Yet it is abundantly clear to me that historical data devoid of the socio-ethnic context of the people who make history is pseudo-knowledge.

The primary function of myth is to provide cultural identity for man. It is in our mythical assumptions from Genesis to the Apocalypse that we are able to embrace mankind as a whole in one ideal history. The rational comprehension of history is also a part of our mental landscape. We are like the Roman god Janus; we have one face that is rational and chronologically orders the past but we also have another face that is irrationally seeking to be one with our ancestors.

Since my commentary is on literary texts and not religious scripture, it is important that we recognize that we are dealing with structures derived from myth and adapted to literary ends. However, there should be no doubt that the literary text is clearly dependent on the validity of the myth as internal history of belief in the people about whom the novelist writes.

The reader upon opening *La muerte de Artemio Cruz* by Carlos Fuentes, if he is of a reflective disposition, finds himself confronted with very puzzling questions, for many of which his previous readings of fiction will not have prepared him. The initial questions raised by the text fall naturally into the three groups formed by the language of the first, second, and third person narrators which alternate again and again for a total of thirteen times. No one of these narrators can be considered in isolation, because each is intimately bound up with the other two. Respect for the text leads me to take them in the order in which they are written and thereby consider their cumulative effect as well as their unique characteristics.

The novel opens in the voice of the first person narrator, who is barely regaining consciousness, sense impressions, and memory:

Yo despierto ... Me despierta el contacto de ese objeto frío con el miembro. No sabía que a veces se puede orinar involuntariamente. Permanezco con los ojos cerrados. Las voces más cercanas no se escuchan. Si abro los ojos, ¿podré escucharlas? ... Pero los párpados me pesan: dos plomos, cobres en la lengua, martillos en el oído, una ... una como plata oxidada en la respiración. (Mexico: Fondo de Cultural Económica 1962, p 9)

I wake ... the touch of that cold object against my penis awakens me. I did not know that at times one can urinate without knowing it. I keep my eyes closed. The nearest voices cannot be heard: if I opened my eyes, would I hear them? But my eyelids are heavy, they are lead, and there are brass coins on my tongue and iron hammers in my ears and something, something like tarnished silver in my breathing.

The extreme limitation of the narrative gradually emerges. The first person narrative is the stream of consciousness of a very sick man hovering between awareness of external reality and unconsciousness. The associations made by the narrator in his mind are a dizzying kaleidoscopic torrent of what he hears, feels, remembers, and thinks, as well as the names of his most intimate motifs:

Sí: el cura se hinca junto a mí. Murmura sus palabras. Padilla enchufa la grabadora. Esucho mi voz, mis palabras. Ay, con un grito. Ay, grito. Ay, sobreviví. Regina, me duele, me duele, Regina, me doy cuenta de que me duele. Regina. Soldado. Abrácenme, me duele. Me han clavado un puñal largo y frío en el estómago; hay alguien, hay otro que me ha clavado un acero en las entrañas: huelo ese incienso y estoy cansado (p 12).

Yes: the priest kneels beside me. He murmurs. Padilla plugs in the tape-recorder. I hear my voice, my words. Ay, with a cry. Ay, I cry out! Ay, I survived! I survived. Regina, I hurt. I hurt, Regina, I discover that I hurt. Regina, soldier: I hurt, embrace me. They have nailed a cold long dagger in my stomach. And someone, someone else has driven a spike into my guts. I smell that incense and I'm tired.

The significance of this intimate language will not be fully understood until we have read more than eighty-five pages.

The second person narrator enters as soon as the first person loses consciousness. The language is of a strange hermetic quality.

Tú, ayer, hiciste lo mismo de todos los días. No sabes si vale la pena recordarlo. Sólo quisieras recordar, recostado allí, en la penumbra de tu recámara, lo que va a suceder: no quieres prever lo que ya sucedió. En tu penumbra, los ojos ven hacia adelante; no saben adivinar el pasado. Sí; ayer volarás desde Hermosillo, ayer nueve de abril de 1959, en el vuelo regular de la Compañía Mexicana de Aviación que saldrá de la capital de Sonora ... (p 13).

You, yesterday, did the usual things, just as any day. You don't know if it's worth remembering. You would prefer to remember, there lying in the half darkness of the bedroom, not what has happened already but what is going to happen. In your half-darkness your eyes look ahead, and they do not know how to foresee the past. Yes: yesterday you will fly home from Hermosillo. Yesterday, the ninth of April, 1959, you will fly back in the regular flight of the Compañía Mexicana de Aviación, leaving Sonora's capital ...

The future tense is employed to narrate the past. The direction of the narrative is relentlessly aimed at the first person. We are thus now in the inner recesses of the subconsciousness of the man whose stream of consciousness we have just experienced. The immediate impact of the second person narrator on the novel is the imposition of a moral tone of prosecution. In this first appearance the second person reviews the adult life of Artemio Cruz as an accused person. The norms implicit in the second person's narration, we realize, are used as a part of a general condemnation being pressed upon the accused, neither as past nor as future but rather in an arrested immediacy of what Paul Tillich has called the present of moral judgment.

The hostility the second person feels toward the first person is the prelude to open warfare that will ensue, with the first person increasingly on the defensive and the second person ever bolder in his assault of the other. The closing words of the second person open up the third dimension of the narrative. For it is implicit in the opposition between the conscious and the subconscious mind that there is a unity to this polarity in a man who acts and participates in the world.

Bostezarás: cerrarás los ojos: bostezarás: tú, Artemio Cruz, él: creerás en tus días con los ojos cerrados (p 18).

You will yawn ... You will close your eyes and you will yawn. You, he, Artemio Cruz, who will believe in your days without seeing them.

The third person narrative voice is a hidden, privileged unobtrusive observer of behaviour and of the thoughts behind the acts. The third person narrator is the only one who narrates with an ordered sequence of discourse. This narration will begin throughout the novel with a precise date, the day of the month and year, and will contain a mounting mass of apparently irrelevant detail.

no decían nada nada hasta que vieron aparecer a la patrona y entonces la madre, que tenía esta idea de las conveniencias, fingió que continuaba una conversación que nunca se había iniciado y dijo en voz alta: ' ... pero ese modelo que parece mucho más lindo. No sé qué pienses tú, pero yo escogería ese modelo; de veras que está muy bonito, muy muy lindo.' La muchacha asintió, porque estaba acostumbrada a esas conversaciones que la madre no dirigía a ella sino a la persona que ahora entraba y le tendía la mano a la hija pero no a la madre (p 19).

they did not speak until the proprietress came into sight; then the mother, who had this notion of appearances, pretended to be carrying on a conversation that had never been begun, and said in a loud voice: 'but that one seems to me much the more beautiful. I don't know what you think but that is the one I would choose if the choice were mine. Really, it's very lovely.' Her daughter nodded, accustomed to these conversations that were not directed to her but to the person now entering, who took the daughter's hand but not the mother's.

The third person's narrative slowly expands before the reader as an eminently verisimilar world with specific historical events, a specific sociological context of the character in his thought processes. Finally, the reader is given something recognizable to hold onto and the comfortable narrative illusion of mimetic analogy is in operation.

Unfortunately for the comfortable reader the third person narration has a duration of some ten pages, after which the novel plunges forth again through the sequence of first, second, and then third persons in their established order. Thirteen times the spiral is repeated but each one is different from the previous one.

A mechanical view of this novel's structure becomes unavoidable. We read on in fascination but with the ever-growing feeling that this sequence of thirteen spirals of *yo, tú, él* is contrived. In spite of this annoyance, a world is taking shape and the parts are falling into place. The gratuitous images of the *él* begin to symbolize the plight of the person. The first principle of the structure of this novel should now be upon us. This mechanism I have been describing is the operating framework for the loom of our imagination. We are indeed moving in two separate directions: one vertical, *yo* moves us up against *tú* and then on to *él*; and yet we also move on a horizontal plane, for the *yo* of one sequence is only removed by some fifteen pages from the next *yo* and so on through the novel. Further, the horizontal plane of the *yo* is sequential; it is the empirical reality of the dying man and we are witnesses to the process of death from the initial stroke, to the hospital, to the operating room to the end. The *tú* is also sequential in that it is set in an intensifying pattern of assault on the reserves of the *yo*. Thus as the novel unfolds the *yo* is weakening and the *tú* is breaking through. Since the third person narration of *él* is dated we can slowly put the pieces together and reconstruct the chronology of his life.

It is obvious that this structure is, by its very nature, founded on the reader's double movement: the vertical, which we can call association and the horizontal, which is based on the continuity of memory. We in a very true sense have been given an imaginative loom and are weaving the tapestry of the life of Artemio Cruz.

Let us take a closer look at this tapestry we have woven. The events depicted are unmistakably in the course of modern Mexican history from Santa Ana to López Mateos; the colours are all authentically Mexican as we recognize that the sociological context of modern Mexico and the principal figure of Artemio Cruz is, in the profound sense of the term, a social symbol since he is an individual who reflects his society in his values, fears, delusions, and aspirations. Unravelling the fabric thread by thread will not add to our understanding of how it is that we amateur weavers have attained such depth of vision. There is one clue in the last statement of the dying *yo*:

Yo no sé ... no sé ... si él soy yo ... si tú fue él ... si yo soy los tres ... Tú ... te traigo dentro de mí y vas a morir conmigo ... los tres ... que hablaron ... Yo ... lo traeré adentro y morirá conmigo ... sólo ... (p 315).

I don't know ... don't know ... I am he or if ... you were he ... or if I am the three ... You ... I carry you inside me and you will die with me ... the three ... who spoke ... I ... I will carry him within me and he will die with me ... alone ...

The clue is the explicit recognition of the three narrators by the first person. What are the implications of this cosmogony of man? Where did it come from? The answer may appear ambitious but I think I can prove it.

The structure of the novel is based entirely on living Mexican myth, the ideal history of the Mexican people in which contemporary men can still find their identity. The vertical movements were woven into the horizontal movements, that is to say, the mythical identity of Mexicans has been developed in the chronology of rational history. The key questions of the structure are: why this sequence of narrators, and why this arrangement of the historical dates in a non-chronological pattern: 1941, 1919, 1913, 1924, 1927, 1947, 1915, 1934, 1939, 1955, 1903, 1889, 1959. And we must also consider the explication of why there are thirteen spirals or sequences.

Narrative structure as well as specific words may be said to have meaning; indeed, the meaning of the structure seems more fundamental than the meaning of words in much of modern fiction.

The implicit cosmogony in the representation of man through three voices has rested at the very centre of the Mexican myth of creation.

The high civilization of the Toltecs, founders of Tula and heirs of Teotihuacan, gave all the nations of Meso-America a common mythology of Quetzalcoatl, whose image, the plumed serpent, had for the Mexican people the same evocative force as the crucifix for Christianity. Even in the later Aztec epoch of the thirteenth to the sixteenth centuries, Quetzalcoatl was still venerated although his teachings were betrayed.[9]

What interests me here is the myth of Quetzalcoatl as the creator of man, which was deeply rooted in the Mexican people before Cortés and which survives today in folk religion and in this novel implicitly in the structure and explicitly in the voice of the unconscious mind.

The teaching of Quetzalcoatl explains that the heart of man is a centre in which cosmic opposites could be reconciled and united, that the nature of these opposites are mind and matter but that man is a composite which does not easily allow for reconciliation.[10] According to this myth the person has two intimate faces and one external face.

The myth of Quetzalcoatl shows that to unite matter, the body, and spirit, the mind, of which he is made, individual man must keep up a lifetime of painfully conscious struggle; he is a battleground in which the two enemies confront each other pitilessly. The victory of one or the other will decide whether he lives or dies; if matter conquers, his spirit is annihilated, for when the body perishes, he will have become a dog; if the spirit wins, the body will die but a synthesis will have been achieved that will shine like the sun in the hearts of other men. The symbol for the victory of spirit over matter is Xochitl (flower). This flowering war is life itself, and the battle is fought constantly but is summed up in groups of three.[11]

According to the myth, the chosen one of the gods is the dying man whose body is disintegrating and who thus has the opportunity of reconciling the opposites. In this myth it is the individual who brings about universal salvation. The danger threatening the Sun, life itself, is inertia and only the movement taking place in man's heart in this struggle between the contraries will maintain creation. The quality of life depends on the degree of harmony man is able to achieve in his struggle of contraries.[12]

As I have mentioned before, the myth of Quetzalcoatl is brought into the novel by the *tú* voice, the unconscious, in its second appearance:

Y si serás una cosa, y no la otra, será porque, a pesar de todo, tendrás que elegir. Tus elecciones no negarán el resto de tu posible vida, todo lo que dejarás atrás cada vez que elijas: solo la adelgazarán, la adelgazarán al grado de que hoy tu elección y tu destino serán una misma cosa: la medalla ya no tendrá dos caras: tu deseo será idéntico a tu destino (p 34).

And if you become one thing rather than another, that will be because in spite of everything you will have to choose. Your choices will not negate the possibilities remaining to you, or anything that you will leave behind by the act of choice: but those possibilities will be weakened, attenuated to the degree that today your choice and your destiny will become the same: the coin will no longer have two faces: desire and destiny will be one.

And more explicitly we have the mythical concept of man's destiny in the third speech:

desearás: cómo quisieras que tu deseo y el objeto deseado fuesen la misma cosa; cómo soñarás en el cumplimiento inmediato, en la identificación sin separaciones del deseo y lo deseado (p 62).

you will desire, and how you will wish that your want and its object might be one and the same; how you will dream of instantaneous fulfilment of the identification without separation of desire and that desired.

Finally the direct incorporation of the myth comes as Quetzalcoatl the man-god looked into the smoking mirror and discovered the meaning of life on seeing himself as his enemy; the second person speaks:

te convertirás en tu propio enemigo para continuar la batalla del orgullo: vencidos todos, sólo te faltará vencerte a ti mismo: tu enemigo saldrá del espejo a librar la última batalla (p 92).

and then you will become your own enemy, that the proud battle may go on: all others conquered, there will remain only yourself to be conquered: you will step from the looking glass and lead your last attack.

In the myth, man discovers egoism after carnal knowledge of woman as Artemio does after Regina. And also in the myth, memory of one who has lived spiritually flowers in the heart of man as the memory of his son Lorenzo does in Artemio's second person voice:

tú recordarás tu juventud por él y por estos lugares y no querrás decirle a Lorenzo cuánto significa para ti esta tierra porque de hacerlo quizás forzarías su afecto: recordarás para recordar dentro del recuerdo (p 168).

this place and his youth will let you remember your own youth, and you will not want to tell him how much this land means to you, because to do so might perhaps influence his feeling for you: you will remember in order to remember within your memory.

Once we have established the intimate relevance of the Quetzalcoatl myth to the novelistic structure we can make short work of the questions which otherwise would remain enigmatic.

The order of dated, third person narrations follows the Toltec horoscope for one born on 9 April 1889. I have worked out Artemio Cruz's horoscope according to the Toltec calendar for divination, the *tonalpohualli*.[13]

Artemio Cruz was born under the sign of Tecpatl, the stone knife. Virility characterizes one born under this sign. These people are gifted with great physical vigour and a great capacity for work. They shall be great entrepreneurs whose energy will appear to be inexhaustible. They are physical people who enjoy sexual love physically but not spiritually. They are rich in imaginative invention but are eminently practical people who have no use for sentiment. They will not hesitate to use physical force to get their own way. They thus have strong personalities and are audacious in the pursuit of their intended goal.

Each of the third person's narrations is the dated reading of the horoscope for one born on 9 April, 1889, that is, the sign of Tecpatl. These passages are the realization of his destiny.

The organization of the dated narrative follows the general pattern of the battle of the body (tiger) and the spirit (eagle) in sets of three. In the first set we move from Artemio at fifty-two years to thirty and then to twenty-four. We move into the past in quest of the meaning of Catalina, the wife who feels superior, and Regina the *soldadera* who loved him. The unknown character of Catalina and the memory of Regina become key motives in the isolation of Artemio Cruz.

The second set consists of Artemio at age thirty-five, thirty-eight, and fifty-eight. Now we move in the opposite direction as we encounter the mixture of cowardice and audacity that leads us to the image of alienation as Artemio looks into the mirror.

The third set presents Artemio at ages twenty-six, forty-five, and forty-nine, when his son is killed in Spain. Artemio Cruz escapes bodily death through daring but is unable to attain spiritual freedom. He is becoming a prisoner in his own hell of the material. His son Lorenzo is killed by an airplane, the eagle, and with him die Artemio's hopes of redemption for his own loss of ideals. The last set moves again in the counterdirection from age sixty-five to thirteen to birth as the last trajectory is made of the lifelong battle. The thirteenth part is the final synthesis in death. Artemio Cruz has no flowering in another; he dies his own victim. In being the most successful abuser of others he has abused himself most.

The thirteen divisions of the novel are established in keeping with the Toltec calendar of divination, which divides the cycle of life into thirteen periods which are dominated by a variable number of the twenty signs of the Toltec horoscope. It is therefore accurate to say that the structure of this novel is mythical.

The historical detail which abounds throughout the novel has its own chronological order which governs the rational external pattern of existence in the novel and in life. The novel is of course not concerned with political manoeuvers in Mexico, but rather with one Mexican's relations to his country and his people. The historical penetration of the power struggle under Calles in November 1927 is an exceptional passage because the life of Artemio Cruz is here enmeshed with the political power of the nation.

I have thus far considered what I believe to be the two main forces by which this novel is shaped. I have considered each in isolation, without due regard to their interrelations. But these interrelations are very important and very interesting. Myth has in various ways contributed to the development of history as an ideal history of the individual's identification.

If most of us were asked to distinguish history from myth, we would most likely claim that history ought to have a certain objectivity, a disinterested reconstruction of the facts about the past. To be objective usually means a rational ordering of details into a consistent explanation of the past. But if we accept such a premise for historiography we are forgetting that the historian is grounded in his subjectivity and, what is more, one of the principal values of reading history is to consider the subjectivity of reflection in the historian. Objectivity in history is limited to the methodology about which agreement is accessible. In the words of the Dutch historian Pieter Geyl:

> History is infinite. It is unfixable. We are always trying to state past reality in terms of certainty, but all that we are able to do is to render our impression of it. No book can reproduce more than a part of that reality, even within the confines of its particular subject; and each book contains something else, which gets mixed up with historical truth in an almost untraceable manner – I mean the opinion, or the sentiment or the philosophy of life, of the narrator; or in other words, the personality of the historian.[14]

This is exactly the point I wish to make. The group identity of the historian is available through the ideal history of myth.

The Mexican revolution is the epicentre of modern Mexican history and it is also a myth in the minds of Mexicans, a myth of national identity in which the Mexican wishes to believe, in spite of the facts which daily tell him that the revolution is dead. A myth which is fed from the inner spring of the myth of Quetzalcoatl. The betrayal of this myth is the theme of this novel and the price that is paid is alienation. The tragedy of Artemio Cruz is to have been born a Mexican and not discovered what this meant until his death.

Cien años de soledad was first published in Buenos Aires in 1967 and by 1970 had gone through twenty-seven printings in Spanish and three printings in the first year of its appearance in English. It is the fourth fictional publication of García Márquez and his first full-length novel.

Colombia may be regarded as consisting of two regions: the one an area of extreme jungle and wilderness occupying some sixty per cent of the country and having about two per cent of the population; the other the high mountain regions of temperate climate and awkward access through mountain passes and containing most of the population. The history of Colombia has been shaped to a very large extent by the geography of the land. Until the coming of the airplane, communication was clumsy at best and often impossible. The central fact of Colombian national life therefore has been exaggerated regional isolation.

Cien años de soledad is set in the mythical city of Macondo, but in the midst of the geographical reality of the Guajira peninsula, which has the sea on three sides and an infested swamp on the fourth land bridge. The principal town is Riohacha on the coast, but it is two days' travel through the swamp to Macondo. The narrative consists of twenty unnumbered chapters and as the title indicates covers one hundred years of history – the life span of Macondo, from Genesis to Apocalypse – and features the lives and fortunes of the founding family Buendía.

The narrator is privileged and unobtrusive as he allows the characters to search for meaning and maintains himself in an established position of chronicler. Nothing he narrates, no matter how unusual or extravagant, will cause even the slightest response in him. This is simply the way things were in Macondo, he is telling us. The opening lines of the novel set up the pattern that is to prevail throughout the ensuing 350 pages:

Muchos años después, frente al pelotón de fusilamiento, el coronel Aureliano Buendía había de recordar aquella tarde remota en que su padre lo llevó a conocer el hielo. Macondo era entonces una aldea de veinte casas de barro y cañabrava construidas a la orilla de un río de aguas diáfanas que se precipitaban por un lecho de piedras pulidas, blancas y enormes como huevos prehistóricos. El mundo era tan reciente, que muchas cosas carecían de nombre, y para mencionarlas había que señalarlas con el dedo (Buenos Aires: Sudamericana 1967, p 9).

Many years later, as he faced the firing squad, Colonel Aureliano Buendía was to remember that distant afternoon when his father took him to discover ice. At that time Macondo was a village of twenty adobe houses, built on the bank of a river of clear water that ran along a bed of polished stones, which were white and enormous, like prehistoric eggs. The world was so recent that many things lacked names, and in order to indicate them it was necessary to point.

The first line immediately situates the narrative that is to follow as remote memory even for the characters themselves. The process at work here is what I shall define as the creation of cosmogonic dimension. The second sentence ends with a most significant simile: 'un lecho de piedras pulidas, blancas y enormes como huevos prehistóricos.'

This interpretation of the rocks is exactly the same as that made by C.G. Jung in his analysis of a painting of rocks by the seashore made by one of his subjects of study:

I had not overlooked the fact that the boulders had surreptitiously transformed themselves into eggs. The egg is a germ of life with a lofty symbolical significance. It is not just a cosmogonic symbol – it is also a philosophic one. As the former it is the Orphic egg, the world's beginning; as the latter, the philosophical egg of the medieval natural philosophers, the vessel from which, at the end of the *opus alchymicum*, the homo nuculus emerges, that is, the Anthropos, the spiritual, inner and complete man.[15]

In this novel the search for the philosophical egg is the quest which dominates the thematic development.

The third sentence of the opening paragraph is the first clear indication that the narration is mythical, that it is an ideal history which is inseparable from external history because the narrative voice does not acknowledge a difference.

Time in the novel is the cosmogonic time of the complete cycle. The first line anticipates the moment in chapter 7 (p 115) when Aureliano Buendía faces the firing squad. After this moment has passed the narrative progresses in an apparently chronological time until the end of chapter 9. However, chapter 10 begins with the following words:

Años después, en su lecho de agonía, Aureliano Segundo había de recordar la lluviosa tarde de junio en que entró en el dormitorio a conocer a su primer hijo (p 159).

Years later on his deathbed Aureliano Segundo would remember the rainy afternoon in June when he went into the bedroom to meet his first son.

These words now anticipate chapter 17 (p 300). From chapter 17 on, time extends to the end of the novel in what appears to be a sequential pattern, only for us to discover that the entire temporal process from beginning to end was not chronological time at all, but rather the perfect timelessness of the circle where there is no beginning and no end, only now. The only sequence has been ours in reading, not Macondo's. Macondo is always there as the mythical Eden waiting for a reader to take it to the final dissolution.

The quest for the philosophical egg which will occupy the days of José Arcadio, the patriarch of the family, José Arcadio Segundo, the great-grandson of the patriarch, and Aureliano Babilonia, the great-great-great grandson of the old man, is the explanation of space in the novel. Macondo is the mythical egg of creation, as I shall discuss presently.

Finally, the narrator is the character Melquíades himself in his timeless knowledge, as he narrates for Aureliano so that he may discover who he is and what Macondo is. He is the microcosmos and Macondo is the macrocosmos and together they are creation from beginning to end.

The reader may now quite correctly ask himself what all of this has to do with history. I can best answer by quoting from García Calderón's account of the history of Colombia written in 1913:

In Colombia men have fought for ideas; anarchy there has had a religious character ... A Jacobin ardour divides mankind; the fiery Colombian race is impassioned by vague and abstract ideas ... These sanguinary struggles have a certain rude grandeur ... In Colombia exalted convictions are the motives of political enmities; men abandon fortune and family, as in the great religious periods of history, to hasten to the defense of principle. These men waste the country and fall nobly, with the semitic ardor of crusaders. Heroes abound in the fervor of these battles. Obedient to the logic of Jacobinism, Colombia perishes but the truth is saved.[16]

What García Calderón is referring to is the chaotic struggles of Colombia between the Liberals and Conservatives. In the civil war of 1899–1903, which the Conservatives won, there were more than 100,000 men killed.[17] What were they fighting for or against? Central government versus states rights, a union of church and state versus a separation, and other such speculative issues. What model of mankind could these men identify with, we may enquire; or, better yet, what sort of man was Aureliano Buendía?

El coronel Aureliano Buendía promovió treinta y dos levantamientos armados y los perdió todos. Tuvo diecisiete hijos varones de diecisiete mujeres distintas, que fueron exterminados uno tras otro en una sola noche, antes de que el mayor cumpliera treinta y cinco años. Escapó a catorce atentados, a setenta y tres emboscadas y a un pelotón de fusilamiento, Sobrevivió a una carga de estricnina en el café que habría bastado para matar un caballo. Rechazó la Orden del Mérito que le otorgó el presidente de la república. Llegó a ser comandante general de las fuerzas revolucionarias, con jurisdicción y mando de una frontera a la otra, y el hombre más temido por el gobierno, pero nunca permitió que le tomaran una fotografía. Declinó la pensión vitalicia que le ofrecieron después de la guerra y vivió hasta la vejez de los pescaditos de oro que fabricaba en su taller de Macondo. Aunque peleó siempre al frente de sus hombres, la única herida que recibió se la produjo él mismo después de firmar la capitulación de Neerlandia que puso término a casi veinte años de guerras civiles. Se disparó un tiro de pistola en el pecho y el proyectil le salió por la espalda sin lastimar ningún centro vital. Lo único que quedó de todo eso fue una calle con su nombre en Macondo. Sin embargo, según declaró pocos años antes de morir de viejo, ni siquiera eso esperaba la madrugada en que se fue con sus veintiún hombres a reunirse con las fuerzas del general Victorio Medina (p 94).

Colonel Aureliano Buendía organized thirty-two armed uprisings and he lost them all. He had seventeen sons by seventeen different women and they were exterminated one after the other on a single night before the oldest one had reached the age of thirty-five. He survived fourteen attempts on his life, seventy-three ambushes, and a firing squad. He lived through a dose of strychnine in his coffee that was enough to kill a horse. He refused the Order of Merit, which the President of the Republic awarded him. He rose to be Commander in Chief of the revolutionary forces, with jurisdiction and command from one border to the other, and the man most feared by the government, but he never let himself be photographed. He declined the lifetime pension offered him after the war and until old age he made his living from the little gold fishes that he manufactured in his workshop in Macondo. Although he always fought at the head of his men, the only wound that he received was the one he gave himself after signing the Treaty of Neerlandia, which put an end to almost twenty years of civil war. He shot himself in the chest with a pistol and the bullet came through his back without damaging any vital organ. The only thing left of all that was a street that bore his name in Macondo. And yet, as he declared a few years before he died of old age, he had not expected any of that on the dawn he left with his twenty-one men to join the forces of General Victorio Medina.

Obviously Aureliano Buendía is not the type of fictional character we are usually treated to. For we do not get the usual verisimilar view of appearance and mind; we are witnesses to a hero and to a heroic role and not to a personality. Aureliano Buendía is not a fictional character, he is an archetype of myth, as are all the personages of this novel.

Before we examine the roles played by the characters, it must be emphasized that the mythical dimensions of this novel are in no small part owing to the extraordinary language usage of García Márquez. A detailed analysis of his rhetoric would reveal a number of figurative devices of immense sophistication. Exaggeration of commonplace objects like magnets, false teeth, physical prowess, or natural phenomena is not a device of distortion, but rather of magnification, of expansion to greater-than-life dimensions which subsequently bring about an incompatibility of a conflict of dimensions. One recalls the queues outside the only toilet in the house when Meme brings home for a visit her entire school.

Another device used frequently is that of enumeration in groups of three and six. There is a sensual rhythm to the enumerations and a constant admixture of the physical and the imaginary. Still another important rhetorical device is the circularity of repetitions of events which creates the illusion of a frenzied activity. Together the rhetorical devices of García Márquez bring about a radical change in the referentiality of narrative discourse. In our reading of narrative discourse, the usual pattern has a dual reference. In part the reference is self-reference by the narrative voice to himself and in part it points beyond the immediate context to an implicit context of world. In vivid contrast to this process, García Márquez has created a narrative where the entire referentiality moves toward a centrifugal point which can only be identified at the end of the novel. Consequently, what normally would be self-reference on the part of the narrative voice is here reference to the timeless point of revelation, and what usually would be a reference to world is here reversed. The explicit context of world history and geography where empirical reality reigns, that is, the reader's sense of the real, now becomes a continuous regression toward the greater-than-life primeval source in myth. The novel is at the centre and all things refer to it.

There are six archetypes in the novel. First, the temptress, destroyer of men, like the sirens. There are four women who participate: Amaranta, Remedios la Bella, Renata Remedios, and Amaranta Ursula. Second, the mother, giver of life and nest builder; there are four women here also: Ursula, Pilar Ternera, Santa Sofía de Piedad, and Fernanda del Carpio. Third, the female as goddess of life and death. The two are: Rebeca, who symbolizes death, and Petra Cotes, who symbolizes life. The male archetypes are also three. First, the hero as warrior, with José Arcadio son, his brother Aureliano, his son Arcadio, and his brother's son Aureliano José, that is, the two brothers and their sons. Second, the hero, seeker of truth; we have already mentioned these three: José Arcadio, the patriarch, José Arcadio Segundo, and the last Aureliano. Third, the archetype of hero as lover is represented by two characters: Aureliano Segundo, who loves women, and José Arcadio the fourth, who loves young boys.

The roles of the men and women of this novel, viewed together, are a strange admixture of commonplace, natural, and supernatural facets. But taken separately we have a fuller grasp of their unity. Thus we have three roles for women: mother, temptress, and symbol; and three roles for men: warrior, lover, and philosopher. But all the characters of the novel share a common world. It is in this world that they must play their role, and it is in this role-playing that we can understand their significance to each other and to us.

The cycle of war is anticipated in the first line of the novel although it is not developed until chapter 5. In this cycle we have the hero as warrior, foremost of whom is Aureliano Buendía. The two brothers José Arcadio and Aureliano are initiated to sexual union by the same woman – the happy, outspoken, provocative Pilar Ternera, who asked nothing and gave openly her love and understanding. The brothers go through the initiation with opposite results, one leaves and the other stays, but both have sons by Pilar Ternera. These four shall be the warriors of the novel, but only Aureliano shall die a natural death. The hero as warrior is, therefore, Aureliano Buendia, who having become a man through sexual initiation moves into a life of a succession of trials he must somehow survive. Through it all he is supported by the prophecy of his second mother Pilar Ternera.[18] He leaves Macondo only when he is to begin his cycle as warrior, and Macondo as the birthplace of the hero becomes the source for the hero, the quietest place on earth, which is described in Siberian myth as 'the place where the moon does not wane, nor the sun go down, where eternal summer rules and the bird everlastingly sings, there where the warrior came to consciousness.'[19]

But, wherein lies the heroic stature of the warrior who only knows defeat and even surrender? His heroic deed is survival. He outlived all of his sons to die in the extreme solitude of a standing tree. Aureliano Buendía has been blessed by the augury of Pilar Ternera so that neither water nor fire, iron nor anything else should ever do him harm. And through these trials his heaviest burden becomes life itself, so that he can say that one does not die when he ought to but when he can. His hero-deed is to endure life in solitude. In his old age he makes the fish of gold with the ruby eyes only to melt them down again and begin anew. His is the cycle of life in its continuous regeneration. Macondo, as I shall discuss, is one full turn in the cycle from Genesis to Apocalypse that Aureliano's fabrication of fish symbolize.

The other warriors in the novel are not heroes because they do not endure. The temptresses Amaranta, Remedios la Bella, Renata Remedios, and Amaranta Ursula are lures that destroy men like Pietro Crespi but they are harmless against the hero warrior. The temptress serves once again to separate the common man from the hero.[20]

The next archetype relationship that is created in this novel is that of women as cosmogonic symbols and men as lovers. As I have indicated above, there are two pairs of characters to be considered.

Rebeca is not a Buendía but is taken into the family. In her youth she is obsessed with the eating of earth and is possessed by the spirit of her dead ancestors. She grows in beauty and acquires conventional ways, but in a time of stress she will revert to her former ways. She becomes a dark symbol of the earth-mother as she represents death and everything that dies. She is the dark side of the moon that claims all that lives to death so that the process of regeneration can go on. She dies with a return to the embryo.

Rebeca murió a fines de ese año. Argénida, su criada de toda la vida, pidió ayuda a las autoridades para derribar la puerta del dormitorio donde su patrona estaba encerrada desde hacía tres días, y la encontraron en la cama solitaria, enroscada como un camarón, con la cabeza pelada por la tiña y el pulgar metido en la boca. Aureliano Segundo se hizo cargo del entierro, y trató de restaurar la casa para venderla, pero la destrucción estaba tan encarnizada en ella que las paredes se desconchaban acabadas de pintar (p 292).

Rebeca died at the end of that year. Argénida, her lifelong servant, asked the authorities for help to knock down the door to the bedroom where her mistress had been locked in for three days, and they found her on her solitary bed, curled up like a shrimp, with her head bald from ringworm and her finger in her mouth. Aureliano Segundo took charge of the funeral and tried to restore the house in order to sell it, but the destruction was so far advanced in it that the walls became scaly as soon as they were painted.

The opposite symbol to Rebeca is not Amaranta, her partner in the love-hate duel of adolescence, but rather Petra Cotes, who is the light symbol of mother earth, the world creatrix. She encompasses all life and through her fecund spirit nourishes all and generates life. Her status as symbol is enhanced by the fact that she does not give birth to a child. Hers is the fecundity of life itself. When the world is worn out she loses her lover.[21]

The fertilizing male is Aureliano Segundo, whose love-making bouts with Petra are symbolic rituals of fertilization of the world as all things multiply through the couple's action. Aureliano Segundo has no other function in life than that of the sexual union with Petra to regenerate nature and with his wife Fernanda to regenerate the family. He, as representative of male fertility, also has an opposite, not his twin brother

José Arcadio Segundo who shall be of the philosophers' cycle, but his son José Arcadio, the degenerate lover of boys, who represents sterility. In this second set we again see the theme of generation and regeneration of life but within a larger grouping which I have already identified as the cycle of Beginning to End, for each generation moves closer to dissolution.

The last grouping of characters is fundamental to the theme of the novel. The central figure is Melquíades as the archetype of the wise old man, father knowledge.[22] The followers of this eiron figure are the three generations of Buendía men who relentlessly pursue the quest for the philosophical egg. The first is José Arcadio, the patriarch, the second is his great-grandson José Arcadio Segundo, and the last is Aureliano, the last survivor of the clan and the discoverer of the secret.[23]

José Arcadio begins the search for the philosophical egg in the garden of Eden, which is Macondo at the beginning. His was the age of innocence but he was not able to go beyond the mediaeval period in his search back through other ages. He finally reached the keys of Nostradamus and was so moved that he could only speak in Latin. As a would-be philosophical hero he is condemned in death to the tree of life for not having found the source of all. The patriarch's fatal error is not to look for the answer in women. The woman represents the totality of what can be known, but it is the hero who shall come to know. As he progresses in the naïve stages of innocence, Ursula is constantly undergoing the transformation of life for him. She is never ahead of him, although through her activity she always gives him more than he can comprehend. She provokes, guides, encourages him to break through; she reaches the outside world and like Pandora releases the demons of the twentieth century on an unsuspecting Macondo. The age of innocence ends when Ursula returns, but José Arcadio cannot find the sought-for unity and must die in solitude. Ursula's eyes fail; as the primordial woman of all myths of quest she is sustained by her eyes of understanding, but her task has ended. Ursula dies in chapter 17, after having lived out her experience of innocence, plentitude, decline, and at the time of her death, the Minotaur, the monster half-bull, half-man, is killed as a symbol of the end of a period.

José Arcadio, the great-grandson, has turned to the quest with unshakable determination after having suffered the massacre of the banana workers. But for all his dedication his ultimate achievement is only to serve as a bridge between the work of the first of the Buendías and the last.

The last of the Buendía family is Aureliano, the son of Renata Remedios and Mauricio Babilonia. He is the final incarnation of the quest for the cosmogony of Macondo. The revelation that comes on the last pages of the novel is central to all myths of all peoples. It is in the most direct sense of the word a universal of man's search for meaning.

Aureliano and his Sanskrit manuscripts written by Melquiades stand there facing each other: the seeker and the found. We are at the culmination of the search. It ends when Aureliano understands that he and his goal are the outside and the inside of a single mystery which is life and which is the mystery of all life, that is, of Macondo.

The great deed of the philosophical hero is to come to the knowledge of the unity, implicit in multiplicity and then to make it known.[24]

As the philosopher hero the last Aureliano is in the apocalypse of his cycle as a man, but he is also now the one who reveals the significance of life. His wisdom is far deeper than that of the hero as warrior personified by the first Aureliano. The symbol of the first Aureliano is the virtuous sword, of the last, the book. The adventure of the first is to win life, to endure; the adventure of the last is to win knowledge.

The manuscripts of Melquiades are cryptic, written in Sanskrit, and internally coded because they are the guardians of the cosmic egg. The inspiration needed to break through the last barriers comes to Aureliano as he sees the body of his dead son inflated to the shape of an egg. He at once symbolizes the beginning and the end of life, genesis and apocalypse, birth and death. And this finally is the meaning of life. Men are born, live, and die, and they create worlds that are born, live, and die, but beyond them lies the unity of all in a singular, unitary moment and this is the cosmic egg. The last lines of the novel require some comment:

pues estaba previsto que la ciudad de los espejos (o los espejismos) sería arrasada por el viento y desterrada de la memoria de los hombres en el instante en que Aureliano Babilonia acabara de descifrar los pergaminos, y que todo lo escrito en ellos era irrepetible desde siempre y para siempre, porque las estirpes condenadas a cien años de soledad no tenían una segunda oportunidad sobre la tierra (p 351).

for it was foreseen that the city of mirrors (or mirages) would be wiped out by the wind and exiled from the memory of men at the precise moment when Aureliano Babilonia would finish deciphering the parchments, and that everything written on them was unrepeatable since time immemorial and forever more, because races condemned to one hundred years of solitude did not have a second opportunity on earth.

The narration of the Buendía family and of Macondo cannot be repeated from the beginning of time and for always because it always is; there are no second trials for man. We live only once, but as each lives his life and as each society goes its way both man and his creation are walking a well-worn pathway to oblivion and destruction.

The sacred text which Melquiades knew and was paraphrasing in its Colombian incarnation is the Buddhist scripture on the end of the macrocosm-society: 'Sirs, after the lapse of a hundred thousand years the cycle is to be renewed; this world will be destroyed by flood and by wind.'[25]

But the closest depiction of the dissolution of the world is in the old Norse *Voluspá*. The chief of the family asks the wise old one what will be his fate and that of his family. The wise man allows him to hear the verses of doom:

> Brothers shall fight and fell each other
> And sisters' sons shall kinship stain
> Hard is it on earth, with mighty whoredom
> Ax-time, sword-time, shields are sundered
> Wind-time, wolf-time ere the world falls.[26]

The point I am making here is a basic one. *Cien años de soledad* is rooted deeply in myth as ancient as man's need to know and partakes of this universal reality freely.

We have come to the end of the analysis and interpretation of these two complex novels and a few words of summary are in order.

What has been given to use in these narrative worlds by these myths and symbols, by this search for the lost unity of man himself and of man's world? The primary truth is that man as represented by these fictional characters has a profound dissatisfaction with his situation, with that which Malraux has called the human condition. These men feel themselves to be torn, separated, and somehow locked into solitude. Most men cannot explain even to themselves what it is that they are separated from, since they have no precise memory of the separation. Man's memory and, consequently, man's records of reality make up the substance of history. But the historian himself cannot say why he has been driven to capture the past.

Deep within the essence of human awareness there are echoes which Jung has called the collective unconscious which are expressed in the sacred texts of all civilizations. This primordial awareness is an awareness of the split that has taken place in man himself and in his world. This is the substance of all myth. If you want more concrete terms, I can say that myth is the built-in nostalgia in man for a lost paradise that he has never seen but feels as a unity of oppositions. Religion has usually called this nostalgia the need for God. Unamuno has called it 'hambre de Dios.'

The life of man, viewed from a detached perspective, is but an insignificant thing in comparison with the forces of nature.

Artemio Cruz was a slave to material power. He worshipped the material world because it was greater than anything he found in himself and because all his conscious thoughts were of things. The essence of Artemio Cruz's mind is self-ignorance and self-deception. We must be able to see him as an archetype in which we all share, for our conscious views of what life ought to be seldom correspond to what life really is. We as men refuse to acknowledge within ourselves and our friends the raw power of the instinctively carnivorous surge of energy that the organic cell is. We colour the whole affair in a pleasant fable of untruth.

The truth is that Artemio Cruz, and men generally, are made up of this hungry power for growth which history records, but he is also that inner awareness, so belatedly recognized by him, that urges man to look into the mirror and see himself. Aureliano through the intercession of Melquiades finally understands that life is a struggle against solitude.

Alienation to Artemio Cruz, solitude to the Buendía family, it means the same, isolation and separation and the loss of unity which can be found in the love of another.

In conclusion, therefore, I propose that the real reader is the implicit reader of the text when he has mastered the structure of the novel. Differences in interpretation among various readers can be fruitful to all if the readers are competent. This conclusion means that the common base for discussion among readers is the verifiable analysis of the internal distance of the novel. If this common base is not present it is not possible to speak or write about the reality of the novel, for each reader will be locked within the confines of his own subjectivity without any point of reference. The novel as an intersubjective experience presupposes the rational capacity to examine, understand, and communicate with others and the affective capacity to associate the text with our own *Lebenswelt*.

On the preceding pages I have transcribed the intersubjective experience of reading *La muerte de Artemio Cruz* and *Cien años de soledad*. These commentaries have not been organized in accordance to a formal method of analysis, for to have done this would have necessitated my having a system of analysis which was fully integrated to interpretation. These commentaries represent the first stage in a complete hermeneutics which seeks to establish the deepest ties between symbolic language and self-understanding. The purpose of these initial commentaries has been to conquer the remoteness, the distance between the text and myself. By overcoming this distance I have appropriated the texts' meaning to myself. Symbolic language is essentially irreducible to univocal meanings, but what I do hope to accomplish in subsequent chapters is a reflective presentation which will give my reader an analytical guide to the reading experience. In other words the common base for interpretations will be provided.

6

The critic

On occasions when literary critics have written of the aims they pursue they have without exception revealed the aesthetic premises of which they depend. For example, it is not uncommon to read a critical statement of purpose which maintains that there is a dark side to the literary work and that the function of criticism is to cast light on this dark side, to explain to the reader what is not clear, and in general to act as an interpreter between the text and the reader. To be sure, there are a number of statements of purpose which differ in detail or in substance with this one.[1] Critics as a rule do not ask the question which must come before the functional query. Why explain, if that is what the critic is to do, literature, and not history, philosophy, or some other body of writings? The value, if there is one, of literature is not a self-evident truth; a value must be established before the critic can go on to fix his position in relation to literature and readers of literature.

Literature has two fundamental values which are the justification for its existence and its study; it is of value as language, as the most elaborate expression of a language community's identity, and as one of the most direct forms of self-knowledge attainable for those who read and those who write. Certainly self-knowledge has been the quest of philosophers and religious teachers throughout history, but the basic difference between literature and philosophy is that in literature the full realm of subjectivity is freed to engage itself in its conception of reality, and the difference between religious teaching and literature is that religious thought depends on faith, which is sometimes unavailable. We must not lose sight of the fact that both religion and philosophy often merge into the literary work. The truth of literature is a subjective and an intersubjective truth and it cannot purport to describe an extrasubjective reality. The modern novel has been used as a sociological document by a number of contemporary investigators; nevertheless its validity does not rest on the information it provides about the world depicted within. It is valuable as a social document in the sense that the novel expresses the intrasubjective structures which operate within a given community.

If the value of literature is subjective and intersubjective it follows that the aims of criticism should also be related to these values. Consequently, the statement of purpose we considered above, which I believe is the prevalent one today, must be changed and redirected to the reader. In this way we can restate the aims of criticism as directed to the reader himself in his subjectivity and not to a text whereby an objective status is presupposed. There is not a dark side to the work of literature, but there are deficient readers of literature. Therefore the aims of criticism are to regain imaginative perception for the readers, and in the case of the novel to open the imagination to the inner distance of the novelistic structure so that the reader's relationship with the text can be examined and understood.

This critical activity thus aims at producing a certain necessary competence in the reader. A second and higher aim of criticism is to engage in the critical dialogue with the tradition of literature as we have inherited it. This second aim seeks to attain a cultural participation for us. The highest aim of criticism, however, must be enrichment of our awareness as readers. To improve the quality of life has always been an aim of human activity and literary criticism is no exception. The competence of the reader is an attainable goal if the readers are willing to share the text directly with others and explain the basis for their observations. Most literary critics engage in this dialogue of readers, but only those who share their method of reading can contribute much to the reading of others.

Another kind of critic is the scholar critic, who is largely concerned with the cultural participation. This indispensable member of the intellectual community on the whole assumes that he is addressing competent readers who have mastered the texts in question, but who have not yet fully appreciated the specific works within the tradition of civilization. The historical dimension is consequently the scholar's background against which he examines the text. The danger which lurks in the wings of historical criticism is the assumption that the historical dimension of the text is or should be part of the reading experience. The reader's historicity is the only valid historical base; we in the twentieth century can only read a seventeenth- or twelfth-century work from our historical position. We cannot separate ourselves from our historical ground. The participation in the cultural tradition consists of an acute awareness of distance and of the universal bonds which transcend the distance between the text and ourselves.

The critic whose aim is to enrich the reader's experience is concerned not only with the competence of the reader and with his cultural participation but also with seeking to open the reader's awareness to his own subjectivity. When the reader can recognize the paths which his subjective response to the text has taken in the reading experience he is engaging in hermeneutical interpretation. There is an ultimate reintegration of the reader's thoughts on the text when he takes on the attempt to share his experience with others.

In chapter 10 I will examine the problems of the genre as we know it today. A scheme of synchronic-diachronic division of narrative fiction is there proposed as a means of facilitating critical discussion. This rather complex organization of narratives is needed only if the critical aim is the full intersubjective study of the reading experience.[2] Obviously the competence of the reader is attainable only with a formal understanding of the work and the more demanding cultural participation can be achieved through the diachronic knowledge of the changing modes and developments in the history of literature. The third aim of criticism – enrichment of the reading experience – demands an open form of classification which can integrate the formal and historical aspects of the works. This necessity is unmistakably pressing because the realm of enquiry is the intersubjective structure of the reading experience and not the isolated text nor the historical milieu. As I have pointed out on several occasions, an intersubjective study operates on basic principles of the self's life-world. The principles of awareness between the reader and the text are the four outlined in chapter 10: (1) that the purported reality of the narrative world is analogous to the reader's reality because of the axiom that the real has a common unity (parallel narrative world of action, character, and space); (2) that the purported reality of the narrative world expands beyond the reader's reality because of the axiom that rational order has its own common unity (expanded narrative world of action, character, and space); (3) that the purported reality of the narrative should conform to the rational order of the narrator and the implicit author because of the axiom that reality is rational (transformational narrative world of action, character, and space); and (4) that the purported reality of the narrative world is temporarily determined by the reader because of the axiom that reality is entirely temporal (becoming narrative world of action, character, and space).

All four aesthetic principles are viable and all are equally valid since each expresses a basic and ancient way of thinking about reality. When Heraclitus, for example, stresses that the world is one, to all who are aware, he is expressing the notion which is basic to our first aesthetic principle.[3] Similarly, when Parmenides proposes that thought and the thinker make up a single unity, he is formulating a metaphysical ground for the second aesthetic principle of imaginative expansion.[4] The third aesthetic of transformation of the real in order to conform with the rational order of man is based on the belief that man is the dominant centre of the universe and with time can accomplish what he wills. One of the most ancient expressions of this anthropomorphic universal is in the fragments of Leucippus, who states that nothing happens by chance, but rather according to rational necessity.[5] Since man is the only rational creature it follows that man can know and do what he wills. The fourth aesthetic principle is found expressed throughout the philosophy of Heraclitus, who sees reality as a flux and as the constant realization of potentiality.[6] So it is that the reader can be more than the imaginative medium of actualization; he can become a full partner in the creative act by providing not only the referential fulfilment of discourse, but also the very context through his associations.

After this preview of chapter 10 we can return to the questions of critical aims and practice. If the critic is dedicated to the greater enrichment of the reader, then it follows that he must seek to attain understanding of all aesthetic positions without granting one dominance over the others. When an abstract concept of purported truth is the guiding light by which the critic operates, he substitutes dogma for reality, which is the reading experience. Thus it may now be seen clearly that I was not merely rewording the critical aim of clarifying the text. I propose a complete redirection of the critical purpose from the text to the reader.

A first observation on human activity which can be our base for an ethics of criticism is that, taken as a whole, man's personal actions constitute a continuous effort at expression. 'Living' for the individual can thus be considered as a continuous but faulty process moving from personal intentions and aspirations to partial realization.

A second observation is one which I have made before: that the human perception of reality is constituted within a value structure. Consequently an expression of values is present in everything we do. In every human act there is an explicit or an implicit expression of value. The world as that which is to be perceived appears to be given without values in an established order which we have but to comprehend, but the world which we encounter is not this established order at all. We see our world within our order of discriminations, needs, and urgency. A table to the furniture salesman, the craftsman, the freezing man in the mountains, the drowning man in the sea, appears very differently because of the personal context of values. Consequently we can say that value to us is the mode of perception, implicit in our action, through which we encounter the world and appropriate it to ourselves. Let us therefore ask ourselves now, what is the value of literary criticism and even before this question, let us ask the primary one; what is the value of literature?

In a recent interview George Steiner was asked what relation literature has to ethics. His response can serve to further our consideration of values:

I had been brought up in a world that believed that if people read good books, went to museums, subscribed to the opera, and loved symphonies, certain decencies would follow. There was a deep belief that human savagery and hatred and killing were caused by lack of education. People who read won't believe in stupid murderous slogans. People who love Beethoven are not going to do certain things to other people. People who spend their lives reading Virgil or Goethe or Shakespeare or Racine will understand each other across disagreements. If we can say with a cold laugh today, 'How stupid. We should have known it wouldn't work,' well, we are the poorer for that knowledge. It was a very reasonable thing to hope for and a very noble hope. I desperately wanted to find out what went wrong. Why did this deep, tremendous house of culture go over like a house of cards the moment it faced political terror and violence?[7]

Steiner's ensuing discussion presents the frustration and failure of humanistic education, but without finding the reasons why these expectations proved to be false. What was mistaken in the ideal concept that man can substitute dialogue for violence? Let us examine the question within the context of literary criticism and the novel.

The traditional answer, which was echoed in Steiner's views, is based on the theory that value is a personal judgment and reality is objective, separate, and valueless. With such an approach it is almost inevitable that a liberal individualism would propagate the concept that the value of literature is the making of the educated man whose cultural sensibility demonstrates that he is at the pinnacle of civilization. Similarly the traditional view has been that the value of literary criticism is in the aid it provides in the education of the élite man. I propose that the traditional view of these values is mistaken because the premise of the opposition between value and reality is an error.

Reality to each man cannot be conceived as valueless. The universe for each individual is the cohesive unity brought about by his value structure.

The moment we appropriate a thought or a thing it enters into our value structure and it takes on the value which is the priority of the encounter. Thus, instead of a theory of opposition between value and reality, let us begin with a radical unity. We know the feeling of satisfaction precisely when our value system is in accord with our milieu. This is to have what we need and desire when we need it and desire it. What, we may ask, is the value of literature and of criticism based on this concept that man's experience at all levels is a value experience? The only answer is that literature has value only if it promotes and satisfies the needs of the reader, and criticism has value only insofar as it also fosters the satisfaction of the reader.

I have consistently sought to avoid a pluralistic subjectivism throughout this book by focusing attention on the intersubjective common ground of man, and this I must insist upon again in this discussion. Beyond the subjective exigency of the value we must search for the intrasubjective structure of value to all readers. For each reader, value is an anticipation of some measure of fulfilment in the reading experience in which he is about to engage himself; it is in this sense the project of reading itself. Consequently if he does not find that the experience has justified his value anticipation, he will judge the activity to have been deficient.

We can now turn our full attention toward the question of value in the literary critic's activity. If the critic refuses to grant the work an objective reality divorced from the reader his undertaking can only be directed to the reader. The value of criticism presents itself not as the lucid and sometimes brilliant observations of the critic, but rather as a dedication to the human reality of the reading experience, his own and that of other readers. This is a concept of mutual enrichment which has been with us for a long time as the ideal of the teacher-learner, but unfortunately has been overlaid with countless layers of self-promotion.

Thus the individual reader must remain the beginning and the end of criticism, for the value of criticism is to be found in the enrichment of the personal reading experience. The experience of this value is an experience of shared subjectivity. The value concept of enrichment of the reading experience must be explored further in order to recover its practical sense within the framework of action. We have established the dual references of language in the reading experience in quest of a theory of interpretation. It is necessary to bring these basic concepts into the present discussion so that the action of reading and the value of enriching the reading can be properly identified. Because there are two referential aspects to the language in the reader's experience, there are also two aspects of value. First, we have knowledge in the third person. Here the language refers to an exterior world and there is an openness and a receptivity in the reader. The world appears as a unity of objects proposed for action. The effort here is to determine as clearly as possible the milieu of the novel in relation to the milieu which surrounds the reader. We try to fix the meaning of words in our discourse with the novel, for we are engaged in trying to understand the world in relation to our own. We thus seek a pattern which we can grasp as social reality. We hope to triumph over diversity by unity, over unrelated incidents by pattern. This form of knowledge is the domain of our participation in life as social beings. The greater enrichment of the reader's social being is achieved through dialogue with other readers, and the critic in this context is a reader's reader who seeks to engage him in dialogue.

In addition to third person knowledge we also have first person knowledge. The self-reference discussed as a fundamental aspect of the narrative's language ultimately comes to bear on the reader's self-knowledge. As readers, we are mostly scattered amid the narrative world-exterior world relationship. The reference of most narrative worlds is away from ourselves and into the third person's world, but we also have the language of self-reference by the narrator which elicits a language of self-reference in the reader. The reader's awareness of his own presence in the literary work comes from an intuition of actualization as it happens. When the reader becomes aware of his relationship to the narrator and the narrative world he has achieved a radical self-awareness as a reader and as a producer of the experience which is the novel. The ultimate achievement of this radical self-awareness as the agent of actualization is self-knowledge.

Thus we have two aspects of enrichment as the literary value. One is the enrichment of the reader as a social being and the other is the enrichment of the reader as self-knowledge. These are not opposed to each other; indeed, they are complementary facets of the central concept of reality as the experience of world through the subjective value structure. Thus these two versions of value are interdependent as the social and personal sides of reality.

The critic as a reader's reader shares the same experience and participates in the same value. The only difference is that the critic seeks openly to engage in the dialogue of interpretation that will bring forth with clarity the position of the reader and will make the reading experience itself the object of attention. Consequently, by achieving an enrichment of the reading experience for himself as a social man and as a person, the critic has fulfilled the same function for other readers.

Criticism can never rival the literary text without denying it. If criticism overshadows the original text, the critic has become an author and has substituted his text for the original. The critical act is devoted to the original text and to an analysis of it in order better to understand the experience of reading it.[8] In conclusion, therefore, the critic serves other readers by first establishing the internal distance of the text and second by exposing his own subjectivity in response to the text in search of an intersubjective dialogue with other readers. The general divisions of the critical activity are therefore analysis and interpretation. Each part has its own logic, its own laws of operation, and its own aim, but they are part of the same integral activity, which pursues the greater enrichment of the reading experience as knowledge of social participation and as self-knowledge.

The ethics of criticism are broadly defined as the activity of seeking the greater enrichment of the reader because of a mutual respect. Just as we can never have true dialogue without mutual respect, we will not have a genuine enrichment of the reading experience without respect for the reader.

The double path of enrichment is open to all critics whatever their specific function among the multiple facets of criticism, for it is an ethical goal and not a method which I have described in this chapter. An ethical sense of literary criticism comes from the consideration of those radical questions: why study literature? and, for whom do we write our commentary? There are other goals than those which I have described, but in my opinion there are insufficient grounds for giving serious consideration to them. The ivory tower concept of the pursuit of truth and beauty becomes meaningless if we objectify truth and beauty. The only meaning of these words which I have been able to understand is that of a human value judgment born out of dialogue with another.

At this stage let us be reminded once again that the premise of this book places the reader at the centre of literary criticism and not on the side as the consumer of the literary text. If my view of the function of the literary critic be a modest one, it is owing to my appreciation of the reading experience. I offer the following pages not as a model of literary criticism, but as an illustration of the function of criticism as I perceive it. My commentary is on the narrative fiction of the Spanish author Benito Pérez Galdós and the Argentine Julio Cortázar.

INTERMEDIATE COMMENTARY: CRITIC'S GENERALIZATION

There are certain imaginative occurrences we are in the habit of calling realistic. Among these we may take as typical a scene of the commonplace or a pattern of behaviour we recognize and acknowledge as plausible human behaviour. The more exact definition of the word 'realistic' will, I trust, emerge as this commentary proceeds; for the present, I shall mean by it whatever occurrences would commonly be accepted as a fully recognizable aspect of life by a majority of readers.

I wish to analyse as fully as I can what it is that takes place in a work of literature to induce the reader to call it real or realistic. And I also wish to distinguish between the real that most readers would agree on and the literary convention that has been called 'Realism.'

Before embarking on our analysis of the real in Galdós, we shall do well to note certain requisites which every literary study should acknowledge but few do:

(1) In the reading of literature we are dealing entirely with a mental appropriation by the reader; this is a 'making-mine' activity to which we are induced by the written language in the text.

(2) In prose fiction – generally called the novel – we are immersed in a convention of a purported world, that is to say, a world that we know is not, but which we accept as given.

Benito Pérez Galdós has been, with the typical fate of the Spanish writer, praised and condemned with equal lack of critical sense. It is only in the last two decades and indeed in the last few years that serious attempts have been made to demonstrate his technical achievement. My possible contribution to this venture is quite limited. The novels I shall consider in part are *El amigo Manso, Miau, La incógnita, Tristana, Nazarín*, and *Misericordia*, that is, a representative selection of his fiction from 1882 to 1897. I have used Galdós' *Obras' completas*, vols IV and V (Madrid: Aguilar 1950).

El amigo Manso is the work of an accomplished and experienced craftsman, yet there are aspects of this work which bothered its first readers and continue to bother us today. I am referring to the first and last chapters. We cannot take them seriously or, even worse, we do not know what to make of them. The novel is narrated in the first person, but what an unusual first person! Paradoxically, he begins *to be* by telling us that he does not exist.

Yo no existo ... Y por si algún desconfiado, terco y maliciosillo no creyere lo que tan llanamente digo, o exigiese algo de juramento para creerlo, juro y perjuro que no existo; y al mismo tiempo protesto contra toda inclinación o tendencia a suponerme investido de los inequívocos atributos de la existencia real (p 1172).

I don't exist ... and if any sly, stubborn and suspicious person does not believe what

I'm so clearly saying or demands an oath in order to believe it I swear on a stack of Bibles that I don't exist; and at the same time I firmly protest against any inclination or tendency to assume that I be invested with the unequivocal attributes of true existence.

In the next paragraph our narrator goes on to say that although he does not exist he nevertheless *is*:

Soy – diciéndolo en lenguaje oscuro para que lo entiendan mejor – una condensación artística, diabólica, hechura del pensamiento humano (*ximia Dei*), el cual, si coge entre sus dedos algo de estilo, se pone a imitar con él las obras que con la materia ha hecho Dios en el mundo físico; soy un ejemplar nuevo de estas falsificaciones del hombre que desde que el mundo es mundo andan por ahí vendidas en tabla por aquellos que yo llamo holgazanes, faltando a todo deber filial, y que el bondadoso vulgo denomina artistas, poetas o cosa así (p 1173).

I am – saying it in obscure language so it be better understood – an evil, artistic condensation, an artifact of human thought (*ximia Dei*) which if it can grasp some style between its fingers will set itself to imitate with it those works which God by using matter has created in the physical world; I am a new specimen of the kind of man-made falsification which, ever since the world began, has been peddled by those I call bums, lacking any sense of loyalty and whom the good-hearted populace call artists, poets, and the like.

The narrator ends this most unusual of opening chapters with this enigmatic statement:

Poco después salí de una llamarada roja, convertido en carne mortal. El dolor me dijo que yo era un hombre (pp 1173–4).

A little after I emerged from an incandescent flame, I turned into mortal flesh. Pain told me I was a man.

In the last chapter of the novel the narrator dies, but continues to narrate the story. He explains his death as simulated death, simulated because he has never existed. The narration reverts to terms similar to those of his entry into simulated life:

Al deslizarme de entre sus dedos, envuelto en llamarada roja, el sosiego me dió a entender que había dejado de ser hombre (p 1298).

When I slipped between his fingers enveloped in a red flame, the calm made me understand that I had ceased to be human.

Before being tempted to dismiss the novel as one of playful fantasy, let us be reminded that the forty-eight chapters in between the first and the last are so rich in detail and so convincingly presented as life-like observation that we do indeed grant Máximo Manso simulated life. As we read these chapters we are progressively drawn into a closer and closer appreciation of the protagonist narrator. Rarely has a fictional man been so clearly drawn as a model of fully recognizable humanity. We would thus not hesitate to say that Manso is real in the initial meaning of real we have determined. That is, we would say the Manso who narrates for us from chapter 2 until 49 is real. What then are we to make of the protagonist in chapters 1 and 50? The willing suspension of disbelief which we so generously give to all writers, geniuses and hacks alike, has been thrown back in our face.

Galdós has written a novel on two levels of reality. The first and last chapters form a frame for the narration proper and that framework is made up of our reality, the reality of the readers. We are being obliged to face up to the fact that a fictional character is not a man of flesh and blood, which is to say he does not exist, but on the other hand we have also been pulled into the narration in tacit acknowledgment that a fictional character does have a realm of being and that realm is our imagination. The reality of the frame is based on our awareness of our physical world. We exist, the character does not. The central body of the novel, however, also has reality and it is based on our awareness of our imagination. I ask the reader to keep in mind that reasons, laws, beliefs, wishes, fears, and many other aspects of life have no corporeal substance yet they most certainly are a part of our reality. Similarly, Máximo Manso appears to exist, but in truth he is only in our mind as a part of our mental reality. We are therefore as persons invested with a duality of empirical and spiritual reality.

Extraordinary as these levels may be, they do not give any clear indication of the craftsmanship that went into the making of the novel. Let us take a closer look at the main body of the novel. We should keep in mind that there is no source other than that of the first person narrator telling his own story in his own words, thereby creating his illusory world without any intervention or evaluation from an omniscient story-teller. His pattern of telling the story is commonplace. First, he informs us of where he lives, what he does, who he knows, and how he thinks. He is one of the meek of the beatitudes who are supposed to inherit the earth. By the end of chapter 7 we have received the essential facts and background of Manso and his world. Consequently, chapter 8 is the beginning of a specific story, that is, the plot. As Manso gradually is involved in the practise of living and not speculation, discrepancies begin to appear between what was happening and what he thought must have happened. Once this unreliability of judgment becomes obvious, the reader is alerted to the most subtle kind of irony implicit in many of Manso's observations. A few examples will suffice: at the end of chapter 7 Manso narrates the following encounter with Irene:

mas ella, como avergonzada, se recató de mí haciendo como que no me veía, y volvió la cara para hablar con la verdulera. Respetando yo esta esquivez, seguí hacia mi cátedra, y al volver la esquina de la calle del Tesoro, ya me había olvidado del rostro siempre pálido y expresivo de Irene, de su esbelto talle, y no pensaba más que en la explicación de aquel día, que era la *Relación recíproca entre la conciencia moral y la voluntad* (pp 1192–3).

but she, as if ashamed, hid from me pretending not to see me and turned her face away to talk to the market woman. Respecting this aloofness I went on towards my lecture room and as I turned the corner of Tesoro St I had already forgotten the expressive face of Irene, always pale, her slim figure, and thought of no more than that day's lecture which was *The Mutual Relationship between Ethical Consciousness and Will.*

Manso interprets the actions of the girl on pure speculation without a shred of tangible evidence which is, of course, his habitual deficiency that will prove to be his undoing. In short, he sees what he wants to see and not what another disinterested observer would have seen. Irene in fact does not see him for she is near-sighted, and figuratively speaking she is only faintly aware of his presence on the margins of her milieu, which can be accurately designated as that of 'la verdulera.' But the irony comes in the last line of the passage I have quoted. Not only do we get treated to an extended portrait of the girl who was supposedly so easy to put out of his thoughts, but we are told that he could now think only of his lecture: 'La relación recíproca entre la conciencia moral y la voluntad.' A layman's translation might be the relationship between what we want to see and what we think we see.

I have been describing an activity all too common to us in our everyday life. Technically it is a perceptual appropriation of external reality, in ordinary language it is jumping to conclusions. The high point of this activity by Manso comes in chapter 13, where he believes he has discovered the inner woman in Irene. She is transformed into an ideal goddess of beauty and wisdom who disdains the frivolous for the great and noble ventures of mankind. There is, of course, not the slightest relation between this ideal and the young girl who reveals herself to Manso in chapter 42. The ideal of beauty and wisdom is Manso's creation, his appropriation of the visual, his imaginative perception of what he wants to see. The essential point to be made is that Manso creates his world through perception and thought and is only subsequently enlightened about the error of his interpretations.

Now we can ask the question: was the Irene of chapter 13 real? Was the Irene of chapter 42 real? The answer in both cases must be yes. The Irene we have met in chapter 13 is the reality of the young girl in the mind of the protagonist-narrator. This view of the girl is altered radically by her conversation with him and we thus have a new sense of reality which supplants the first. But is this the ultimate real? Not at all, for Manso's interpretation in chapter 42 is still subject to error; it is merely what he thinks the real to be at that moment. One may now be able to see where Galdós has led us in this strange novel. There is no doubt that his craftsmanship led us to accept the world of Manso as real, but the fantastic frame has rudely awakened us to the fact that it was an illusion. Therefore we have a parallel situation. Just as Manso is forced to acknowledge the illusory nature of what he thought was real, so the reader is forced to accept the obvious: that the main part of the novel was an illusion.

At this point I should like to sum up what we have discovered about the real.

1 The real for us is based on what we experience through our senses and how we interpret it. We may all agree that the object in front of me is a table, but we shall all differ on what it means to us depending on whether we want to write or simply get out of the room, or are tired and would like to rest.

2 The real in a novel is based on the reader's capacity to make an analogy between the imaginative world and his own world.

3 The power of this analogy should never be underestimated; it can overcome the most fantastic packaging, as in *El amigo Manso*.

4 By bursting the bubble of our imaginative analogy and revealing the novel as a novel, Galdós is calling our attention to that realm of our reality which is our mental appropriation of what we see. For example, a young man who meets the same girl on his way to work every day but does not know even her name can certainly give her a fully developed personality in his imagination. Our reality is made up of such images. Some of these images correspond well to external reality, some do not, and a special kind take place only in the mind.

I trust that the more specific use of real is now before us so that we can review the ways in which Galdós refined it in his mature period. Let us now move forward six years to 1888 and the publication of *Miau*. We must regrettably pass over some of Galdós' longest and best-known novels – *El doctor Centeno*, *Tormento*, *La de Bringas*, *Lo prohibido*, and *Fortunata y Jacinta*.

Miau is one of Galdós' best-structured novels. There are three characters who dominate the novel: Luis, the sickly young boy; Abelarda, his young aunt; and Villaamil, the grandfather and father respectively of Luis and Abelarda. The tragic figure of the old man is the focal centre in the novel.

This novel depicts Spanish society with extreme deliberation. Each of the main characters achieves his own sense of the real as he responds to external reality. Consequently, we have a detailed depiction of external reality for the characters but each of them in turn creates his own version of the real.

The child's organization of reality is quite simple. It is merely a question of having more or less of everything. An insatiable urge to possess is the viewpoint from which he sees the world. The supreme symbol of possession is God, who appears in his dreams.

Abelarda's view of reality is more complex. Her agony is her sense of inferiority and insignificance and her conflict is caused by her widowed brother-in-law, who leads her on with talk of love. This cruel game erupts in a fit of madness as she attacks Luis. Her dream of marriage and position are her colouring of the real.

Finally, the old man, Vallaamil, is the tragic figure in the novel. He views the real with eyes of despair. He has lost his position in the Department of National Revenue a few months before his retirement with pension, and throughout the novel is gradually reduced by the bureaucracy until he commits suicide at the end. His tragedy is greater in our eyes because we have followed his descent. The human condition is depicted in this novel through the three generations. Each has his own sphere of activity, his own lens through which he sees life, his own conflict, but it is the old man who is worn down and destroyed. The words from *King Lear* are applicable:

> The oldest hath borne most: we
> that are young – shall never
> see so much nor live so long.

The structure of the novel appears to be a seamless unity of world and characters. But this is only a superficial gloss owing to the technical achievement of Galdós. Underlying the plot, Galdós has had to face one of the most difficult challenges of his creativity. I have already emphasized how each of the central characters has his own private sense of the real and how in spite of this there is a concrete external world common to all of them.

Let us approach these claims critically. If the characters are to have their own perspective of reality they must in some way be independent, and if this external reality is to be common ground for all of them, the narrator must be able to present it unchallenged. In any case these would be the standard ways of achieving the 'individual-world' dualism outlined above. Galdós, however, is radical in his writing of this novel.

We have a narrator of strong opinion who presents the most intimate thoughts of his characters and who knows the story of their lives as one who has experienced them himself. Further, he presents himself as the writer of this true story and tells the reader that such and such an event or character will be treated presently. At times he presents thoughts and dreams of characters, but at others he cannot tell who is in the next room. A very deep paradox thus emerges in this novel: how is it possible to make the reader aware that he is reading fiction and still maintain his belief in what is being presented? Galdós, by deliberately reminding the reader that he is reading fiction, has again forced the hand of his reader. Either one acknowledges the reality of fiction in the imagination or one gets out and stops reading the novel.

Consequently, Galdós' narrator has pleaded common cause with the reader and has struck up a compact of mental experience with the powerful implication that this story can claim to be *true* if the cause and effect of man responding to the world is convincing. The reader thus becomes the ultimate judge of this social truth claim.

La incógnita was begun by Galdós before the publication of *Miau* and was published in the following year, 1889. In this novel he tries his hand at the epistolary form. This had been a favourite of the Romantics like Goethe, Hölderlin, and Sénancour and had been used with success by Juan Valera in part of his *Pepita Jiménez*.

Galdós, like Valera before him, uses the letter writer's perspective ironically. *La incógnita* consists of forty-seven letters written by Manolo Infante to his friend Equis in Orbajosa. In contrast to Valera's novel here there is only the correspondence of Manolo Infante, who progressively reveals himself to be biased and generally unreliable as a source of information. The novel presents the intrigues of the characters and indeed the characters themselves from a most unreliable source. Objective reality has been banished from this novel. In the companion novel, titled significantly *Realidad*, Galdós gives us the facts that in *La incógnita* must be seen as opinion and speculation.

With these two novels Galdós has made his idea of reality not only convincing but virtually irrefutable. He presents our common idea of reality to be only our conjecture about the real based on perception that may or may not be accurate and is by necessity limited and organized by our rational faculty, which may or may not be in error. Thus what we call reality is but the superficial and external appearance of the real. Further, when we have a privileged perspective of the real in literature, as when we are permitted to be witnesses to a character's thoughts, we are dealing with a literary convention which is, of course, illusory. The Galdosian paradox is now before us if we have the wits to meet its challenge. Is there anything more unrealistic, he is telling us, than the fictional representation we call realism?

It is in these years that Galdós parts company with all of his Spanish contemporaries like Pereda and Palacio Valdés. And it is at this time that Galdós achieves a depth of vision that would not be appreciated for another half-century. Life as we know it is an illusion of the senses as we encounter the external world. And, similarly, life in fiction is an illusion, but in this case an illusion of the imagination.

There was no turning back for Galdós after this breakthrough; in subsequent novels he plunged further into that uncharted sea of the human imagination. *Angel Guerra* was published in 1891 right on the heels of *La incógnita*, *Torquemada en la hoguera*, and *Realidad*, all published in 1889. And in 1892 another radical step was taken in *Tristana*.

This novel has a traditional development of reconstructed past and dramatized past ranging over a limited number of years and a limited physical setting. It is a representative Galdosian novel because the world of the central character expands gradually until the end of the novel. The narrative concentrates on the theme of freedom as it is discovered or lost in the two principal characters of don Lope and Tristana. Tristana is the young orphan taken in by the aging don Lope only to be converted into his mistress. She accepts her role as 'la esclava' until she meets a young man, Horacio. Tristana falls in love with Horacio and her battle for freedom from the old man begins. The young man is obliged to go to Valencia and for eight chapters the young lovers live through and for their correspondence. During this time Tristana becomes ill and has a leg amputated. Horacio returns and both lovers discover that they have changed and break off their relationship. Don Lope has finally succeeded in having the girl to himself. He only half-heartedly resists the demands of his family that he marry the girl. They marry and live together their remaining days.

These are the bare bones of the plot and will serve only as signposts to re-enact the very profound reality of Galdos' novel. I have said that the principal theme of this novel is the search for freedom. This, of course, is a universal theme which has been treated by writers of differing ability throughout literary history. But the extraordinary development in this novel is that the theme of freedom is used to reveal the Galdosian real.

The narrator begins the novel as a witness to the story he is about to tell and consequently presents the characters, Lope and Tristana, as we would describe someone whose life we were recalling. This manner of remembering the way the character was establishes a pattern of living which we immediately recognize and accept as life-like, that is, 'real' in the ordinary but vague sense of the word. However, no sooner have we gotten comfortable with the idea of a completely recognizable image of persons when we are surprised. As soon as the characters begin to have experiences, we find that they have an individual and unique mind which is not at all commonplace. Let us consider the situation of don Lope. He is an aging gentleman of means who lives his life according to a strict self-imposed code. It is a curious chivalric code which demands extreme action. When a friend is in need the gentleman must go to the rescue even if by so doing his own well-being is jeopardized. Thus, when one of Lope's friends finds himself in financial want, Lope reduces himself to poverty but nevertheless persists in his attempt to save the friend. There is, however, one exception to this chivalric code and that is women. All women are objects of Lope's lust for self-gratification. He therefore shows no compunction when he makes the orphaned child of his friend his mistress.

What we have in this novel is an intricate duality, for the Galdosian narrator gives the world of the novel as a series of events in time and space, but he also gives us the unique mind of the character. Thus, the character responds to some things and events in a predictable manner, but to others in a most unconventional way. When an older lecher gets his hands on a nubile attractive girl the results are predictable: he will seduce her, but when that same old lecher is faced with complete ruin because of the financial aid he is giving a friend he responds in the un-usual way of accepting ruin rather than deserting his friend in need. This duality has the immediate effect of transforming the 'real' in the novel into the 'real' in our experience. This means that the world as an external mass of things, sounds, tastes, and images is given in precisely the same terms as we experience it. But the character in the novel is not held to this general presentation of external reality. He is quite free to see and understand what he sees in his own way. The fundamental doctrine of reality which Galdós so brilliantly arrives at is Cervantes' presentation of reality in *Don Quixote*.

The technical problems which face Galdós at every turn are formidable indeed. Let us take up the central problem. How is it possible for a narrator who is remembering the past to give us the necessary intimate insight into the minds of the characters? Cervantes' model of multiple authorship is not a feasible solution for Galdós in the nineteenth century. Galdós' answer is the creation of a highly complex narrator; one who is remembering the world of the characters but who can step aside at the right moment and permit the characters to function independently. Galdós designed the character of the girl on the pattern developed for the old man.

At the beginning of the novel Tristana is a passive submissive young girl who accepts her position in don Lope's household. The narrator constantly refers to her as 'la esclava' and we have no cause to dispute the label. The situation, however, begins to change as the novel progresses. Slowly at first and then at a faster pace Tristana begins to adopt the pattern of perception of her master. Before we fully realize it we are faced with two and not just one independent mind in the novel. We are told by the narrator that Horacio Díaz is an ordinary looking young man who has the varied background which is the lot of diplomats' children. After losing his parents he was brought up in an atmosphere of near slavery by his paternal grandfather. The narrator tells us this in a concise paragraph without comment and then gracefully bows out and lets the character Horacio present his autobiography to us but also to an avid listener, Tristana. As the recounting of the past continues the narrator comes back in, to comment not on the life of Horacio but exclusively on the reaction that this story is having on the young girl.

ésta lo escuchaba con deleite, confirmándose en la creencia de que el hombre que le había deparado el Cielo era una excepción entre todos los mortales, y su vida lo más peregrino y anómalo que en clase de vidas de jóvenes se pudiera encontrar; como que casi parecía vida de un santo, digna de un huequecito en el martirologio (pp 1558–9).

She listened to him with delight, strengthening her belief that the man Heaven had provided for her was exceptional among all other mortals and his life the most unusual and anomalous any young person could find; it almost seemed a saint's life, deserving a small place in the book of religious martyrs.

The narrator thereby allows us to witness the cause which is Horacio's retelling of his life and the effect in the mind of the young girl. With delicate subtlety Galdós reminds us that appearances are deceptive, that we more often see what we want to see rather than what is there confronting us. Describing the landscape next to the cemetery of San Idelfonso, the narrator comments on the cypress trees 'que a media luz parecen más elegantes de lo que son' (which in the twilight seem more elegant than they are). The ironic language follows with the same subtlety as the young lovers come upon oxen by the road and the narrator draws attention to the huge horned animals:

bestias inofensivas a fuerza de cansancio, y que, cuando las sueltan del yugo, no se cuidan más que de reposar, mirando con menosprecio al transeúnte (p 1561).

harmless beasts through exhaustion and when unleashed from the yoke do not care for anything but rest, regarding passers-by with indifference.

Tristana then goes up to the beasts in a manner clearly reminiscent of 'el Caballero de la triste figura' in his adventure of the lions. She turns to her lover and states triumphantly:

Desde que te quiero ... no tengo miedo a nada, ni a los toros ni a los ladrones.

Since I love you ... I fear nothing, not even brave bulls or thieves.

Let us not miss the central point of the Galdosian novel: what the character sees and what is there to see are closer or further apart depending on the character's frame of mind. Tristana sees in Horacio a most extraordinary human being, a hero of almost superhuman proportions. There is always the danger that the difference between Tristana's heroic Horacio and the Horacio we see will be realized by her through a change in her awareness of reality. The danger is circumvented when the young man goes to Valencia and thus Tristana is left with memories and letters which are her imaginative sustenance. We can thus anticipate that the gap between her viewpoint and the realities of the young man will be unbridgeable by the time he returns. But the supposed shock of the clash of realities is completely dissipated, for Tristana has moved beyond her need of a hero by the time he returns. She moves successively through four ascending planes of spiritual dedication. From Horacio she passes to the creativity in painting. Next she moves to music, which she finds superior because of its transcendence of the corporeal, and her final phase is that of an almost mystical dedication to God.

It should not be surprising to find that Tristana's path of ascending spirituality is inversely proportional to don Lope's descent from the spirituality of chivalric code. Don Lope, like don Quixote before him, loses his ideal and awakens to find himself merely an old man seeking comfort for his remaining days.

I stated at the beginning of these remarks on *Tristana* that the theme was freedom and slavery and it is important to understand how this theme is related to the awareness of reality.

The last two chapters of *Tristana* make the thematic statement very emphatically – freedom is to be found in complete devotion to an ideal greater than oneself. And, consequently, slavery is depicted as the surrender to the world and one's material needs.

The novel began with don Lope, a free man to the extent he was true to his ideal of the *caballero*, but enslaved with his weakness to sexual demands. Near the end of the novel Tristana is free because of her devotion to God and because of her disdain for the things of this world. But don Lope is now completely enslaved as a prisoner of physical needs. Galdós ends the novel on a most ambivalent plane with Tristana now devoted to making pastry. The irony of life's cycle is implicit.

Obvious though it may be, let us sum up what this novel has added to our concern with the real in fiction.

1 The characters think they know reality when in fact they only know what they see and they see largely what they want to see. In other words, Galdós' characters have the same access to reality that we have.

2 The theme of freedom and slavery is expressed in the novel through the perceptive autonomy of the characters. Thus the more aloof the characters are from the external world that surrounds them, the greater their freedom, and the closer their ties to materiality the greater the enslavement.

3 Because the characters can only speak for themselves and their views have little weight outside of their perspective, the world can only be given by the narrator.

I should now like to turn to another novel written only three years later, in 1895, *Nazarín*. I shall not linger long on this well-known novel but only point out the contributions it makes to our enquiry into the real.

It is my opinion that the problem of presenting reality in the novel reaches its most profound implications in *Nazarín*. In fact I shall go as far as to say that whether or not Galdós thought of his ideas as philosophical – and I doubt that he did – he had now developed a highly refined philosophy.

The basic technique he uses is the same one that he has been using from the beginning. The technique I call the relationship between narrator and character includes not only attitudes, sympathy, antipathy, and other emotions but, most significantly, establishes the internal and the external domain of the character so that each important character can make his own world. What I am saying is that the modern dualism of mind and matter which had been implicit in Galdós' novels becomes explicit and stated in *Nazarín*.

Galdós is now building a narrative structure that exemplifies the contrast between the reality of the mind and the empirical reality of the world.

The reader can quite rightly ask what is Nazarín – charlatan, madman, disguised bishop, or saint. Galdós' answer is: all are true for each of these views has been held by a character and insofar as that character was concerned his view was the true one. On a higher level of enquiry Galdós informs his reader of the obvious, that he is reading prose fiction, but then almost in the same phrase states unequivocally that this is a true story. The answer is important for us. The story is true because we have made it ours through reading and imagining. What we have read is fiction, but fiction is true, it is as true as our sense of the real in our own experience. Galdós has reached out to our imagination and has stated openly that the novel is a reading experience. This means that the novel is a mental reality and it takes its place within the mind along with all other images which are removed in time and space from their efficient cause.

The last novel I wish to consider is one of Galdós' acknowledged masterpieces, *Misericordia*, of 1897. The story as told by the Galdosian narrator is an intriguing tale of human kindness and illusions. The principal character, Benina, spends part of each day as a beggar in order to support her mistress and a growing number of persons in need. This plot appears to be patterned on an intensifying path of increasing difficulty for the alert Benina to make ends meet. The essence of the novel, however, lies in the presentation of reality, which, I can now say directly, is the negation of the literary convention we call realism.

Realism as a literary convention for the novel had come to be in the nineteenth century by the use of two laws of narrative writing: (1) the story in the novel was to be placed within the history of nation, class, and thought; consequently it was through the deft usage of historical events and a minute observation of period details that the historical identification was made; (2) the organization of action, that is, of the behaviour of the characters, was made to be in keeping with the universal patterns of environmental and class inheritance as they were understood at the time.

These techniques of novelistic realism can be summed up by the terms historicity and behaviouralism. Galdós began to write at the time that these laws were being elaborated and he himself participated in his earlier work and in the *Episodios nacionales*. Galdós felt that all of his work responded to these directions. But he was too great a writer to stop with a formula; he continued to develop and as he developed he went beyond the laws of realism and gave us the novels of experience that we have been studying.

Let us return briefly to *Misericordia* in order to conclude these observations. I have said above that this is a novel of charity, hunger, and illusions. That is as precise a definition as I could state in a single line, for this novel begins with an established dualism for reality: there is on the one hand the physical need to survive in a hostile world, but there is also on the other the imaginative fancy of these persons which mitigates their desperate situation. The high point in the novel comes when the illusions of the characters Benina and Paca become realities. If the reader is still insistent on approaching the novel historically he will find these experiences unexplainable and may be tempted to dismiss them as contrived fiction. The truth claim in this novel is that the spiritual dimensions of the mind can change matter insofar as the individual is concerned. Matter itself is characterized as being beyond our grasp. Matter as we know it is a product of our perception and of our interpretation of what we perceive, thus the old adage that faith can move mountains takes on new depths in this novel. We are given to understand (a) that the narrator is a creator by telling the story, but (b) that the character is also a creator by imagining her own answers, and finally (c) that the reader is the ultimate creator for he has imagined all that he has read.

Galdós is at pains to make these points obvious and yet to end his novel effectively. His solution is nothing short of brilliant. At the end of *Misericordia* Benina is visited by Juliana, who has had her cast out of the home she served with such devotion. Before Juliana comes we have begun to witness a metamorphosis in Benina. All those around her believe she is a saint, but she and the reader know that she is not a saint. She becomes a minister for faith. Galdós achieves this by utilizing the spiritual words that he could anticipate were common to his readers and these are the words of the common of the Roman Catholic mass. Through the last ten pages we begin to attend mass with Benina as priest. We go from the prayers at the foot of the altar as Benina's thoughts, to the lavatory as the priest prepares himself to handle the host. Benina washes, we are told, so that she may be purified. Next we have the song and incense of Almudena, which were a part of the mass as Galdós knew it. The words of Benina and Almudena continue to echo the prayers of the mass. The high point is the arrival of Juliana as the penitent who cannot enter the house of the Lord, that is, the house where Benina the priest has consecrated herself. On Juliana's second visit she humbly pleads that she has sinned and is not worthy, but she believes, for she has come to ask for divine intercession. Benina the priest tells her: 'Ahora vete a tu casa y no vuelvas a pecar.' That is to say, 'You are absolved, go and sin no more.'

Galdós eventually denied realism because he created a novelistic world that was not an imitation of the empirical world but rather a separate intimate creation of his reader's imagination and this creation of the imagination is real, for all that we know and all that we believe are joined together in our minds and this is what we call reality when we share it with someone else.

I would like to conclude this chapter with two general observations. First, it has become commonplace for contemporary artistic and intellectual endeavour to contradict the public's sense of reality. However strongly the reader or perceiver's empirical sense of appearances resists the work of art, he has been convinced that his misgivings with the new forms should be kept private or suffer the consequences of appearing to be a philistine. Second, owing to the fact that the writer of prose fiction seeks to engage not only the public arbiter of taste – the journalistic critic – but also the private person, the novel has become an extraordinary aesthetic battleground.

There was a time when the novelist could strike a compromise by the use of deftly placed symbolic clues and maintain the general appearances of empirical reality while developing an inner current of figurative expression. This period has now generally been termed 'realism' and ceased to be a viable force in art by the end of the nineteenth century.

The twentieth century ushered in a strong reaction against the compromise of mind and world, by emphasizing the inner meaning to the detriment of the external world. The cult of psychological interpretation flourished as a consequence. The novel was no longer to be trusted to the mere reader. The reading experience was now thought to be the mere crude raw material from which the cultist would hope to reach meaning under the guidance of the master interpreter. Of course most readers just gave up and certainly not all writers danced to the tune of the piper, but enough did to make it a fashion and turn the novel into an inverted reflection of itself which completely excluded the reader's sense of the real. In a Spanish context the novels of Azorín, Ramón Pérez de Ayala, and Benjamín Jarnés come readily to mind.

Outside of Spain the neo-allegory was moving forward at such a pace that the culmination of the process was in sight, the non-novel. It would be: a title-page, chapter headings, and blank pages accompanied, of course, by an instruction manual on how the blank pages were to be interpreted.

In Spanish America the late nineteenth-century novel lingered on into the twentieth century until the sudden eruption of creativity in the last twenty-five years. Precisely in the late 1950s, when fashionable literary circles in New York were speaking of the demise of prose fiction as a contemporary vehicle of creativity, the birth of the new Spanish American novel was taking place.

The central value of the contemporary Spanish American novel is that it gives the novel back to the reader.

I propose to outline the principal factors of some very old aesthetic considerations in ultra-modern dress as we find them in the Argentine novelist Julio Cortázar's *Rayuela* (Buenos Aires: Sudamericana 1959).

I consider *Rayuela* to be a parody of nineteenth-century realism in Spain and Spanish America, but also a rejection of early twentieth-century literary aesthetics, especially those in vogue in France and to a lesser extent in Argentina among the *ultraistas*.

A powerful iconoclastic sensation hits the unwary reader when he opens this book. I shall not go into detail in describing the mechanics of this well-known work. Let it suffice to point out that the tripartite division of '*Del lado de allá*' (From that side) plus '*Del lado de acá*' (From this side), and finally '*De otros lados*' (From other places) subtitled 'Capítulos prescindibles' (Chapters which can be left out) exists only for the '*lector hembra*' (female reader). It is this kind of reader who reads in the traditional manner by turning one page at a time and the irony of it all is that the most important part of the novel, the third part, does not fit into this reading.

Let us assume we are all imbued with *machismo*, at least as readers of fiction, and we accept Cortázar's challenge and read the novel according to the zig-zag plan announced on the first page. What kind of structure do we have now? Like so many aesthetic concepts it is deceptively simple to state but complicated to explain.

The structure of *Rayuela*, all of it, is the game from which it takes its title. The reader accepts the invitation to play the game by reading in the prescribed manner. If at first we think we are playing a solitary game, we are soon reminded that the author is also playing along with us. We turn as many as 515 pages at a time in order to continue reading and we arrive to find that singular clue of reference to the next assignment in our odyssey. It soon becomes very much like the adventurer following the pirate's map to the buried treasure. We have the distinct feeling that someone has been there before. But as if these were not sufficient complications we turn to passages which unnerve as if our thoughts were being added to the text. Chapter 102, for example, states:

Así como había visto cierto día con un vidrio de aumento la piel de mi dedo meñique, semejante a una llanura con surcos y hondonadas, así veía ahora a los hombres y sus acciones. Ya no conseguía percibirlos con la mirada simplificadora de la costumbre. Todo se descomponía en fragmentos que se fragmentaban a su vez; nada conseguía captar por medio de una noción definida (p 520).

Just as I had looked at the skin on my little finger in a magnifying glass one day, something like a field with furrows and hollows, so I looked at men and their actions now. I could no longer perceive them with the simplifying look of habit. Everything was breaking down into fragments which in turn were becoming fragmented; I was unable to grasp anything by means of a defined notion.

This extraordinary passage does not merely echo the reader's thoughts as he reads through the labyrinth, but also those of the character, for it is a note taken from Hofmannsthal purportedly found by one of the characters. Consequently, this passage is in essence an interpolated document, but it is also a part of the fiction because the character has read it and, more significantly, because we have read it in the new context of the novel.

A common cause has been struck in the creation of this novel between the narrative voice, Morelli, the characters including Morelli as a character, and the reader. The common cause is to play the game and create the novel. The principal technique used by Cortázar to reduce the conventional distances between narrator, character, and reader is the use and manipulation of the interpolated document. The entire third part of the novel consists of documents to be interpolated according to plan among the plotted chapters. In general the documents fall into two separate functional categories. The first is the document from an acknowledged source that is quoted completely out of context and consequently interrupts the flow of development in the novel. I shall call this the document of interruption. The second general category consists of those documents which comment on the aesthetic premises of the novel we are reading. I shall refer to these as documents of interior revelation. The immediate question before us is to determine the function which both types of documents serve in the realization of the novel.

The documents which I have designated as interruptions in the reading of the novel are for the most part short quotations taken from such diverse sources as the *L'Express*, *Almanaque Hachette*, *The Observer*, *London Times*, *British Medical Journal*, and authors as diverse as Gombrowicz, Octavio Paz, Malcolm Lowry, Clarence Darrow, Anaïs Nin, Lezama Lima, Meister Eckhardt, and Lévi-Strauss. The immediate effect is to stop the development of the plot and to add an external and extraneous commentary to the text. But what is the nature of the context formed by these interpolated passages? It is not enough to say that the narrative thread has been broken unless we are to assume that the interpolated passage is meaningless. It is my contention that not only are the interpolated passages always meaningful in themselves, but that the only way to read them is as part of a new context with the ongoing narrative. The new context inspired by the relation of the narrative and the interpolated passage is based on the principle of figurative writing we refer to as metaphor. The range of expression through metaphor is only limited by the reader's ability at imaginative association and transference of characteristic. Consider the following line:

El mar baila por la playa,
un poema de balcones
(F. García Lorca, *Obras Completas* [Madrid: Aguilar 1954], 365).

The sea dances along the beach
a poem of balconies.

The meaning of the line is so much more than the subject matter. It is evident that the reference is to the sea breaking on the beach, but the metaphorical element is the essential expansion which takes place due to the juxtaposition of the extraneous objects and activities of *poema, balcones,* and *bailar.* Consequently, the metaphorical meaning includes the transference of characteristics in the mind of the reader; thus, we have an expanded and expanding consciousness where the sea is merely the starting point. The movement of the sea is seen as an activity of expression like the dance.

Now returning to the interpolated extraneous passages in *Rayuela*, chapter 34 is one of a number of textual manipulations which irritate some but interest most readers. All but the last paragraph of the chapter is written in alternation line by line with a passage from *Lo prohibido* by Pérez Galdós. Line after line we read the Galdosian novel, a book belonging to Maga, but now being read and commented by Horacio. The chapter ends on a pathetic note as Horacio characterizes their life together as 'haciendo su dibujo, danzando para nadie, ni siquiera para ellos mismos, una interminable figura sin sentido' (p 233) (making its drawing, dancing for no one, not even for themselves, an interminable figure without meaning). Our thoughts of Horacio and his obsessive self-analysis are abruptly cut off as we turn from page 233 to 468 to read chapter 87. This chapter reports on a 1932 recording by Duke Ellington called 'Baby when you ain't there.' The lines of the blues are given and then are followed by this commentary:

¿Por qué, a ciertas horas, es tan necesario decir: 'Amé esto'? Amé unos blues, una imagen en la calle, un pobre río seco del norte. Dar testimonio, luchar contra la nada que nos barrerá' (p 468).

Why is it so necessary at certain times to say: 'I loved that'? I loved some blues, an image in the street, a poor dry river in the north. Giving testimony, fighting against the nothingness that will sweep us all away.

The apparently unrelated comments of Horacio as he looks over Maga's reading matter (chapter 34) and the Duke Ellington blues (chapter 87) have been forced together into a contextual relationship in a manner analogous to the words *mar* and *baila* in the verses discussed above. The difference is that in *Rayuela* we are dealing with prose contexts rather than single words, but the result is the same, a creation of metaphorical expansion by the reader. To reverse the argument I should like to propose a metaphorical meaning of these passages from *Rayuela* in verse:

El garabato absurdo
de nuestra vida
se convierte en memoria
para existir
testigo, lucha, nada.

The absurd scribble
of our life
becomes memory
for being
witness, struggle, nothingness.

Horacio's introspection has as its final phase only one possibility, which is the anticipation of annihilation. The clash of contexts liberates the imaginative scope of the reader from the plot into the kind of reflection which is the essence of literature but the hallmark of poetry.

The second class of documents which I have identified as interior reflection of the novel can also be grouped under the title of *Morelliana*, which is used in some chapters. These passages consist of the arguments for the techniques being employed by Cortázar as well as the aesthetic suppostions on which they depend. One of the most useful is chapter 109, which according to the reading plan is the fifty-fifth instalment:

En alguna parte Morelli procuraba justificar sus incoherencias narrativas, sosteniendo que la vida de los otros, tal como nos llega en la llamada realidad, no es cine sino fotografía, es decir, que no podemos aprehender la acción sino tan sólo sus fragmentos eleáticamente recortados ... dar coherencia a la serie de fotos para que pasaran a ser cine (como le hubiera gustado tan enormemente al lector que él llamaba el lector-hembra) significaba rellenar con literatura, presunciones, hipótesis e invenciones los hiatos entre una y otra foto (p 532).

In some place Morelli tried to justify his narrative incoherencies, maintaining that the life of others, such as it comes to us in so-called reality, is not a movie but still photography, that is to say that we cannot grasp the action, only a few of its eleatically recorded fragments ... giving coherence to the series of pictures so they could become a movie (which would have been so very pleasing to the reader he called the female-reader) meant filling in with literature, presumptions, hypotheses, and inventions the gaps between one and another photograph.

The most complete statement of the aesthetics of *Rayuela* is in chapter 79. In the forty-third instalment we read:

Intentar en cambio un texto que no agarre al lector pero que lo vuelva obligadamente cómplice al murmurarle, por debajo del desarrollo convencional, otros rumbos más esotéricos. Escritura demótica para el lector-hembra (que por lo demás no pasará de la primeras páginas, rudamente perdido y escandalizado, maldiciendo lo que le costó el libro) ... (p 452).

To attempt on the other hand a text that would not clutch the reader but which would oblige him to become an accomplice as it whispers to him underneath the conventional exposition other more esoteric directions. Demotic writing for the female-reader (who otherwise will not get beyond the first few pages, rudely lost and scandalized, cursing at what he paid for the book).

And a few lines below he adds these remarks:

Método: la ironía, la autocrítica incesante, la incongruencia, la imaginación al servicio de nadie (p 452).

Method: irony, ceaseless self-criticism, incongruity, imagination in the service of no one.

These self-revealing documents fulfil their basic function as the most destructive elements to confront the novelistic convention. As readers we can take all manner of extraneous interruptions and still cling to our comfortable insistence on a closed world unfolding before us. But the novelistic convention is jolted and I think fully challenged by the direct revelation of the inner workings of the writing as it is addressed to the imagination of the reader. Cortázar's use of interior duplication to challenge the reader has been used by novelists before and after, but as a weapon of confrontation only John Fowles in *The French Lieutenant's Woman* can match the Argentine writer.

Cortázar's fiction is made up of a zig-zag pattern as a narrative quest for identity and meaning by the central character is interspersed with the documents of metaphorical context and those of interior revelation. The result is that the reader becomes the accomplice of the author in the manufacture of the novelistic world. The reader joins in the quest actively and participates in an unprecedented manner in imaginative creation. The reader is not only the recipient, he is also the associate creator.

Although the language and narrative technique appear to be radically new, I submit that they are as old as the modern novel in western literature. The interpolated document used to create a new and richer context as well as the commentary on the novel within the novel itself were initiated and still have their classic expression in *Don Quixote de la Mancha*.

Let us review what I have written about the novels of Pérez Galdós and Julio Cortázar in the light of the aims I have identified for literary criticism.

In chapter 5 I referred to the competent reader as the reader who mastered the internal distances of the text. In this chapter I have referred to the critic as the reader's reader, for the critic is not only a competent reader, he is a reader with a purpose. The functions of criticism in a phenomenological perspective are twofold: to disclose the reader's relationship with the language of external reference and to identify the dimensions of self-reference in the text which ultimately involve the reader himself. In my commentary on Galdós' novels I concentrated on the language of external reference, what we usually call the reference to the 'real world'; and in the study of *Rayuela* I emphasized the elements of self-reference in the text. These novels have been selected because they contain a number of features which facilitated a brief presentation of these functions, but the point I have been making about criticism would be lost if I gave the impression that the aims of the undertaking are not determined by the critic. In my view it is only the clear conscious choice of the critic to pursue these goals that separates criticism from language games. Interpretations, rival interpretations, if you will, cease to be language games when they are grounded in a particular existential function. In this chapter I have argued for the existential functions of criticism as I understand it.

7

A structure of enquiry

No theory of interpretation is adequate unless it is applicable to the needs of students as well as to those of specialized scholars.[1] Theorists are mostly writing for other theorists. If they do delve into practical criticism, they are simplifying their elaborate schemes for a general audience. Some have written books on specific authors and their art but without, as a rule, having had to face the problems of the general reader. My main point was made by Northrop Frye in his 'Polemical Intoduction' to the *Anatomy of Criticism* (Princeton 1957): 'If criticism could ever be conceived as a coherent and systematic study, the elementary principles of which could be explained to any intelligent nineteen-year-old, then, from the point of view of such a conception, no critic now knows the first thing about criticism. What critics now have is a mystery-religion without a gospel, and they are initiates who can communicate, or quarrel, only with one another' (p 14).

A work of literature, besides being a subject of study and the result of a creative effort to communicate, is also the product of these enterprises; a verbal construction. This product is complex, but I think it can be studied on three interdependent levels. The first is the description of the reading and primary identification of the parts. The second is the explicative interpretation by the critic. The third is the aesthetic realization of basic principles of imaginative expression. The aim of this theory of interpretation is to integrate and explain the interdependence of these fundamental levels.

Among my contemporaries, the study of literature usually begins with the close reading of the text and almost inevitably ends in a normative commentary by the critic based upon his ideological convictions. The genuine beliefs, though not usually the professed precepts, form the essence of the critical study. The issue is not whether the critic should indulge in direct normative interpretations, but rather that he should be aware of the ground upon which his intelligence and erudition have taken root: even in enquiry of the most disinterested form of knowledge, when the overwhelming aim is simply to know, a value system is in operation.[2]

Literary interpretation is a normative leap of the imagination. It is in the first instance an imaginative experience that is subsequently described, explicated, formulated, and synthesized, but it remains an achievement, if successful, of inductive reasoning as an inspired plunge into an uncharted area of knowledge seeking to understand the initial experience. The critic who recognizes the personal foundations of his commentary has only to extend the same privilege to his reader. Consequently the self-conscious critic is addressing the reader about an analogous experience the two have had in reading the same text. Literary interpretation is thus an inductive form of enquiry[3] moving imaginatively from one level to another in pursuit of knowledge of the whole. At each step reason tests the interpretation for coherence. As Popper, Gotschalk, and others have noted, this form of enquiry is always a series of calculated leaps beyond the evidence. It is therefore imperative that the testing apparatus of the system be fully developed.

Two well-established principles of interpretation[4] have been the explication of the meaning of the text and the elaboration of the significance thus established. These two principles, which cover a great area, are not by themselves sufficient where an elaborate literary text is concerned. Understanding the text's meaning, in the literal sense of acknowledged communication, is obviously not the only object of reading a work of literature, but it is certainly a requirement. As for the significance of the imaginative construction, the imagination is, to begin with, essentially hermetic: it turns the reader away from all avoidable interference from the outside and fuses the literary images with the private world of the reader. My position is that the rational study of meaning must be made a corollary to the imaginative rendering of significance. In our domain reason or literary analysis is primarily the giver of facts and the tester of validity; the leap of imagination or interpretation is the force which motivates us toward a figurative knowledge of the whole. We can ill afford to be taken over by one without the other. Analysis is essentially an acute distinguishing process and requires some positive concepts of what constitutes a poem, novel, or drama. If it stands on its own, however, it leads nowhere. In itself it is the blind earthworm constrained to an aimless descriptive accumulation.

And, although interpretation is the object of the critic's enquiry, it must be an informed leap. Interpretation alone is a butterfly, colourful but transitory for lack of proven substance.

In summary, in any successful theory of interpretation, one can distinguish the levels of application as those of the reader's analysis, the interpretation, and the aesthetic correspondences. In this theory these three are served through the same phenomenological enquiry. It is only the scope that changes from the words to the functional relationship and to the aesthetic principles. Criticism is a discipline; it is also a way of thinking, and, at least in my case, it is based on a philosophy.

The demand for analysis[5] in literary criticism is fed by the same spirit that sustains it in other disciplines. Knowledge is the goal, which in this context means making the reader the master of the textual construction of the work. This is true; but if it be taken as disposing of the question, it is inadequate. It fails to account for the importance of individual thought and most significantly for the importance of the reader's imaginative experience. The question now before us is the role of analysis in criticism and its validity per se. If we consider the reader's imaginative experience as a whole, including the accumulation of similar experiences from the past as well as those immediately present, there can be no doubt that analysis is the means to gain control over the linguistic and conceptual structure of the work. Analysis is to criticism what mathematics is to the understanding of an architectural masterpiece. Thus the value of analysis in criticism is entirely functional; it is a means to the advancement of these higher goods that belong to the life of the mind. I would like to specify the kind of analysis I have in mind.

'A word is a microcosm of human consciousness.'[6] It is with words that we are first engaged in the study of literature. Each word in the literary context forms part of a larger category of imaginative communication, but out of context it is a part of an image, metaphor, or symbol only potentially. The first encounter involves meaning. To analyse the meaning of words[7] we usually distinguish between denotations, or reference, and connotation, or description. Thus 'green' refers to something of this colour but it also connotes the colour itself. We can of course have words with connotation but no denotation or hidden denotation such as 'greenness.' The opposite is just as likely in literature. The first time we read the name of a character whom we do not know, we have denotation but no connotation until we get to know him. As we read a literary text, the words appear and reappear in an established order. The position of the word in the text is as important as the semantic function just described.

Obviously the position of words in a poem has much greater importance than in a novel or a drama, and the analysis in each case will be designed to cope with the problems of the text. However, in general the analysis of vocabulary establishes the primary meaning of the text and also the sequential order with which we discern the fabric of the text. We must leave more detailed remarks on methodology of analysis for studies on each of the literary forms.

The grammatical organization of literary language, to a large extent, determines style. Although the conclusions drawn by stylisticians range over a wide spectrum from descriptions of technique (Hatzfeld) to inferences about the 'soul' of the author (Spitzer), they share a common focus on the peculiarities of the language in the text. The examination of syntax is part of the analytical enquiry and together with diction may be considered the linguistic base for the description of figurative language. Inferences of significance cannot result exclusively from the study of the linguistic apparatus without falling into the same impressionism meted out by the journalistic arbiter of taste. The description of syntactical relations such as length of components, tense and mood of verbal forms, relative position of predicate and complement, use of co-ordinate versus subordinate constructions in the paragraph, and so on, all point toward the elaboration of a unique linguistic system of signification. Anyone who has studied a literary text recognizes the linguistic system very early in his examination as the context of the work. It is common to use terms like 'meaningful in its context' or 'give me the context and I shall give you the meaning.'

The clear description of the elements of context is essential to the analytical enterprise because the central concern with figurative language rests on the supposition of an understanding of context.

Analysis of a literary text also entails the examination and description of the make-up of the literary image, metaphor, and symbol. I shall limit my remarks here to the general directions of the analytical enquiry.

Images[8] in the text form a basic and distinct category of literary language, for they are as much linguistic entities as psychological constructions. The analysis should describe the position and function of the imagery within the work. The sequential order of images is the principal means by which the author creates a pattern of responses in the reader. A second analytical category in the study of imagery is the inner consistency and function which is realized in the work. This phase of study, which we could call the inner logic of the image, is based on an elementary concept, namely that the images be consistent in creating the same inner meaning in the work. Images also have a capacity for description of an object or state of affairs that can serve the general function of object-awareness for the reader.

The metaphor[9] is a complex linguistic resource because of its diversity and its great capacity for imaginative expansion. The inner consistency of metaphors is of an exceptional nature for it is not a logical order that is being invoked, but rather one of mutual support and total effectiveness. The capacity for description through metaphor is almost unlimited as long as the reader is adept at imaginative expansion. In other words, the metaphor does not merely describe a given object or situation. It gives much more than is required in description; it links, expands, and creates a new sense of the object or situation which is not available through a report. Let us consider the following sequence of words: 'Lanterns shone in the dusk; a thousand silver tambourines wounded the day.' The first half of the line describes the physical characteristics with sufficient clarity to provide understanding to the reader, but the second half of the line expands the description in an evocation of properties of dramatization and violence which are beyond the scene and belong to the reader's reaction to the scene. In brief, metaphor begins where description ends; it moves the reader into an imaginative situation.

I have written above that each word is a potential symbol.[10] This potentiality lies in the capacity that words have to enlarge and develop our awareness until it begins to reach the most obscure corners of consciousness. With the discussion of the symbol we can sum up the general forms of enquiry we have been treating as literary analysis.

The literary symbol is a specific artistic form of a much larger facet of reality. Ricœur[11] identifies symbolic signs as 'opaque, because the first, literal, obvious meaning itself points analogically to a second meaning which is not given otherwise than in it' (*The Symbolism of Evil* 15). The principal distinction we must make between symbols in general and literary symbols is that the literary symbol is one of higher potentiality and availability. The reader has in most cases a series of highly developed symbolic levels in the text which, if correctly read, enlarge and develop his awareness of reality.

Let us first review the sequential order of symbols.[12] As the reading experience progresses, the reader is receiving each symbol in the order in which it is written. Of primary interest to us is the determination of his associations and relations from this sequence as he reads. The resultant order is not always the dominant one in the literary experience, but it is of great importance in determining the private apprehensions and scope of the work for the reader.

The second order I have been discussing is the rational demand for consistency.[13] This order is accentuated in works whose tone is critical and is obviously diminished in works of high lyric evocation, but there is a sense of the demand for consistency in all literary symbols, since the reader feels the need to know that the arrangement is free of contradictions in its total structure.

The third order I have been treating is that of basic recognition.[14] This is what we generally express when we say that something has 'meaning' for us. The symbol thus described has registered a given awareness in the reader. This does not mean basic understanding of the symbol, for that most certainly is the first requirement of analysis. Recognition of symbolic terms is a form of imaginative assimilation by the reader so that literally the symbol becomes the reader's mental causeway from recognition to expansion of awareness. When this happens it is due not only to the predisposition of the reader, but also and perhaps essentially to certain properties in the symbol, such as key words of high associative potentiality.

Analysis of literary language gives way to the higher demands of literary structure, wherein the work is examined and described in terms of functions of voice, time, space, and persona. The discipline of observation, study, and description which I have outlined in the analysis of literary language applies also to structure.

Analysis of literary structure is an essential part of the study of literature, for only through the rigorous examination of the literary dimensions and their explicit functions can the critic have access to the whole of the work; the problem is much more acute in longer works of literature. The structure of a novel, poem, or drama is composed of implicit or explicit dimensions of time, space, literary persona, and voice. Consequently the analysis of structure consists of detailed observation and explication of functions of these basic components. The questions involved in structural analysis vary considerably from one text to another; nevertheless we can observe the general characteristics of this kind of enquiry. Time in literature is like a bifocal lens. The reader is constantly being asked to focus the eye of his imagination on the broader temporal dimensions with their beginning and end in the work and at the same time to be conscious of the immediacy of the scene before him. The variations of the temporal dimension can be most intricate, especially in the modern novel. Literary space, like literary time, is related to external reality and to inner significance. For example, we can have a varied empirical world depicted in a novel, but its significance to characters, and thereby to readers, can be a monotone of sorrow with no variation visible; or, in a lyric poem, space may be entirely made up of associations based on the observation of commonplace things. The point I wish to make here is that the method of examining space is consistent with our program of analysis. The reader observes, notes the development of the basic dimensions, and then moves on to describe the literary function of space. Literary personae can be independent literary entities or merely figures in a broad panorama; they can also be central or marginal to the work, but in each case the role they play has been determined by an accumulation of detail amid which they emerge. The literary voice is the central concern of structural analysis, since the reliability, personality, scope, and situation of the literary source must be identified and described in order to achieve knowledge of the whole structure. I would like to conclude this commentary on analysis with a general argument for the necessity of analysis and analytical methods as a basis for interpretation.

There are three things that analysis provides the critic which, in my opinion, are necessary for the realization of systematic criticism: first, technical training in the mechanics of the literary text; second, self-discipline in accepting the primacy of the text over the impressionism of undisciplined interpretation; and third, the possibility of criticism of the whole work and not the piecemeal reflections of memory.

I should like to begin this central and controversial phase of criticism with a clear statement of my position on criticism. Unless we presuppose the unity of the reader, the presence of data within a reader's experience, the creative capacity of the imagination, the judgment and verification of reason, the presence of memory, the reality of time and of the reader's world as well as an objective world which is there when not observed or verified, there is no literary reality. In summary, a complex of limiting factors converges in the formation of the cognitive structure we call literature. To read is a human activity and the reading experience is a human product; therefore we must assume that it is deeply marked and coloured with the singular human traits of character and circumstance. I am not saying that interpretation is a plunge into the hopelessly closed world of personal subjectivism of each reader. What I am stating, however, is that knowledge is a human achievement, and knowledge of literature distinguishes itself only because of the extraordinary use made of the imaginative faculties of the reader. Just as the full meaning of a symbol – literary or merely linguistic – is not clear unless the singular situation of the use and function of the symbol is clear, so also the reader must be considered in all his assumptions and limitations for a full understanding of literature as knowledge. The objective reference for readers and critics is always the text. The shared symbolism of the literary work establishes an intersubjective consensus grounded in the semantic demands of the text. Consequently interpretation[15] is the study of the intersubjective relationships of the work; analysis, as we have seen, is the study of the verbal ground which is the text.

Interpretation is a study of distances; these are moral, intellectual, ideological, and sociological distances, invoked and manipulated between the reader and the literary text. The lyric and dramatic genres offer fewer problems to the critic because they are more direct experiences for the reader. The relationship between the lyric voice of the dramatis personae and the reader is one of direct consequence in imaginative creation. Narrative, however, is more complex for the critic because of the variability of the narrative voice.

The critic distinguishes himself from the general reader not in the nature of the literary experience, but in the self-awareness of why and how that experience has been realized. Interpretation is an enquiry by the critic into what happened to him as he read a literary text. Each text demands specialized treatment so that only a brief, general outline of the enquiry can be given here.

Literature to a greater or lesser degree offers the reader the possibility of identification with the literary reality. Identification with a literary character or voice that results in certain cases, especially drama and fiction, is neither good nor bad per se. Clearly this situation can be carefully planned for and constructed by a talented writer. The potential identification is realized only through the reader's recognition of his own world in the imitation. It is a Pandora's box which, once opened, unleashes a torrent of emotional and psychological forces and consequently is impossible to control. Yet identification is at times quite desirable in order to achieve an intimate understanding of the literary world being depicted.

A work of literature which explicitly or implicitly carries a truth claim is to a large degree dependent on the belief induced in the reader. There are many ways to convince a reader that the imaginative situation he is experiencing reflects the external objective world. This aspect of the reader's belief is directly related to the question of realism and the reflection of the external social, political, and economic world. The writer who captures the essence of some aspect of the external world moves the reader into a quiet surrender of any scepticism he might have had and obliges him to accept the literary world as an accurate re-enactment of the reader's own world. Belief in the truth claim is most effective when the reader is not readily aware of the writer's techniques.

There is also a third form of interpretative distance in the internal relationship of the work itself which we can see exemplified in the novel by distance between character and narrator. The distance here is one of support or correction from a position of greater to one of lesser authority. The body of ideas of a work is largely constructed in this internal distance. Let us say, for example, that the narrator in a novel supports the opinion of the protagonist by commentary and by corroboration. Further let us say that the character becomes convinced of a certain ideology and takes steps to live up to his convictions. Since the narrator has already predisposed the reader to believe in the sound judgment of the character, much more has happened than the mere conversion of the character. The shortened distance has made it possible for the narrator to demonstrate that the conversion was honourable, just, and so on. Thus the ideology has been presented as clearly as if it had been explicitly stated.

One of the master subtleties of prose fiction is the establishment of ironic distance. An unreliable narrative voice, for example, commenting on the significance of a character's behaviour, inverts the normal effect. An unfavourable assessment can thus constitute support while favourable remarks can induce a negative response in the reader.

Inner distances are also used in the other genres to create a precise tone. For example, in drama, the isolation of the protagonist from the social group is one of internal distance. In lyric poetry, distance is expressed primarily in the personal metaphor separating or uniting the lyric voice of self to his world.

In short, interpretation is an integral part of the critical commentary whether the critic recognizes it or not, and it is treated openly, not implicitly, in the best criticism.

I have thus far based this chapter on the premise that literature is a phenomenological experience which exists in the mind of the reader and that this intersubjective reality is the material we study. It is, therefore, necessary to give some attention to the knowing subject in order to avoid any misinterpretation of the methodology here proposed. Why does one read? There is an almost limitless array of idiosyncratic reasons for reading anything, be it a newspaper, a legal case, or a novel; however, the general aim of the activity we call reading is to gain awareness of a situation or of specific items in the situation. How do we then distinguish the reading of literature? Like any other human domain of knowledge, it is a specific enterprise and as such has it own rewards and difficulties for the reader. It is a discipline of the imagination that results in an imaginative awareness of the reader's own world. The metaphorical generalization which the reader assimilates into his own experience is a unique human creation and has its historical origins in man's search for an explanation of the world through myth. The imaginative assimilation of the metaphorical statement is also the primary criterion for measuring the value of the reading. When a reader declares that a given work of literature 'says nothing to me,' he is expressing in ordinary language what the critic states in more elaborate professional language. This judgment merits acceptance in direct proportion to the abilities and previous disposition of the reader. The reader who knows himself as the knowing subject and who is aware of his function as he reads is one who will be a reliable source of the intersubjective value of the work. On the other hand, the reader who associates literary value with personal taste has nothing to say except that his private taste runs in a certain manner.

The reader with critical self-awareness is like Janus facing two ways. He casts what he reads toward a diversified universe which contains all things, and he faces inwardly toward a knowledge of self.

It should now be evident that the aspect of knowledge we treat, imaginative knowledge of self and world, is not an innate, ready-made form of cognition; it is primarily a creative activity. Imaginative knowledge is not acquired by passively permitting an influx of sensations to enter the knowing mind; it must be constructed. It is the product of awareness operating more or less openly through a multitude of associations. Knowing is an original and natural part of living and imaginative knowing is the reader's sustained effort to attain all, to be all, and still to be oneself.

The creative process of reading literature begins with the initial recognition of the written symbols, but instantly becomes a recording of internal associations as well as external items of the world within the consciousness of the reader. This process is a reconstruction of the external model through a system of realized symbols. Only secondarily and very superficially is the literary experience ever an acquisition of prefabricated facts from social sources. I think this is the basic mistake most social science programs have committed when they have attempted to incorporate literature into the study of an area like Hispanic America. The roots of the reading experience lie deep inside the reader's personality, and in every case, if the work of literature is recreated, it comes to be in the original version of the reader. I do not deny the importance of the social context in forming the literary experience of the reader, for he is clearly a product of his civilization. In fact, if the literary experience is treated as a primary form of knowledge, it can be of service to the specialist interested in the make-up of a civilization. The central concept I am pressing here is that the literary experience begins with the reader, with his transformation of the linguistic symbols before him into a system of communication which thereby creates a world within a world.

The critic is a reader's reader since his principal function is to make the work of literature more accessible to the reader. The critic who traffics in arbitrary pronouncements of interpretation and value is a critic in name only.

I consider literary criticism to be an intellectual discipline dedicated to the study of knowledge of the imagination. It thus demands of the critic certain distinctive qualities of mind and disposition. It should now be clear that the study of literature is being considered only as an intellectual endeavour and not as a lesser enterprise for entertainment. To the critic, literature presents an intellectual challenge with inescapable questions about self, world, and, most of all, human creativity. Man is born into a world he did not make, into a process over which he has no control. His primordial need is to understand the physical and the spiritual complex that surrounds him. Although his understanding is partial and temporary, it does provide insight and enlightenment. Literature as a manifestation of man offers the critic a unique document of man's concept of reality. There are numerous substitutes for literature, which in some cases are the predecessors of literature, such as magic, ritual, folk myth, and primitive religion. The critic thus has the opportunity to delve into man's inner conceptions of his world. Not all critics, of course, take up the intellectual challenge, and some indeed give the impression that they consider literature a decorative art for the embellishment of civilization. However, let us not be concerned with those who do not recognize the depth and significance of literature in favour of those who do.

The critic works for an expansion of awareness. To him criticism is more than an activity; it is above all a contribution to what we have come to call the humanities. The highest reward to which the critic can aspire is to open the work which previously was closed to the intellectual reader. There is a myriad of specializations and perspectives in literary criticism, as there should be in a discipline that is dealing with an intersubjective reality. These words do not, however, imply a lack of guidelines in the practise of criticism. It is merely an acceptance of plurality as a fact. I believe in the seriousness and necessity of the enterprise; therefore, I have criteria of what constitutes valid criticism. First, the critical structure must be well organized; it must be free of inner contradiction. If coherence is lacking, any insight gained in one part may be eliminated by a contrary proposition. Second, the critical structure must be sufficient to the literary work being studied. The critical structure must consider and treat all of the components of the work. Nothing necessary to the work can be omitted, and no more need be added for the sake of clarity. Thus, although I make no claims of superior methodology, it is clear that the argument for the combination of analysis and interpretation in the manner I have described is based on these criteria of validity. In my view, the critical goal is not personal satisfaction, but rather increased awareness by the reader of the literary work. Only if this occurs is there ultimately an attainment of the knowledge which justifies the enterprise.

Analysis and interpretation of an aesthetic reality have been my concern in this chapter. By way of conclusion I wish to outline briefly the philosophical thought on which these remarks have been based and on which a system of criticism may be found of practical significance to intellectual readers.

My work is indebted to phenomenological philosophy and criticism. I consider a work of literature to be an anthropological situation with a history. The study of the history of literature is not only useful but emphatically an essential part of literary studies. However, the historical study of an author and his time is not the critical study of literature. The work of literature exists as an imaginative experience in the reader and not as an historical event in the past. Therefore, the task of the critic is to explain neither the genesis of the work nor the formative influences, but rather to make it explicit, to reveal the symbolic language, open the structure, and interpret the themes: in brief, to make it part of the reader's existential domain.

The logical beginning for the enquiry is with the language. Literature is available to the reader only through a mastery of the inner circle of the symbolic system we call literary expression. The second step is the historically informed understanding of literary structure with its implicit development of themes. The third step is the interpretation of the work in terms of the reader's reality. In criticism a novel is not a thing; it is an experience.

The search for the recoverable historical sense of a work and the time, language, and so on in which it was written is to me a very marginal enterprise to one who is concerned with literature. The central justification for literature is that it is an open source for self-realization and fulfilment by the reader, and it is to this endeavour that I am dedicated.

8

A method of enquiry

My main problem in developing a critical method for narrative based on textual analysis and intersubjective interpretation has been reconciling methods of enquiry which often seemed to be moving in opposite directions. The first impulse is to try to integrate the two or, if this fails, to choose the better of the two. The reality of the reading experience is not simple and we must be able to establish the internal and the external distances of the intersubjective structure. The essence of the method, I shall propose here, is a dialectical relationship which first appears in dialogue. It is the dialectic of language and experience.

Textual analysis and intersubjective interpretation can be seen as having inverted patterns of operation in which each must leave out an essential part of the other because of its very point of departure. Thus a dialectic between the two poles suggests the possibility of a more complete method of enquiry. The problem we seek to investigate is therefore defined as the relationship of experience to language; the two dialectic poles from which we shall approach the problem are analysis and interpretation.

Analysis begins with a description of the textual language and structure; and, consequently, moves from language toward experience but stops short of it. The knowing person, in our case the reader, is a necessary assumption which cannot be reached through analysis of language. On the other hand, interpretation approaches the language-experience problem through the expression of subjectivity. Thus the movement here is from an expression of experience itself toward the explanation of the subjective response to the literary language. However, the literary language cannot be reached unless the investigator is prepared to move beyond the limitations of his subjective response. The literary language itself is the necessary assumption for interpretation.

The dialectic relationship exists as necessary movement toward an assumed pole. In this way we can conceive of analysis as the description of language which is actualized only in experience and similarly we can think of interpretation as the expression of subjectivity which is based on language. Both are always present in the process of understanding a text, each is implied in the other, and each is the necessary pole of the other. It follows therefore that a method of enquiry which seeks to fulfil the reader's experience must be dialectic in theory and in practice. Let us consider the preconditions for the elaboration of this method.

First, we must find and identify the limitations of both analysis and interpretation. Analysis of the literary text bypasses experience and plunges the enquiry into the language of literary discourse. The reading experience is always implied but never treated directly. The undeniable limitation is the reduction of experience to a unitary supposition of actualization. The more complete the analysis of literary language becomes the more pressing the need to know how the reality of experience takes place and how it realizes the literary expression. Interpretation seeks out the intersubjective common ground of the reading experience. Within the circle of experience the relative distances from the text are established as that which is basic reference to the exterior world and that which is a secondary construction of self-reference. Within the circle of experience, interpretative theory cannot grasp the organization of the text itself.

Second, we must establish the logical procedure for a dialectic method. The enquiry progresses through a series of inversions. The emergence of knowledge through a dialectic methodology is possible only if we accept cognitive unity as a synthesis of the two opposed approaches of enquiry. The forces of analysis and interpretation are exclusive of each other outside of the dialectic. Within the method, however, we experience the inversion from one to another and thus use both. The answer to the general question of where the two methods meet can already be anticipated in this second precondition of methodology; the two sides of any inversion meet in the phenomenon itself and in our case the phenomenon is the reading experience.

Third, we must outline the successive inversions of the dialectic method. The enquiry begins away from the immediate experience in order to penetrate into the fixed external basis of meaning – the text. It is necessary, however, to recognize the antithesis of this inversion even while we are pursuing it. Therefore a radical questioning of the questioner himself must follow immediately.

This process of controlled inversions of questioning will be repeated in successive stages of an enlarging enquiry. Within each stage the direction of the questions is to be fully understood only in the light of the inversion which follows. Since these directions, analysis and interpretation, are the two sides of the methodological inversion, each is implicit in the other. I have designed the method of enquiry in five stages, each with its own inversion. They are: (1) fictional language, which approaches the text first from the direction of analysis and then from that of interpretation; (2) fictional structure, which is also examined first from analysis and then from interpretation; (3) fictional context, which is the last of the three stages to move first from analysis and then from the perspective of interpretation; (4) reader distance, which reverses the order of the first three stages: here we begin with interpretation and follow with analysis; and (5) intersubjective value, which is the last stage of the method and like the fourth stage also begins with interpretation and concludes with analysis.

My central argument on methodology can now be stated in more detail. I propose that the inversely related procedures of analysis and interpretation must be joined into one dialectic method if we are to attain a full understanding of the literary reading experience. Literature is distinguishable from other forms of expression in its vastly expanded referential aspects which make the reading experience one of immensely broad and diverse enrichment. I am therefore proposing a dialectic method which incorporates both analysis and interpretation in inverse movement to each other. The goal is to open up the reading experience first to the reader himself and then to the community of readers who have shared the same text in an analogous experience.

My theoretical basis on methodology can be found in the writings of Miguel de Unamuno, Edmund Husserl (published and unpublished), and principally in the philosophy of Paul Ricœur. Ricœur points out the following insight into the problem of expression and experience: 'In Husserl's first works consciousness is defined not by perception, that is by its very presence to things, but rather by its distance and its absence. This distance and this absence are the power of signifying, of meaning ... Thus consciousness is doubly intentional in the first instance by virtue of being a signification and in the second instance by virtue of being an intuitive fulfilling. In short, in the first works consciousness is at once speech and perception' (Ricœur, *Husserl* 204).

The literary work is in this theory always and at the same time language and experience, and the method I shall outline here is an attempt to examine this phenomenon without reducing its multiplicity to any formula, but rather with respect for the intentionality of the text within the subjectivity of the reader.

In my reading of Ricœur's hermeneutical theory I have identified five basic presuppositions underlying the interpretation of a literary text:

1 The sentence is the fundamental unit of discourse wherein metaphor and symbol are constituted as event and meaning is discerned.

2 The actualization of written language in a text differs radically from that of spoken language in that the event (writing) is fixed and reference to the author's intentions and world are suspended. Textual reference on the other hand operates as a possible mode of *being in the world*. Consequently the audience of the text is generalized, anonymous, and unprivileged.

3 Meaning in a literary text can be described as movement from *sense* to *reference*. There is an implicit epistemology here and a central question is the analysis of movement as dialectical tension.

4 The text is constituted as an ordered, singular, and generic totality, consequently the interpretation of metaphorical referentiality must be mediated by the text as a whole. The ultimate limits of referentiality are set by the text itself.

5 The primary task of interpretation is to reveal the intentionality of poetic language. The intentionality of poetic language is to predicate a metaphoric meaning which can be understood in terms of a dialectical tension between mimesis and poiesis, which can be characterized as the common utilization of a collective meaning (communication) and the unique moment of the imagination (metaphoric creation).

Let us first consider the applicability of Ricœur's hermeneutics to poetry before developing its possibilities for narrative study.

A phenomenological theory of literature approaches the literary text as the facilitating basis for performances by the reader which are variations on a theme. A fundamental corollary of this principle is that the intentionality of the text itself is variational. This idea takes into account an implicit inventiveness in the text which must be put into play if it is to be actualized. The essential activity of the writer and of the reader is therefore the creative engagement of language as expression.

These general observations on the inventiveness of realizing variations of the text are not contrary to the Aristotelian dictum that poetry (texts considered as literature) is ultimately more true than history, for it is only by exploring the possibilities of the mind's free play that discovery and creativity can be examined.

Ricœur's theory of dialectic tension is best depicted as the intersection between two spheres of discourse. This intersection of the separate spheres can be understood if we recognize that their difference is based on separate modalities of each discourse. Consequently the intersection is the encounter which is possible because of the oppository relationship implicit in the semantic aims of each discourse.

Metaphor is taken by Ricœur as a paradigm of the creative encounter of the spheres of discourse. The active metaphor yields a gain in meaning and this gain is inseparable from the multiple levels of tension present in the metaphor. These levels are identified as (a) tension in the terms of the statement or ultimately of the text which can be focused through the question: *What does the text say?*; (b) tension in the formal structures of the text which we can characterize with the question: *How does the text speak?*; (c) tension in the referentiality of the text which can be understood with the question: *What does the text speak about?*; and (d) the final tension between the text's autonomy and the requirements of the reader's appropriation; the question here is: *How have I read the text?*

The gain in meaning is not a synthesis, for it remains caught in an open dialectic without an absolute. This gain is at the moment of appropriation when there is an intersection of two separate movements. One movement aims at determining more rigorously the conceptual traits of reality while the other movement aims at making referents appear. This is the encounter of the capacity of logical abstraction with the capacity to imagine, concretize, and apprehend the given.

The essential characteristic of the poetic text is thus a creative gain which Ricœur examines through four levels of tension operative in the reading of the text. In ordinary language an analogous situation occurs when a speaker attempts to express a new experience; he must do so in words which he must appropriate for the occasion. Thus the speaker seeks a formulation capable of carrying his intention from the network of meaningful expressions he finds already established. The first two levels of dialectic tension in the text are accessible through critical description and analysis while the third and fourth levels are primarily levels of interpretation.

Let us for the moment assume careful description and analytical rigour, the question still remains how this data is to be tied to the interpretative enquiry of referentiality and appropriation.

The metaphorical utterance in the poem stands before us as a statement expressed in specific formal patterns. Ricœur holds that the utterance is about something and the enquiry into what this is, is the task of interpretation. The metaphorical utterance functions in two referential fields at once. This duality explains how two levels of meaning are linked up in the same symbol. Put somewhat differently, two energies or force fields converge, because of the gravitational pull exerted by a second referential field (experience) the first and familiar one (language) is forced to leave its place of origin and move toward an encounter. The dynamism of metaphorical meaning is seen as an unstable convergence of the referential field of experience as it moves toward expression, and the referential field of language is forced out of the familiar where it begins and moves toward experience.

HERMENEUTICAL COMMENTARY

The poem 'Concorde' was written by Octavio Paz in 1968 and published in the book *Ladera este* (Mexico: Joaquín Mortiz 1969); in 1968 he also published the poem in a graphic design *Discos visuales* (Mexico: Era 1968). I shall make reference to both versions of the poem.

Concorde

A Carlos Fuentes

> Arriba el agua
> Abajo el bosque
El viento por los caminos

> Quietud del pozo
El cubo es negro El agua firme

El agua baja hasta los árboles
El cielo sube hasta los labios. (p 11)

Concorde

To Carlos Fuentes

> Water above
> Forest below
Wind on the roads

> Quiet well
Bucket's black, still water

Water coming down to the trees
Sky rising to the lips.

The text presents three related verbal contexts developed in three stanzas. The first context establishes a situational relationship of spatial opposition for the nouns 'agua' and 'bosque,' but with an implicit sense of movement in the line 'El viento por los caminos.' The characteristic of 'viento,' which is movement, is heightened by the preposition 'por' and the plural 'caminos.' However, movement is only implicit.

The second context takes up stillness and posits the opposite of movement. Consequently, the absence-presence relationship of opposites is operative. The 'quietud' of the well implies the possibility of 'agitación' which is absent. Stillness is further linked to the blackness of the well and the firmness of the water. The first verb is introduced here and it is the copula of identification of blackness-bucket and by parallel structure of water-firmness.

The third context releases the movement which thus far has only been implicit or posited in absence. The movement is presented in an oppository pair and also in opposition to the first context. Here water moves down and the sky (reflected in the bucket's water) moves up. There is a completed cycle insofar as the water which was above has come down to meet the trees (forest) which were situated below in the first stanza. But it is the final line that is the fulfilment, for here the sky (implicitly reflected in the water in the bucket) goes up to the lips of the poetic voice whose presence is finally revealed. The play of opposites has been utilized to reveal an absence-presence relationship of the poetic voice and the poem.

The concrete text is set up in four cycles of the disc. The first establishes the basic organization of oppositions by countering the first two lines of the text. The second cycle isolates the implied movement of the third line. The third cycle balances the stillness of the well with the blackness of the bucket and the firmness of the water. The fourth cycle posits the final opposition of countermotion.

The second level of enquiry responds to the question: how does the text speak?

The basic structure of this poem is derived from dichotomous paired opposites. The original dichotomy is 'up-down' and into this network the poet inserts water and forest, which are in opposition only because of their linguistic relationship to the true dichotomy. The opposition of water-forest is one of implicit spatial situation.

The second basic structural element is derivative of the first: the explicit brings the implicit into the text. The wind through the roads implies the verb and of course implies movement.

The two basic devices are maintained and developed as the separate spatial realms of 'up-down,' everything is still in place: the well, the bucket, the water. But stillness ('quietud') implies agitation and we wait.

The dichotomy is exploited as the implicit movement becomes explicit and what was up moves down, but the surprise is that what comes up is something new, it is the reflection of above (sky) but now it comes up to a new entity, the lips. We can recognize that the structure of the poem is the ultimate dichotomy of absence-presence.

As we turn the disc, the oppository relationship of words suggesting a spatial relationship is graphically represented in an ideographic situation. It is significant to recognize that there is an axis which joins and separates at the same time and a single image centre toward which the design points. Consequently, in the fourth cycle trees and lips are in proximity to each other and it is the water which is coming (down) toward the centre as the sky is coming (up) toward the same centre where trees and the poet's lips await.

The third level of enquiry responds to the question, What does the text speak about?

On the surface the poem is simple, clear, and accessible. There is an easy familiarity of the words in their contexts. The poet is utilizing the most basic spatial dichotomy available in language: up-down. The oppository pair is enlarged and given spatial significance; thus water becomes an oppositional partner with forest because of its spatial situation.

The playfulness of the poem is enhanced by omitting the verb and yet implying movement through the third, fourth, and fifth lines. Words have become properties and each is in its assigned space and its separateness. We are awaiting. The familiar poetic properties are awaiting the coming of movement. Finally it comes as suddenly as rain bursts from the clouds. With the coming of movement we have the revelation of the hidden but implied presence. The experience of being present is symbolized by the emergence of the poetic self through the appearance of his lips. With the movement of the bucket up the well we have the reflection of the sky coming toward the lips. And the sky in the water reaches the lips and there is the metaphorical truth of concord as the poetic self emerges as the centre of the poem.

This is a poem of becoming, a metaphorical variation on the theme of movement in the endless dialectic between absence and presence. It is poetry of absence which culminates in presence with the powerful revelation that this is a fleeting moment when the elements come together, making it possible to be.

The reading of the poem is an experience of epiphany. The text stands autonomously as an endless source of variations. The reader comes to it with a hermeneutic search for poetic truth and a historical appreciation of the poet's work in *Ladera este* and *Discos visuales*. In the reading experience the text's multiple variations resist a facile sense of closure. It is only when the text's dynamism is understood by the reader that the final revelation of the poetry of becoming emerges as truth.

The fourth level of enquiry responds to the question, How have I read the text?

The language of the first stanza imparts a concrete enunciation of situation.

> Arriba el agua
> Abajo el bosque
> El viento por los caminos

It creates a structure wherein names are positioned in a specific relationship for movement of the third stanza to operate.

The language in the second stanza is attributive and assigns the qualification of the objects.

> Quietud del pozo
> El cubo es negro El agua firme

Here we receive the physical properties of sound, sight, and touch. The situational position of the first stanza receives qualified objects in the second stanza, which together create the metaphor when movement is added in the third stanza:

> El agua baja hasta los árboles
> El cielo sube hasta los labios

The centre of the metaphor is the absent concordance which is the self who perceives acts and whose absence is turned into presence as the missing but necessary centre of this lyrical structure.

It would be naïve in the extreme to assume that this system of reference is not related to other texts. As a system it is closely tied to Paz's poetry, even his earliest poetry. Consider, for example, 'Salvas' from 1943:

> Torre de muros de ámbar
> Solitario laurel
> golfo imprevisto
> Sonrisa en un oscuro pasillo

andar de rio que fluye
dulce cometa
Puente bajo cuyos arcos corre
  Siempre la vida

Tower of amber walls
Lonely laurel
unpredictable gulf
Smile in a dark hallway
the pace of the flowing river
tender comet
Under the arches of the bridge always runs life

But beyond the poetry of Octavio Paz we hear and see a marked kinship to the poetry of the Mexican, José Juan Tablada (1871–1945), who introduced the haiku and the ideographic poem to Mexican literature. Consider, for example, 'El Cartelón del Circo.'

Hasta la noche, desde la mañana
incesante roncar de la tambora
que al olor del ocote se incorpora
¡Tónica de la fiesta mexicana!

¡Y en su salto mortal hacia el Ocaso
luce en el sol la cara del payaso! (p 480)

From morning, till night
incessant song of the tambour
mixing with the aroma of ocote
Spirit of the Mexican fiesta!

And in its deadly leap towards sunset
the face of the clown glows in the sun!

Or if a further example be needed consider this haiku:

Hombre, árbol
superior
tus brazos, las ramas
tus pies, las raíces
tu rostro, la flor (p 604)

> Man, superior tree
> your arms, branches
> your feet, roots
> your face, the flower

Paz has taken the essentialism of Tablada into a concrete system of internal reference and fused the collective with the personal into a metaphor of the unity of opposites.

The *Discos visuales* also have a clear precedent in Tablada's 'poemas ideográficos' such as 'Luciernagas,' 'Nocturno eterno,' and a host of others which are of no use to us unless we can see them as well as hear them. Tablada's texts are but the beginning of the recognition of traces of other poets. Beyond Tablada there are the Japanese poets of the haiku, Apollinaire with his *Idéogrammes lyriques,* and Mallarmé with his graphic poetic creations.

The essentialism we have found in Paz and traced to Tablada also has deep roots in ancient and classical poetry. The mystical belief that the world can be found through meditation on a grain of sand, or eternity in a moment has both a graphic and a lyrical expression in William Blake. Consider 'The Fly' from *The Songs of Innocence and Experience.*

The point of this excursion into the intertextual thickets is to demonstrate that the core of Ricœur's theory is to disclose the creative power of metaphor in dual referentiality of experience and expression.

I would now like to turn to another poet and a different text than those we have been considering in order to conclude this presentation of Ricœur's theory of literature applied to poetry. I would like to comment on 'Oda a unas flores amarillas' by Pablo Neruda.

Oda a unas flores amarillas

Contra el azul moviendo sus azules,
el mar, y contra el cielo,
unas flores amarillas.

Octubre llega.

Y aunque sea
tan importante el mar desarrollando
su mito, su misión, su levadura,
estalla
sobre la arena el oro

de una sola
planta amarilla
y se amarran
tus ojos
a la tierra,
huyen del magno mar y sus latidos.

Polvo somos, seremos.

Ni aire, ni fuego, ni agua
sino
tierra,

sólo tierra
seremos
y tal vez
unas flores amarillas. (pp 670–1)

Ode to Yellow Flowers

Against the blue, movement of blue,
the sea, and against the sky
some yellow flowers

October comes

And even if it is
so important the sea unfolding
its myth, its mission, its yeast,
on the sand
bursts
the gold
of a single
yellow plant
and your gaze
is chained
to the soil
your eyes turn from the immense pounding sea.

Dust we are, dust we will be.

Not air, not fire, not water
but earth
earth,

Only earth
we will be
and perhaps
some yellow flowers.

What does the text say?

The text consists of five stanzas. The first four stanzas alternate between lyrical descriptive images and brief lyrical statements. The fifth stanza is an extended metaphorical statement.

The first stanza establishes two images of movement: the sea moving its blue against a background of blue and the second image of yellow flowers seen against the sky.

The second stanza is the simple and direct statement of temporality: 'Octubre llega.'

The third stanza returns to the images of sea and flowers presented separately in the first stanza but which are now linked. The linkage consists of 'aunque estalla' in the fourth line. At this point there is the presentation of a new image, the presence of the 'other' to whom the poem is addressed. For the link between the sea and the yellow flower is in the *perceiver* who turns from the sea and concentrates on the land.

The fourth stanza is again a brief statement which links the 'tú' of the third stanza and the lyric voice in the plural 'somos, seremos.' Temporality is expanded from the present to the future.

The sixth and final stanza enlarges on the rejection of the sea in favour of the land by reviewing the four elements of pre-Socratic philosophy, air, fire, and water, which are all rejected in favour of land. The stanza ends with the metaphor of the yellow flowers, which had been one of the initial images.

How does the text speak?

The text is made up of simple parallel structures which set up key images in explicit lyrical contrastive contexts. The first, third, and fifth stanzas have this structure and the single-line second and fourth stanzas serve as breaks or separations for the parallel of contrasts.

The syntactical basis for this structure is the simple syntactical patterns of parallelism:

First stanza – 'Contra ...
　　　　　... y contra;

Third stanza – 'y aunque sea ...
　　　　　estalla ... y se amarran

Fifth stanza – 'ni, ni, ni ... sino ...
               y tal vez.'

The first syntactical structures establish a parallel slot for 'mar' and 'flores amarillas' and it is in this situation that we receive the first contrastive images, blue moving its blue, set against yellow with the sky as background.

The second stanza separates and breaks with the parallel structure of the first stanza. We have here a statement of time with an implicit lyric voice for whom time exists.

The third stanza once again takes up the parallel structure of the first. The sea with its movement is further developed and then contrasted with the solitary 'planta amarilla' on the sand. The contrast is not merely fixed in the text, it is also acknowledged in the text as the 'tú' enters the text choosing the singular plant and fleeing from the massive ever-present movement of the sea.

The fourth stanza is once again an interlude between the parallelism of the third and fifth stanzas. The significant feature here is the first person plural, which effectively unites the lyric voice and the 'tú.'

The fifth stanza utilizes one of the most common parallel structures in Spanish: 'not this but rather that' or 'ni, ni, ni ... sino,' but the stanza ends with the extension of the imagery into a fully developed metaphor – 'y tal vez.'

What does the text speak about?

The poem offers a complex metaphor of human life by means of an elementary syntactical structure. The poem begins describing two basic images in opposition – the sea in movement and yellow flowers.

The dual images are given a temporal dimension of an implied lyric voice, before being enlarged. The sea becomes not only movement but also the important massiveness with its own myth and mission, the implication unmistakably that of eternal and overwhelming power. But the flowers are also featured. Now it is but a solitary yellow plant broken and swept up onto the sand. The implications are in clear opposition to the sea: singularity, fragility, the insignificant residue thrown up on the beach by the all-powerful sea. It is at this point that the human dimension of the 'other' is clearly linked to the plant on the sand, for the eyes of the 'other' are tied to the plant and flee from the power and roar of the sea. The metaphor of sea as universe contrasting with the singularity of the individual plant and the beholder come together.

The poem now unites the lyric voice and the 'other,' thus proposing the singularity of human life as against life in general, for we are dust and it is to dust we shall return. The final development of the metaphor starts with a rejection of three of the four pre-Socratic elements (air, fire, and water) in order to reiterate that man is 'tierra.' Just as the rain merges into the sea in an indistinguishable mass, so our remains (dust) merge with the land, but there is a difference, for man as distinct from all other forms of life has a possibility of giving forth an expression of his uniqueness and singularity which will be seen and will stand out albeit for a limited time as symbolized in some yellow flowers.

How have I read the text?

The Ricœurean hermeneutics aims at the disclosure of metaphor at the fundamental intersection of the spheres of discourse characterized by language and expression. This intersection or the creation of metaphorical truth is the forced encounter of the external referentiality of the language with the internal referentiality of the text.

In Neruda's poem we must be able to incorporate such references as sea, flowers, colours, waves, and sand within a parallel structure which elaborates them in a unique expression: 'azul moviendo azules' and 'el oro de una planta amarilla y se amarran tus ojos.' But there are also the intertextual references, since 'sólo tierra seremos' refers ultimately to Genesis 2:7 as fire, air, water, and earth refer to pre-Socratic philosophy, but there is also 'el mar desarrollando su mito' with its oblique reference to Paul Valéry's *Le Cimetière marin*. The decisive factor in this study of the text is in the recognition of creativity as the fusion of horizons.

Literary criticism derived from Ricœur's hermeneutics starts with the recognition that the text is analytically accessible as distinct from the psychological recesses of the author's intentions. The form brought forth by the analysis of the text is not the hidden meaning, rather it is the requirement for reading addressed to the reader. The interpretation which follows analysis accordingly is a kind of obedience to this injunction which comes from the text.

The concept of hermeneutical circle is not ruled out by Ricœur's shift in hermeneutics. Indeed the hermeneutical circle is formulated but in new terms. It no longer proceeds from an intersubjective relation linking the subjectivity of the author and that of the reader. The hermeneutical program is a connection between two discourses, the discourse of the text and the discourse of interpretation. This connection means that what has to be interpreted in a text is what it says and what it speaks about – the kind of world it opens up, discloses. The final act of appropriation is less the projection of the reader's prejudices into the text than the fusion of horizons which occurs when the world of the text and the world of the reader merge into one another.

Let us now turn to the problem at hand – the elaboration of a method of enquiry for the narrative. If we transform the questions derived from Ricœur's philosophical hermeneutics to categories of enquiry we come up with (1) fictional language, (2) fictional structure, (3) fictional context, and (4) an intersubjective model. The principles of Ricœur's hermeneutic philosophy have been stated on numerous occasions in the last twenty years, but perhaps the fullest treatment is the recent revised version of *La Métaphore vive* (Paris: Seuil 1975) in English translation, *The Rule of Metaphor* (Toronto: University of Toronto Press 1978).

FICTIONAL LANGUAGE

The enquiry begins with the analytical examination of the text. The questions must force the internal design of the language to surface and be identified. Nothing can be assumed as obvious or inherent to expression. Thus a radical enquiry commences with the relations of sound and meaning, sound patterns and the semantic weight of the words. The textual enquiry continues with an interrogation of narrative discourse in its basic grammatical organization and subsequently focuses on the rhetorical conventions of literary language used in the text.

The methodological inversion consists in turning the interrogation from the text to the reader and examining the effect of language in its actualization by the reader. The questions are therefore directed toward the subjective patterns of significance. We identify the specific realization of the patterns of self-reference and the pattern of reference to external reality. Beyond the identification of the referential patterns the questioning further seeks an identification of function in the reading experience.

The illustration below can be seen as a model for the questions of this first stage.

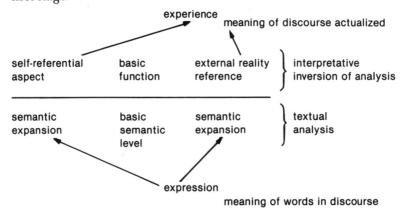

FICTIONAL STRUCTURE

The second stage commences with the enquiry into the internal relationship of interdependence. Questions about the purported reality of the narrative world and about the capacities of the narrative voice are fundamental. However, we must also seek out the situation and the attitude of the narrator in regard to his narration. Subsequently, it is necessary to examine the capacities of the fictional subjects and their setting within the emergent narration.

The inversion in this case moves us into the broader patterns of order through which a narrative takes shape in the reading experience. Once the operational laws are identified, it is necessary to examine their unitary function in the reading experience. In other words, what kind of a world have they established in the reader's actualization of the text?

FICTIONAL CONTEXT

The third stage moves into the broader consideration of the whole of textual intentionality. We are now seeking the answer to questions pertaining to tone, plot, truth claims, and themes. It is not to be confused with the traditional study of content, because we are here concerned with the specific elements of the story within a fully developed strategy of intentionality and not as an isolated examination of elements of plot. The arbitrary division of form and content, even as a rational abstraction used to examine the novel, is suspect because the division expresses only the critic's isolation of certain narrative aspects and neither reflects the intentionality of the text nor the reading experience.

The inversion of the third stage encompasses an enquiry into contextual meaning through an identification of the patterns of causality whereupon we can query their function in experience.

INTERSUBJECTIVE MODEL OF EXPERIENCE

The fourth stage of the method represents a complete change of direction. The first three stages moved progressively along an established projection of expression aimed at experience, but in this stage I shall move from experience toward expression.

The preliminary questions explore the basis for interpretation in the reader himself. Thus we are concerned with the capacities and the limitations of the reader. Consequently we are here examining the role of the implicit reader of the text.

The methodological inversion in this stage represents a direct application of the information gained through the analysis of the internal distance of the novel in order to establish the aesthetic dimensions which the reader's experience actualizes. This level of enquiry represents the broadest interrogation into the external distances based on the internal distance. Thus we are here putting into practise the full intersubjective structure.

The method of enquiry I have been elaborating does not consider the novel in a way commensurate with objective value judgments. I have discussed what the basis of value is for this approach. Let it suffice here to restate that the reading experience is the phenomenon to be evaluated and not a text considered in isolated abstraction. Consequently the preliminary questions on value correspond to a radical self-analysis by the reader of his relationship with the text. The inversion seeks to fix the textual intentionality to the experience of self-knowledge and social knowledge.

If my hypothesis of literary reality is accurate the methods discussed on these pages will help literary study.

AN OUTLINE OF THE ENQUIRY

Fictional language
Preliminary questions on language
  1 Do sound and meaning reinforce each other prominently?
     a Is onomatopeia present?
     b Is vocabulary used for its sound value as with alliteration or assonance?
     c What relation do these features have with the narrative presentation of character or narrative world?
  2 Do sound effects or patterns have any importance in the narrative?
     a Is there rhythmic prose?
     b Is the rhythm metrical or syntactical?
     c What importance does their position have in the sequence of words that comprise the narrative?
  3 Do individual meanings of words need explication?
     a Is vocabulary regional or dialectical?
     b Does the writer invent new words?
     c Does vocabulary belong to a specialized field or profession?
     d What effect do these features have on the presentation?
  4 How redundant or brief is the narrative in the description, characterization, and background passages?
     a How are scenes and summaries used?
     b If there is repetition, when does it occur?
     c Is there a *leitmotiv*?

5 How elaborate is the word choice in the descriptive scenes?
 a What kind (ie, sensory, visual, emotive, etc.) of adjectives are employed in scenes?
 b Is there any evidence of mood manipulation?
6 Is there a predominance of nouns or verbs in any selected passage? What is the effect of this usage?
7 Has there been any noticeable change of position in the grammatical arrangement of the sentences?
8 Has the normal grammatical agreement of number, gender, or tense been altered?
9 Has verbal mood been noticeably used? To what effect?
10 Do textual interrelations of words require explication?
 a Is parataxis (equality among phrases) used extensively? To what effect?
 b Is hypotaxis (imbalance of phrases) used extensively? To what effect?
 c Is there any use of anacoluthon (unfinished thought) in the narrative?
 d Is ellipsis employed? When and to what effect?
11 What type of word order is most prominent in the various kinds of narration which comprise the work?
12 Which rhetorical figures appear most prominently in the narrative?
 a Is there an ornamental design in the narrative?
 b Is there an emphatic sequence and plan of rhetorical figures?
 c Do rhetorical figures stimulate aesthetic communication?

Focal effect of language
 1 Identification of the fundamental patterns of significance
 a Textual self-reference
 b Textual reference to extralinguistic a priori concepts
 2 Identification of the functions of reference
 a correspondence between parallel realities
 b apologetics and the erosion of the reader's resistance to the argument
 c displacement of the reader's reality
 d creation of unique correspondences

Fictional structure
Preliminary questions on structure
 1 How does the story purport to exist?
 a Who provides the information?

    b How does the purported existence of the work equate with the narrative style?

2 What is the point of view of the narration?
    a Is there more than one?
    b How does point of view affect the dimensions of knowledge of the narration?

3 What is the attitude of the narrative voice toward what he narrates?
    a Is the narrative voice reliable?
    b Is he concerned with the fate of his characters?
    c Does he intervene in the story?
    d How does he affect the reader's opinion about the story and its characters?

4 What is the situation in which the narrator finds himself?
    a Does he identify himself?
    b How much does he know? Is he privileged to 'see' into the minds of his characters or is he merely an observer?

5 Who are the principal characters and how are they developed?
    a Are they multifaceted or uni-dimensional?
    b Are introspective techniques used to reveal their personalities and minds?
    c How is dialogue used to present them?

6 What is the setting of the narrative and to what extent is it structurally important?

7 How is narrative time presented and what is its importance in relation to experienced time in the narrative?

8 What are the relationships between the larger textual elements, for example, parts or chapters, and what, if any, is their structural role?

Textual interdependence
    1 Identification of the patterns of organization
        a linear laws of spatio-temporal relations
        b concentric laws of spatio-temporal relations
        c cosmic laws of spatio-temporal relations
    2 Identification of the function of organization
        a narrative structure of action
        b narrative structure of protagonist (character or other narrative agent)
        c narrative structure of space (world)

Fictional context
Preliminary questions on context
1 What is the tone of the narration?
   a What elements of style does the narrative voice use in creating narrative tone?
   b What is the overall tone and the means of its presentation?
2 What is the plot of the narrative?
   a What pattern emerges from the structural elaboration of time and space?
   b What sense of causality appears throughout the plot? Is there a pattern of tensions?
3 What is the main story?
   a Are there secondary stories?
   b What importance does it have in the narrative?
4 What is the narrative idea or ideas which dominate(s) the telling of the story?
5 How is the theme of the narrative created?
   a What role does theme have in the narrative dominated by character?
   b What function does theme have in the narrative of action?
   c How is the thematic narrative elaborated which sets it apart from other narratives? What importance do exterior ideologies have? What pattern of symbols is used?

Contextual meaning
1 Identification of patterns of causality
   a a necessary chain of causality
   b cumulative causality on a limited base
   c multiple causality distinguishable as general or universal forces
2 Identification of the functions of causality
   a a narrative development of climactic resolution with first causes
   b a narrative development of complexity on a singular focus
   c a narrative development with cosmic dimensions of order

Model of intersubjective experience
Preliminary questions on interpretation
1 What is the reader called upon to provide in his relationship with the narrative voice?

2 What is the reader called upon to provide in his relationship with the narrative world?
3 What are the limitations of the reader's participation?

Dimensions of interpretation
  1 an aesthetic of mimetic correspondences
  2 an aesthetic of apologetics or persuasion
  3 an aesthetic of metaphorical displacement
  4 an aesthetic of participation in creation

9

Commentary on *Don Quixote*

The idea that an author's message is transmitted directly through his text to the reader is true only under certain circumstances, as when the interpretative aspect is close to a neutral position in both the author and the reader. Graphically it can be expressed in the following manner:

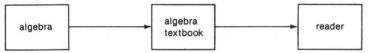

In all situations where the interpretative faculty of the author or the reader is in play there is an indirect transmission of information. A graphic depiction would be:

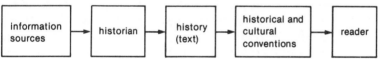

However, in the case of literary texts, that is, those texts which society agrees to treat as imaginative renderings of reality, the situation is far more complex.

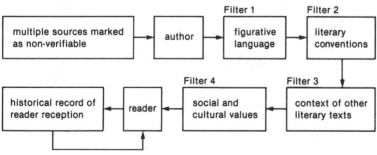

In this case the message passes through a system of filters in the process of being realized or 'decoded' by the reader, and even at this point, there is still the added filter of the synthesis of values which previous readers, including critics and reviewers, impart to the message. In this book so far, I have examined the issues which obtain in a critical examination of the narrative; now it is imperative to organize these insights into a system of analysis and interpretation. By way of demonstration I shall examine the four filters described above as fine redirectioning which together seem to me to form jointly the reality of the narrative text. Consequently the system of analysis and interpretation consists in constructing five levels of enquiry which correspond to the four filters. The four are (1) the analysis of fictional language which examines the first filter of polysemic language, (2) the analysis of fictional narrative structure, (3) experiential context, and (4) intersubjectivity of the text. I shall consider each of the four levels in turn as they apply to *Don Quixote de la Mancha* by Miguel de Cervantes.

FICTIONAL LANGUAGE

Fictional language is as much a matter of linguistic devices employed effectively as it is a general strategy employed for an implied reader. These two sides of the same question are always present, but in describing them analytically one is obliged to take them up one at a time. For purposes of demonstrating the first level of study, I shall use chapter 31 of Volume I.

The subject of this chapter is Sancho's report to Don Quixote on his visit to Dulcinea. The dialogue which ensues covers two-thirds of the chapter and is a continuation of Sancho's last words in the preceding chapter. The linguistic presentation of the visit takes place on different contrasting levels of style which are identified with each of the two speakers. The narrative voice steps aside and is limited to the mere identification of speakers until two-thirds of the chapter has passed. The chapter begins with Don Quixote's enigmatic invocation in the chivalric style of redundancy, circumlocution, alliteration, assonance, and not a few patterns of internal rhyme; this is followed by Sancho's short cryptic pragmatic deflationary descriptions of the physical situation. This exchange is repeated sixteen times until the narrative voice comes in with his own views on the subject of the visit. From the first to the eighth, the exchanges are relatively brief, limited to one or two statements by each speaker. The ninth through the twelfth exchanges increase in length until we have full half-pages taken up by each speaker. The thirteenth to the sixteenth gradually decrease in length until we are back to the brevity of the first exchange. If we were to plot the succession of dialogue exchanges between the two speakers we would find a zig-zag graph gradually increasing until reaching its peak with the expansive twelfth exchange of thirty-six printed lines which is then followed by a rapid decline in length until a minimal four lines is reached in the sixteenth exchange between speakers. The overall pattern of the language, of course, closely resembles a true dialogue situation.

As I said above there are two styles in this passage, each corresponding to one of the two speakers. Don Quixote's style is inflationary and constantly overstates the projection of his imagination; but we must not forget that he is asking Sancho what has happened. In contrast, Sancho's style is deflationary and understates, for he is very reluctantly reporting to his master. We can gain a closer insight into the nature of the dialogue sequence of styles by having a look at a few examples. First, in imitation of the novels of chivalry we are treated to the circumlocutions of Don Quixote as he imagines what might have been the scene as his squire came before the unparalleled Dulcinea: 'Llegaste, ¿y qué hacía aquella reina de la hermosura? A buen seguro que la hallaste ensartando perlas, o bordando alguna empresa con oro de cañutillo para este su cautivo caballero.' (You arrived, and what was the queen of beauty doing? Most certainly you found her stringing pearls, or embroidering something in gold thread for this her captive knight.) But Sancho's response is even more cutting in its cryptic brevity because of the narrator's functional 'respondió Sancho' breaking up his response. Thus from the high-flying fancy of Don Quixote we are abruptly grounded by Sancho's 'No la hallé,' and then with only a slight reduction in shock, we get the rest of his statement: 'sino ahechando dos hanegas de trigo en un corral de su casa.' (No, I found her winnowing two loads of wheat in the barnyard of her house.) A clash of images ensues: on the one hand an exquisite mediaeval princess, on the other a rough peasant girl threshing grain. The immediate question is how such an obvious disparity can possibly lead to further dialogue. But our doubts are dispelled in the second exchange. Don Quixote is not disturbed in the least and urges Sancho to use his imagination. This is the pattern which holds through the first ten exchanges. Again and again Don Quixote recovers from Sancho's undermining of his ideal concept. For example, in the seventh exchange Don Quixote asks Sancho if he were not pleased to have smelled such a delicious fragrance as that of Dulcinea's perfume. Sancho responds that he can give a name to the undefinable which Don Quixote suggests – it was perspiration from the exertion of threshing. But undismayed, Don Quixote goes on, saying that Sancho must have had a cold or could only smell himself.

Such is the nature of this dialogue until the eleventh exchange when Don Quixote enquires how it was that Sancho was able to travel from the Sierra Morena to El Toboso and return in three days. Before Sancho can reply, Don Quixote provides him with the magical solution: the intervention on his behalf by a friendly wizard. Sancho is thus forced to drop his pragmatic counterpoint and to agree to the fantastic, for he can only reply that it must be so. Now that Sancho has implicated himself in the use of the imagination, Don Quixote asks his advice on the situation at hand. Don Quixote's dilemma is whether he should keep his knight's word and serve the princess Micomicona or hasten to the side of his lady Dulcinea. The knight and his squire finally reach agreement that he should first serve the princess and thereby gain Sancho his reward as a loyal squire and then go to pay homage to Dulcinea. The accord is reached only because once again the two make a pact to respect each other's needs as part of reality.

The reader learns to rely upon the observations of the narrative voice, whose references to the empirical world are given as a matter of course. But when from time to time the reliability of the narrative voice is called into question, it becomes necessary for the reader to establish his own patterns of referentiality. In this dialogue the patterns are quite complex. The careful reader is able to discern almost from the outset the dialectical nature of the dialogue. Idealism is identified with an imaginative capacity to grasp the ideal concept which in a platonic perspective is hidden by the gross materiality of appearances. The pragmatic basis for action is maintained by retaining appearances and acting on the basis of pragmatic experience. What better example can we find than the passage presented above. The ideal concept of the lady in the tradition of courtly love equates her perfume to the scent of delicate aromas, but the pragmatic projection of experience is just as clear: threshing grain is strenuous and the thresher will perspire. Throughout this chapter the reader is treated to a contrastive dialogue as courtly love is debated against the empirical reality of the peasant. The world views clash and seemingly are destined to reach an impasse, but this is not to be. The positions of both speakers alter with subtle manipulation of the language. Don Quixote seeks to impose his ideal concepts onto Sancho's report so that it will conform to his idea of a knight errant devoted to his lady.

However, it is not the practical squire but the knight who brings up the most obvious practical impediment to Sancho's trip: the reality of time and space. How could Sancho travel the necessary distance in three days? Don Quixote has thus given tacit acknowledgment to the physical reality of his world. On the other hand, Sancho, who has been insistent to the point of violence on the material effects of physical activity, now finds himself making a pact of recognition and respect for ideal concepts. He has no choice, if he is to have his version of Dulcinea accepted; he must accept some form of intervention in making the trip in three days. Finally, when Sancho questions the validity of the knight's ideal lady and Don Quixote replies that there is an ideal of disinterested love, there is a breakthrough for Sancho followed by understanding. Sancho recognizes that the ideal of courtly love can be equated with love of God. The mutual isolation of the two positions is broken and an accord is reached. Thus it is that the reader, because of the non-authoritative narrative voice, is confronted first with a clash of perspectives and subsequently by an accord between the two. Broadly speaking, a dialogue between two clearly definable positions has led to the creation of a new position for both. This, of course, is not permanent, for it shall be replayed numerous times throughout the novel. But in the background lie the realms of thought and action and their interaction.

The dialogue has no sooner ended than our narrator returns to the fray. Sancho is described as being delighted at an interruption of his report; he was growing tired of lying and feared that the knight might catch on to the deception, for we are told although Sancho knew that Dulcinea was a peasant from El Toboso he had never laid eyes on her. The magnificent irony of the narrator's observations adds a new level of referentiality. Sancho, we are reminded, has engaged in story-telling of his own, based on his conjectures taken from his own way of life and experiences, but of more consequence: the physical existence of Dulcinea is taken as fact by the narrator. The point made is that Sancho has not seen her because he has failed to make the trip but implicitly she can be seen. It must be remembered that the narrator is never a witness to the action; he is narrating a story based on a translation of an obscure historian, Cide Hamete Benengeli, one of Cervantes' most profound jokes.

Where does the reader stand amid all this play of the imagination in conflict with empirical experience and in harmony with ideal concepts? The reader can, of course, also project the narration into a facsimile situation based on his own experience of empirical reality, or he can relate the text to the tradition of courtly love and the ideal concept of disinterested love. He is invited to do both. But these relations take place on two separate levels of referentiality. The first takes place almost without reflection as the reader becomes a witness, indeed a participant, to a dialogue situation which is taking place in the theatre of his reading experience. The textual reference is outwardly directed toward the recognizable situation of persons engaged in dialogue. The immediate effect of this level of referentiality is to establish a correspondence between the reader's sense of world and the textual world. This correspondence can best be described as a structure of parallel purported realities. However, even as this level of referentiality is being established a second level is emerging.

The second level is self-reference recognized by the reader in his capacity as a reader of fiction. This second level of referentiality is subtle, but never, in this novel, too far below the surface. From the outset, the reader and the narrator have made a pact to recognize that the ultimate authority in this text lies removed in the shadowy figure of Cide Hamete Benengeli. In the passage under consideration the opening positions of the speakers establish a dialectic of idealization opposed by a peasant's material reality, but as I have said before, these positions are transcended when Don Quixote is forced to explain disinterested love and Sancho recognizes that this is the stuff of which religion is made. Suddenly, as our omniscient but non-authoritative narrator re-enters the scene, the reader is forced to return to the fiction as fiction and not as dialogue. The narrator informs the reader that Sancho is getting tired of lying, for he has never laid eyes on Dulcinea. The focal effect of this reminder is to nudge the reader into a realization that his own empirical world is often transcended through the imagination. Consequently, instead of a structure of parallel realities, the reader is abruptly made aware of his metaphorical capacity to create unique correspondences for, in a most profound way, Sancho is here a paradigm for the creative reader.

FICTIONAL NARRATIVE STRUCTURE

Any discussion of the fictional structure of *Don Quixote* which I can give here will be inadequate to the task because of the richness of the text. For our purposes a general description of structure is the most we can hope to achieve. The purported reality of *Don Quixote* is history. I write this in full appreciation of the author's remarks in the prologue where he alludes to the literary conventions of the day and to the imaginative making of the character and his story. The key words are near the end of the first paragraph of the prologue, where the author writes: 'Pero yo, que, aunque parezco padre, soy padrastro de don Quijote ...' (But although I appear to be the father, I am but the stepfather of Don Quixote.) Cervantes is the stepfather in two ways: first because in the course of the novel, the character attains an autonomous status whose story demands certain kinds of incidents and rules out others; second, the reality of Don Quixote comes to be only by the free interaction between the narrator and reader. Cervantes' words are clear. It is only because critics have laboured under the nineteenth-century obsession with biographical criticism that so many readers have not been able to understand Cervantes' openness. The purported historical reality of this novel is secured by a number of devices.

The device which presents the story of Don Quixote as the work of Cide Hamete Benengeli does not originate with Cervantes. In fact, we first identify it as another instrument of parody on the novels of chivalry. However, in this novel this stock introduction of sixteenth-century prose fiction takes on unprecedented meaning. Benengeli is, of course, related to the numerous pseudo-authors of Romances, but he is also related in the novel itself to the many intermediaries, the narrators of the interpolated tales as well as the narrator proper and his mozarabe translator. Every reader who has taken up this book has readily accepted the pretence that responsibility for the story must ultimately rest with Benengeli. Consequently, the reader accepts his part in the play of fiction, for this is the highest example of art, consciously presented as art and not life. Cervantes is an extremely careful writer and goes to great lengths to show the fiction as fiction and to involve the reader in this pretense that it is history.

There are two important results to Cervantes' use of intermediaries. First, it creates a situation of authorial distance with all the ambivalence which surrounds this narration since the story is not supported by the traditional unquestionable authority of the omniscient narrator. Second, this device grants unprecedented freedom to the fictional characters. The report of their adventures is an amalgam of conflicting interpretations of what is real and what merely appears to be real. When Don Quixote sees giants instead of windmills, we are told by the non-authoritative narrator that he is out of his mind. At this stage we are induced to follow the narrator's interpretation, because of Sancho's testimony and the obvious improbability of the knight's meeting giants in the fields of La Mancha. However, it soon becomes apparent that each person in this novel sees the world in terms of his needs. Thus when Don Quixote prepares to send Sancho off to deliver a letter to Dulcinea and Sancho discovers that Dulcinea is Aldonza Lorenzo from El Toboso, Don Quixote must teach his squire the difference between a material and an ideal correspondence (Part I, chapter 25).

The extraordinary length of this novel also presents a problem of plot design. The age-old debate of novelistic unity versus artistic variety is of major importance here. The sequential plan of Don Quixote's three trips provides the bare skeleton upon which the novel is built, but we must contend with the interpolated stories as well as the sequential movement itself.

The interpolated stories have proven to be an embarrassment to many commentators of the *Quixote*, especially those who are imbued with an historic concept of artistic unity. In this view a 'digression' must be justified in terms of what it will add to the substance of the principal plot. The problem is made even more complex because of the differences between Part I and Part II. In Part I, it will be recalled that the significant digressions of 'El curioso impertinente' and 'el Cautivo' are clearly structured as tales within a tale, but in Part II the inclusion of such material is severely criticized. How can these two be reconciled? The answer lies in the intricate structure of interior duplication of this novel. The first part begins a parody of the novels of chivalry which is maintained by means of stylistic as well as structural devices. One among many is the use of the interpolated story. Several ends are achieved through the use of this device. First, as we have noted, the same parodic temper which has characterized many of the knight's declarations is continued in the structure itself as the loose form of the chivalric novel is playfully echoed. Second, the change in narrative voice in the interpolated stories sets up a carefully contrived use of intermediaries.

But what about Part II? Here we find that the whole of Part I has been objectivized as a text as well as a story. From chapter 3 on, the various participants of the second part engage in critical commentary on the form of Part I, specifically the use of digression. But when we come to approximately the same place in Part II as the place where 'el curioso impertinente' and 'el cautivo' appear in the first, we encounter the most extraordinary defence of interpolated material as the work of Cide Hamete Benengeli who, we are told, has chosen to enliven the text and to entertain us. Part II then proceeds into the spatial separation of the protagonists and the alternating separate treatment of Don Quixote in the Duke's palace and Sancho on his island. What we have now is the internal duplication of the digression since the separation of the two protagonists is possible only if the text is consciously presented as a text and not as the episodic verisimilitude of sequence. Thus we have a novel whose structure is based on a parodic mirror of literature which is itself mirrored as a literary text. The first part provides the parodic mirror, the second the self-conscious mirror of fiction as fiction. The episodic sequence is interrupted in both parts at the same place (two-thirds through each part) and by breaking the flow of time and space also breaks with verisimilitude and establishes the higher realm of art – the creative imagination.

Scholars have often been struck with the reflective aura which surrounds this comic adventure story. The study of textual interdependence as outlined on these pages offers us a systematic means of describing this anomaly.

The textual interdependence of the parts and the whole in this novel can be studied on two levels: the surface and the deep level. By surface I have designated the narrative pattern as a process of sequential reading. The deep level is the pattern of relationships which links the reader to the narrator and to the characters.

The surface level of *Don Quixote* is that of an episodic sequential process interrupted at various points by digressions. As early as chapter 12 of Part 1 we have the story of Marcela related by the goat-herder as a minor digression, but of course the well-known side roads come in chapters 33–5 and 39–41. The second volume has its main digression from sequence in chapters 44–5 where chapters alternate between the two protagonists. The surface level pattern is therefore broken in both volumes and extended by the interpolated digressions.

The deep level is a function of the surface level. In this novel, it reveals a continuous growth in complexity for the fictional characters mainly through their independence from the authority of the narrator, but also because of the involvement of the reader in their fiction-making.

Thus we cannot fail to recognize that *Don Quixote* as a narrative text constantly fluctuates between the narrative progression of sequential episodes and the growing awareness of the personality of the fictional characters as fully autonomous centres of thought and action. The deep pattern emerges precisely because of the breaks in the surface pattern and the use of reflexive devices such as Cide Hamete's commentary on his sources, or the characters' evaluation of the validity of Part 1. Wolfgang Kayser has called *Don Quixote* the prototype of the novel of character. I easily subscribe to this view, but it is of major interest here to examine the means by which an episodic novel of adventures was transformed into the prototype of the novel of character.

I have identified two levels of operation in the text. The recognition of these two levels will have far-reaching results in the following parts of this enquiry. At this stage let me comment on the surface level of the text as the specific linguistic construction of the writer which by its stability as a written text eliminates an almost infinite number of possibilities and fixes a reduced sphere of terms as the text. The text must not, however, be construed as an unbroken stream of signs which have been selected by the writer. There are all manner of breaks in the stream and these breaks, gaps, or vacancies serve to open up the deep structure of the text, for they constantly and consistently elicit the questions of 'where are we going' and 'why.' In other words the enquiry into the function of the surface organization goes on as the text unfolds. Examples can be taken almost at random from *Don Quixote*. Let us examine chapter 44 of Part II. The knight has stayed at the palace of the Duke while Sancho has gone off to his governing of Barataria. On the surface level there is only one incident to report: Don Quixote's modesty, gentility, and chasteness in refusing any services to his person. Yet in the midst of this display of knightly virtue we are offered an editorial commentary by Benengeli which serves to bring into clearer focus the deep level which is the world view of the character himself. The knight in preparing himself for bed has discovered so many runs in his silk stockings that he is beside himself with consternation. Benengeli declares himself in favour of the virtue of being poor in spirit as advised by Paul in his letter to the Corinthians, but then goes on to generalize about the façade that an impoverished gentleman must maintain for the sake of his honour. In words reminiscent of the squire in *Lazarillo de Tormes* Benengeli obviously places the knight in a sociocultural context. The gaps created on the surface level of the text are filled with an extraordinary and surprising dimension of the knight as a social person which comes not from the narrator nor any of the characters but from the source closest to the action, the purported 'historian of the true adventures.'

We have now come to a central point in this examination of the text. Our third level is concerned with fictional context. The process by which a specific set of signs are *realized* as specific signals is the central task of any critical study, for in this process of *becoming* all of the writer's talent and formal skill is examined in terms of the narrative function. Anyone seeking to systematize this task must find a schematized arrangement for the enquiry. I have designed a five-part arrangement: 1 control indicators of the narrative voice, 2 the plot and its organization, 3 the main and secondary stories contained within the plot structure, 4 the pattern of general ideas in the plot and its stories, and 5 the general theme which pervades the narrative and the manner in which it is developed.

Don Quixote emerges from this type of close examination as a most challenging and complex work. The tone of the narrator fluctuates between open disbelief of the story he is narrating and facile dismissal of the action as the obvious behaviour of a madman. On the other hand, as the novel progresses the knight is given more and more opportunities to counter both attitudes. This delicate counterpoint in tone is achieved by the knight's unerring consistency of manner. Thus when he speaks politely to the lowly of the inn as well as to the duke and duchess or when he strikes out at the muleteers or the priest in the palace of the dukes, his contribution to the general tone has taken on aspects of Platonic dualism. The tone of the novel thus presents a clash of perspectives between the two central forces. It reaches its highest degree of self-awareness in chapter 43, Volume II, where the narrator acknowledges a contradiction but still holds to his interpretation of the knight's madness, albeit a specialized madness brought on by things chivalric.

¿Quién oyera el pasado razonamiento de don Quijote que no le tuviera por persona muy cuerda y mejor intencionada? Pero, como muchas veces en el progreso desta grande historia queda dicho, solamente disparaba en tocándole en la caballería, y en los demás discursos mostraba tener claro y desenfadado entendimiento, de manera que a cada paso desacreditaban sus obras su juicio, y su juicio sus obras.

Who, upon listening to the foregoing speech of Don Quixote's, would not have taken him for a very wise person, one whose wisdom was exceeded only by his integrity? It has frequently been remarked in the course of this great history that it was only when he came to touch upon the subject of chivalry that the knight talked nonsense and that when any other topic was under discussion he showed himself to be possessed of a clear-seeing, unfettered mind, the result being that his deeds were all the time contradicting his own best judgment and his judgment his deeds.

The plot of *Don Quixote*, as noted earlier, is in fact a dual plot. One is the episodic telling of the travels and adventures of the knight and his squire strung out in sequential fashion in time and space. The other more subtle plot is the development of the characters. They seem to move quite easily in the narrative world of inns, windmills, galley slaves, peasants as well as the nobility, but they also transcend this world into a fully developed individual world view. This transcended aspect is not willy-nilly; on the contrary it also is the creation of a specific organization or plot. Sancho's growth as an empirical philosopher goes on unabated but it is tempered with tolerance for the vision of others, and although the knight is ever the platonic believer, and at odds with the interpretations or sense perception of others, as the novel progresses Don Quixote gives every indication of being consciously aware of his uniqueness. The text thus makes an issue of reality, an issue which grows to become central on both levels of plot. The adventures of the mad knight turn on his famous disability. Reality and the perception of it becomes the central concern in the development of the two protagonists. It is clear that every enquiry into the nature of reality begins with some statement – implicit or explicit – of what evidence is admissible as proof of the real. The evidence of the senses has the strength of commonsense appeal to a majority of readers of all times, but not even the firmest mediaeval Aristotelian or nineteenth-century positivist would hold that the senses reveal all. The evidence of the imagination provides a subtle but undeniable presentation of suprasensual values as part of reality. Man, in this argument, is clearly separated from the other animals mainly because of his ability to organize reality according to his needs. The dual plot therefore unfolds on two planes which intersect but never clearly coincide.

The main story has a strong comic bent to it, but the secondary stories do not. Consequently if there were nothing but a funny story in the main focus of the novel, the secondary stories would be little more than the reverse of comic relief – a kind of change of pace. Nothing could be further from the text of Don Quixote. The main story's humour is always mitigated by growing awareness that the knight's ideals are in fact expressions of Renaissance thought with the now familiar utopian concepts of man's place in the scheme of things. The secondary stories are therefore not a mere change of pace but rather a demonstration of man's capacity to create his own worlds.

The narrative idea of this text is one of the richest of our western culture, for it is nothing less than a symposium on the nature of man. Sancho's growth in stature enhances his representation of man's pragmatic spirit and his capacity to cope with the challenges of nature. The knight's growth in self-awareness augments his part of the symposium. For whatever laughter his actions may induce, his quixoticism is unmistakably the expression of faith in the capacity of man to create a world of human values. The central idea is therefore that man is a natural part of the world but unlike his fellow creatures he alone has the capacity to transcend the natural and create the world of spiritual value.

It would be a serious mistake to assume that this narrative idea 'just happens' or that one may pass over it lightly. The theme of the novel creates its unity of meaning, and this unity is available for the entire length of the two volumes if we can participate in the narrative ideas as variations on the central theme, which is the innate capacity in man for the achievement of humanism – an ideal Renaissance philosophy of man's divinity.

The theme of this novel is like an underground stream whose echoes are always in the background and which surfaces from time to time when the knight explains his mission. A representative example, and one of the richest, is the nature of Dulcinea. It will be recalled that as early as chapter 25 of Volume I, Don Quixote explains to Sancho that Dulcinea is an ideal concept of beauty and nobility which must have a bodily representation and for this purpose Aldonza Lorenzo will do as well as any other woman. It is all too easy to see Dulcinea as another manifestation of the knight's madness. To do so is to dismiss a major part of the Renaissance tradition of humanism. Ideal concepts of nobility, truth, and beauty are the very substance of man's speculations about himself and his creation through expression. It must also be remembered that the concept that bodily manifestations of the spiritual substance are but the earthly vehicle of expression is a fundamental part of Roman Catholic theology. The eucharist is but a lowly bread wafer yet it is the *real* manifestation of the body and blood of Christ. The doctrine of transubstantiation looms in the background of Don Quixote's incarnation of Dulcinea. The spiritual nature of Dulcinea is consistently developed throughout the novel. We need only compare the dialogue in the Sierra Morena, to which I have referred, with the dialogue with the duchess in chapter 32 of Volume II. The duchess begins to speak with Don Quixote with the belief that he is a harmless madman at whose expense they can have some entertainment. Owing to the fact that the entire court has read Volume I, she is able to question Don Quixote about Dulcinea. If one believes his story as true, the duchess enquires, what can we make of the Lady Dulcinea, whom the knight has never seen and therefore must be an imaginary lady made up and begotten in the brain of Don Quixote who thus has leave to give her whatever charms and perfections he so chooses.

Don Quixote's response is a statement of Renaissance thought and poetics. 'En eso hay mucho que decir,' he responds, 'Dios sabe si hay Dulcinea o no en el mundo, o si es fantástica, o no es fantástica; y éstas no son de las cosas cuya averiguación se ha de llevar hasta el cabo. Ni yo engendré ni parí a mi señora, puesto que la contemplo como conviene que sea ... ' (On that topic there is much to say. God knows if there be a Dulcinea in the world, or if she be but fantasy. This is not one of those discussions which can be fully resolved. I did not engender nor give birth to my lady, because I contemplate her as is befitting ...)

The question of Dulcinea is, of course, only one facet of the thematic core that is man's perception of reality. The theme defines and in turn is defined by the growth of the two protagonists and their expression of it.

CONTEXTUAL MEANING

The coherence of the narrative context has been usually noted by its absence in works which have been judged lacking. But rarely have critics of the novel identified coherence as the basis of contextual meaning. There is meaning in the context because of some mode of order. There are a great variety of modes of order used in the novel and in Don Quixote two are clearly distinguishable, in keeping with the duality of form I have thus far discussed. The first sense of order is that of the narrator and his accomplices in the art of narration. Theirs is an order of empirical causality. Events are narrated in the sequential historical order in which cognition occurred and the connections between cause and effect are always based on the consensus of sense perception. This mode of order is facile and available to all, but it is also likely to be very unreliable, for there are many incidents which cannot be understood and are as full of uncertainties as they are of surprises. The second mode of contextual order is that of the two protagonists, whose perspective is available independently of the narrator. Don Quixote and Sancho Panza experience the same phenomena but they interpret it differently. This difference is not a random difference; it is a strict complementary difference.

An analogy may be made of how we see an object with one eye, then with only the other, as distinct from how we see with both eyes. Conceptually speaking, Don Quixote and Sancho each represent a given perspective which, fused together in dialogue, give us a symbolic order; the phenomena which unfold in sequence are interpreted by the protagonists according to their own position of platonic knight and empirical squire, but in so doing create a full context for the cognition of reality. This symbolic order creates a sense of the situation for the object under consideration. An illustration may help to clarify this line of enquiry. Don Quixote has spoken at length of how Aldonza Lorenzo is quite sufficient as the human embodiment of Dulcinea del Toboso.

Sancho, who knows the country girl, is amused, and when the need arises he tries his hand at platonic bodily representation of the ideal lady. In chapter 10, Volume II, he tells Don Quixote that his lady is approaching, but the knight can only perceive a foul-smelling peasant girl riding an ass. The series of incidents have been rendered into a very rich fictional context because of fusion of the two perspectives into one symbolic order. In the first incident in the Sierra Morena there was no immediate conflict because both Dulcinea and Aldonza were not objects of perception for the knight; thus the one could serve well as the bodily representation of the ideal concept of perfect beauty. Nor was there any conflict in Sancho's perspective, for although he had seen Aldonza he had never seen her as Dulcinea. Now in the second incident Don Quixote is faced with perception of a girl and since he still holds to his ideal concept of Dulcinea there is a crisis of the inadequacy of the girl to represent the ideal. There is also a conflict for Sancho, who has claimed that the girl in chapter 10 is the representative of the ideal lady. He is now the one who must explain the inadequacy of bodily form. Sancho's joke has involved him in the revelation of ideal concepts in a situation of flawed material phenomena, for the language he uses to address the peasant girl is that of the ideal. The total context which emerges is one of contrast and transformation from one plane to the other.

The function of the order of empirical causality (the narrator) and the symbolic order of Platonic form (Don Quixote and Sancho) is to give the novel a context of universal application with a revelation of deep relationship which the reader experiences. The facts are stated, but the facts must be interpreted and they can be interpreted differently. Instead of granting one interpretation, the text presents two, but fused, as in fact our interpretation of life is.

MODEL OF INTERSUBJECTIVE EXPERIENCE

Don Quixote is known to the reader long before he opens the novel the first time, for he is one of those supreme creations of the imagination who has an existence independent of the work in which they have come into the world. Not only does the English-speaking person have the word 'quixotic' (defined as a person caught up in the romance of noble deeds or unreachable ideals; romantic without regard to practicality), he also has a long tradition of opera, ballet, tone poems, and musical comedy based on the knight of La Mancha. Consequently the reader is strongly predisposed in one way or another. An interesting problem for study is the reciprocal relationship between the extratextual legend of the character and the reader's interpretation of him in reading the text.

The relationship which has developed between the biographies of Cervantes and his masterpiece is one of the most extraordinary of literary history. It is clearly demonstrable that the biographies and the written commentaries directly bearing on the novel have affected each other and have been set on a pattern of convergence from the late eighteenth century to the present. This situation has come about in spite of numerous dissimilarities between the known facts about the author and his novel, in spite of elementary logic which dismisses as fundamentally erroneous that a biographical reconstruction can explain a literary text. It is just as absurd to say that day causes night because it is always followed by night, as to say that a biographical fact leads to a critical truth about the text. Thus, in spite of the twin obstacles of history and logic, we have a clear record of a growing and today almost complete identification of author and narrator and to some extent, of author and protagonist. But ironically, if ever there was a text which impeded the synthesis of author and narrator, it is this one.

Cide Hamete Benengeli occupies a central position in the book's strategy. He stands between the narrator and the story and consequently between the story and the reader. If we line up all the intermediaries from the narrator to his Spanish-speaking translator to Benengeli, to Benengeli's sources and fellow story-tellers, the list appears to recede into a murky shadowland. Yet the reality of Don Quixote cannot be doubted, for in the second part of his story he is a reader of the first part. The most extraordinary side of Cide Hamete Benengeli is that Don Quixote needed a chronicler, invented one, and believed in one much in the same way as with Dulcinea, but in the case of Cide Hamete he comes to be, and proves his existence by the publication of Part I. By implication the difference between what is desired and what is, dissolves. The major effect is that we have two characters who have their own author and who accept him as long as he represents them accurately. Benengeli and the two characters respect each other's independence and relative domain; this respect is based on the fact that they are both fictional. Of course, Cide Hamete Benengeli is a joke but the comical nature of this fictional author should not impede our recognition of his importance to the novel. There is no mistake here. Cervantes has manipulated every means he had to endow Don Quixote and Sancho with as much independence as possible, but he is equally careful to enable the reader to be a participant in this endowment.

There is still another major device used by Cervantes to involve the reader. It appears that Cervantes was writing chapter 59 of Part II when the false second part written by a man calling himself Avellaneda was published. Quite unexpectedly, there is material for still another dimension to this novel. The treatment given to Avellaneda by Don Quixote and Sancho is direct and to the point: they scrutinize this second chronicler on questions of accuracy and detail, but there is a deeper question which takes shape. If this book purports to present events which did not happen to the heroes the implication is that there are impersonators of Don Quixote and Sancho. Don Quixote, who has been playing his part with zest, finds his role threatened. The result is inescapable: the reader must recognize Don Quixote as a self-conscious fictional character.

Two observations of some importance underlie this examination of the reader's relationship in *Don Quixote*. The first has to do with the reality of fiction and its limits. The initial opposition of fact and fiction is illustrated by the repeating juxtaposition of empirical observation on the part of Sancho supported by the commonsense plausibility of the narrator as against the wilful wish-fulfilment of Don Quixote. But all clear boundaries between the two are slowly and carefully erased. As one may recall, Sancho's goats in the Clavileño episode are green, scarlet, blue, and combinations of these colours. Whereupon on the first occasion which Don Quixote has he speaks thusly to Sancho: 'Sancho, pues vos queréis que se os crea lo que habéis visto en el cielo, yo quiero que vos me creáis a mí lo que vi en la cueva de Montesinos. Y no os digo más.' ('Sancho,' he said, 'if you want us to believe what you saw in the heavens, then I want you to believe me when I tell you what I saw in the cave of Montesinos. I need say no more.') Sancho's clearly marked boundaries between the physically real and the real of the mind have been blurred, but what is most significant is that the boundaries between life as a lived experience and literature as an imagined experience have been shown to be indeterminable. The lived experience and the imagined experience are continually interfering with each other. Inherent in this phenomenon is the nature of literature itself, which has its reality because of interference and interaction. Thus, the question we now ask is what happens when fiction is presented as history, but history with a high degree of awareness of its indeterminate nature. My answer is that the reader responds to the implied author as an Aristotelian first principle and the fictional narrator becomes indistinguishable from the historical narrator.

My second observation has to do with the effect of fiction on the reader. In this novel the acts and words of the knight have affected and altered the behaviour of many people, from Sancho to the duke and duchess. But perhaps the most notable effect of this story is to be found in the narrator himself, who begins writing in parody of a popular ballad of the day: 'En un lugar de la Mancha, de cuyo nombre no quiero acordarme, no ha mucho tiempo que vivía un hidalgo,' and concludes with the remarkable statement: 'Para mí solo nació don Quijote, y yo para él; él supo obrar y yo escribir; solos los dos somos para en uno ... ' (In a village of La Mancha the name of which I have no desire to recall, there lived not so long ago one of those gentlemen ... For me alone Don Quixote was born and I for him; it was for him to act, for me to write, and we two are one ...) The narrating persona, our narrator, has found his identity as the re-creative source of the fictional character. But there is yet one more re-creative source whose participation has been openly acknowledged throughout the novel and that is the reader himself. Our question here is: where does the true Cervantes stand in the eyes of the reader? Is he to be identified with the character as the literary historians would have or is he to be identified with the narrator as some scholars propose? My answer is that a biographical view of Cervantes has never been in the text. And that each reader's version of Cervantes is in fact a reflection of the reader looking into this looking-glass game. The ironic Cervantes of the prologue presents the reader with an open invitation to see the author in his own image.

We have seen how the narrator in *Don Quixote* becomes a self-conscious intermediary, and the protagonist becomes a knowing actor of his own adventures, and so it is with the reader, who has been subtly turned into an accomplice of the fiction-making. All the intermediaries, as well as the characters, turn from time to time and cast a glance in the direction of the reader.

Although our participation in the fiction becomes matter-of-fact, when we read the last paragraphs of the book, we, as readers, are suddenly faced with the duplicity of the intermediary authors whom we have helped to maintain.

The reader searches in vain for the author in order to cement his relationship fully. I maintain that the urge to find the author is so great and the tendency to see him in one's own image so strong because of the aesthetic principle of participation which is fundamental to this text.

On the last page of this 1000-page trip through time and space, the narrator addresses the reader directly for the last time in order to say farewell. A strong sense of identification links the reader to the narrator. Since we prefer to have a name for this travelling companion we call him Cervantes, but he is in fact more representative of our own mind than of a late sixteenth-century Spaniard.

I cannot leave the problem without offering some interpretation. As I have suggested, this looking-glass narrator is a very deliberate technical achievement which conceals the identity of the author and reveals that of the reader.

The discussion of aesthetic principles without first mastering the probabilities of the text is not only futile but counterproductive. When we identify a given aesthetic relationship as operative we are establishing the general guidelines for the relationships I have called intersubjective. These relationships are the patterns of the reading experience at its broadest range. *Don Quixote* has been variously called the first modern novel, the prototype of the novel form, the model from which eighteenth- and nineteenth-century fiction would build. But in all of this there is recognition of only part of the aesthetic patterns of the novel. Most certainly there is in *Don Quixote* an aesthetic of mimetic correspondences which is central to the development of the novel after Cervantes. There is, however, another aesthetic pattern deeply fixed within the text which demands a far greater fictive awareness from the reader. This is the aesthetic of participation in creation, that is, in the fiction-making.

I have pointed out some of the devices employed by Cervantes, but it is significant to the reading of the novel to understand how these function in a general pattern of involvement for the reader. Thus we can say that *Don Quixote* has the uniqueness of presenting the prototype of the mimetic aesthetic as well as the most anti-mimetic tendencies of reader participation, which carry a profound scepticism of the commonsense reign of empirical realism. It is certainly true that no theoretical system of literary study can devise methods which can be passed on directly to literary criticism. Every item of method must come from the analysis of the methodology already in practice in the field. But because the field of literary criticism is so diverse, methods which are well known in one part of criticism may be unknown in another or may be so generalized as to be mixed up with barren methods. The explicit formulation of method has in some quarters become a measure of responsibility by the critic and if this practice continues to gain followers it can lead to a greater awareness of direction and aim of the interpretation and may even eliminate the superfluous academic article, but this is perhaps a quixotic dream.

To comment on the aesthetics of *Don Quixote* is high privilege that must be earned by a thorough study of the technique and idiom of the text. The great aesthetic achievement of this novel is the intertwining of the two aesthetic directions in one unitary experience. The two different perspectives we have are nothing less than the perceived world and the perceiver conscious of himself as perceiver or in other terms the world and the knowing self or in more literary terms the story and the story-teller.

The more one reads this novel the richer it becomes, for this reading experience involves the reader's own criteria and sensibility openly in the process of fiction-making. Often a reader may ask whether it would be advantageous to visit Spain and go to the place where Don Quixote and Sancho travelled. The historian might be tempted to add some information on the reality of sixteenth-century Spain. This has been the work of many eminent Hispanists such as Américo Castro, Menéndez Pidal, and Marcel Bataillon, to name a few. But I am not directly concerned in this chapter with the history of Spain nor even with literary and intellectual history; my concern is the reader's experience of the novel itself, and to that end, the historical data of sixteenth-century Spain is but one aspect of the background to the reading experience.

Don Quixote can be read in an annotated edition which brings to bear the accumulated historical enquiry of generations, but it can also be read without this documentation, and what is more to the point the scholarly addendum is at best a peripheral expansion of the text and never affects the narration itself.

The presence of Cervantes in *Don Quixote*, as I have remarked, is illusory and what often appears to be the author more often than not is the reader projecting himself into the reading experience through the vehicle of the implied author.

There are two distinct attitudes on literary evaluation which are predominant today. One, which is text-oriented, seeks to identify value on the basis of some aspect of form. The other, which is reader-oriented, identifies value in terms of the reader's greater enrichment. This chapter has dealt with both attitudes and has openly linked them to different and equally valid assumptions about literature. If we hold that the literary work of art is an autonomous creation of man's genius we shall be led to the formalist attitude on evaluation. If on the other hand we maintain that the life of a literary text depends on its readers whose existence it expands then we are clearly in the reading-experience camp of evaluation. I have been striving to maintain both sides of the argument not only as valid but as dialectically necessary for each other. Consequently in these concluding notes on method I should like to insist that the evaluation of *Don Quixote* is available through both approaches but I also hold, what is of much more consequence, that each of these positions on evaluation presumes the other. It should be clear that if we find and describe the formal aspects of *Don Quixote* as effective and efficient means of communication, we are assuming that there has been communication at least with the critic and his readers and that there will be further communication when these parties return to the novelistic text. In other words, evaluation of form implies evaluation of a reading experience. On the other hand evaluation of the intersubjective basis of reality assumes a constant form which has made this experience one which can be shared among readers.

By recognizing both aspects of value we are merely taking cognizance of the starting position of the encounter between reader and text.

It is my conviction that most serious statements about literary value, whatever the critical biases of the critic, assume the interaction between the text and the reader. Further, I would say when we have a divergence of evaluation between the two approaches it is because the text-experience relationship is a deficient one. In other words the highest literary value must be recorded both in the sign as a sign, that is, text, and in the signification of that sign, that is, the reading experience.

Don Quixote is an inexhaustible masterpiece of literary art because whether we approach it as sign or as signification it is always greater than either one. The literary masterpiece, I am saying, must be the perfect interaction of expression and experience.

The heuristic devices have served their purpose, the construction is complete, the critic has managed to write something more or less significant, more or less informative about the literary text. What stands now is the construction of criticism, which neither replaces the original nor fixes its significance. Without having considered all the difficulties along the way, we have come to the bottom line of rendering an account for the act of criticism on a phenomenological basis. Although the problem suggests another book, we must consider it briefly.

My disagreement with claims to critical permanence has already been expressed. In my view, the systematic description of textual phenomena provides us with a possibility of dialogue with fellow readers who share the same interest in a given text or body of texts; the methods developed for accomplishing such a description are in themselves models of my mode of arranging the universe and indeed they often would suggest themselves to me as models for the treatment of parallel problems in other realms of my experience. But since I do not choose to practise self-delusion I am aware that these methods, models, and descriptions are extensions of my mind. I offer my reader my experiences in reading *Don*

Quixote – that I am a critical reader is self-evident, and I also offer my reader a blueprint of that experience. Such a description seems to me to have a value that is quite independent of the acceptability of my interpretation, for its value is to make critical experience accessible to others.

I have argued that there is no single correct reading of texts available and it does not bother me one whit if some argue that there must be a Platonic ideal reading for which we strive, as long as no one claims to have a measurable way of demonstrating who is closer and who is not. In the realm of experiential reality there is no correct reading, there are only readings which can be verified and readings which cannot. The former enrich us as they enrich the text through the continued participation in the tradition of literary criticism.

10

Heuristic models of enquiry

As speakers of Spanish, English, French, and so on, we are in the habit of calling certain texts *novelas*, novels, *romans*, etc. Beyond the linguistic habit there is, of course, a general understanding of the term that can be summed up as a book-length text of narrative prose. The first task of this chapter is to find a more rigorous definition of a literary class. Second, and of more consequence, is the consideration of the logical suppositions for literary classification which will enable us to construct a phenomenological theory and thus complete the task of introducing a new concept of literary history to Hispanic studies.

Because it is not feasible to designate certain texts as literary and others as non-literary and to base a logic of classification on such a premise, it is necessary to question the basic assumptions of classification itself. Why do we classify texts? Can only some texts be considered as historical? Do we not classify with the very designation of 'literature'? Let us begin with some basic observations. We classify anything we wish to understand ranging from the natural to the symbolic. Second, all texts are historical insofar as they were written and are read in someone's temporal dimension. Third, any text can be a literary text if conventions of literary venue are effectively invoked. Let us keep in mind that some of Ortega y Gasset's finest writing is read today as literature and not as philosophy. The problem at hand thus is to define, as clearly as I can, the concept of literary class and to argue for its place in literary history.

It has been proposed that modern dissatisfaction with generic classification is inevitable because of the very nature of literature as an historically bound expression.[1] It follows, the argument goes, that since literature is determined by the historical forces which are acting upon writers, any classification of one period will be maladjusted when applied to an earlier or subsequent period. The greatest strength of the argument lies in recognition of the fact that the classification of anything depends on the discrimination of some characteristic of the object which is permanent and stable. Consequently a denial of such a basis is a denial of the validity of a class-name except at the most superficial levels of conversation. The flaw in the argument, however, is the assumption that literary class is determined exclusively by historical factors. I shall argue in favour of consideration of both the formal and the historical factors of literature, and if that argument is correct, a literary class is a heuristic tool and is the product of both an historically determined intersubjective experience and a formal strategy of expression. A logic of criticism will have to submit the phenomenological reflection on experience to the linguistic evidence of formal considerations. This reflection will make it possible to go beyond the limitations imposed heretofore by literary history. However, the retention of the formal aspects will enable the logic to achieve the control over literary works which is implicit in classification.

The distinctions between formal and intersubjective aspects which are encompassed in the logic I am proposing can be considered as analogous to the study of modes of composition and modes of reception.[2] The present logic of classification differs from traditional modes of organization in that it is an investigation of an intellectual, heuristic construction, a retracing of the path from experience to the text, only so that we may return to experience more informed of the reading.[3] A narrative text poses an author's strategy as a system of intentionality which we shall study in its concretization as the reading experience. An explication of the implicit logic of this path begins with the understanding that it is a question of the internal shift of focus from intentionality – the text – to its product – the reading experience – and that by shifting our own critical focus we can uncover the links that tie expression to experience.

All narratives as narratives have three fundamental levels of operation: (a) as a formal cause, (b) as historical reflection, and (c) as a reading experience. Let me expand on these three levels. The narrative is comprised of a descriptive unfolding of events in an explanatory mode for the purpose of communication; consequently there is a formal design which is outside of time and which is not yet meaningful but rather only potentially meaningful. Second, narratives insofar as they are composed in a natural language reflect the cultural and social basis of the human collective which is language. Finally, meaning is the product of the reading, which is in the strict sense of the word the actualization of the text as communication. Our logic will attempt to discern the fundamental aspects of form and of historical reflection in a dialectic situation which methodologically simulates the reading experience. Once we have been able to discern the basic outlines of both formal and interpretative considerations we shall be in a position to acknowledge their essential points of conjunction. In this manner we have the emergence of the basic logic of classification.

The primary purpose for literary classification is to establish connections between diverse writers and writings. The characteristics of narrative which shall be examined are more an heuristic infrastructure for our understanding of the history of narrative than fixed generic categories or subdivisions.

Perhaps the most serious impediment to a history of literary form has been the persistence of the notion of unchanging universals as the only basis for classification. The profound breakthrough of Charles Darwin's[4] populational schema seems to have made no inroads among literary historians. In Darwin's terms an organic species is not a permanent entity defined by unchanging essential characteristics, but neither are the members of a species associated by an arbitrary decision of convenience. In Darwin's schema and in our own, species or literary class is an historical entity. By this statement I mean that each class is an individual group whose component elements – all of them – are at all times subject to diversification, but that the group is also one within which selective factors are continually eliminating ill-adapted innovations and accepting others. The key question which underlies this point is how do we recognize the specific continuity and character of such an historical entity, for example, the novel? The operative questions cannot be taken as mere enquiries into the appropriateness of the 'fit' of current candidates for membership in the class, for such questions presuppose the completeness of the class. Our questions all have to do with the balance between innovative and selective factors of the class, for it is not membership which is at stake – we will willingly grant that to all candidates. The issue is how to establish a record of change and of mutation in the literary form. This can be accomplished by placing a synchronic analysis into a context of tradition, convention, and aesthetic reception. My view of genre is that it cannot be conceived of as a rigid system defined by the works imputed to belong to it and others that do not meet the prescribed requirements. Rather, my view of genre is flexible, governed by the need to explore the interconnections which we assume operate within such vast conventional groupings as lyric, dramatic, and narrative.

The above is the outline of my argument; various points in it, however, have to be examined and expanded before it can be considered fully. In the first place, to assert a rigid definition of a class such as 'novel' would defeat rather than fulfil my aim of furthering an understanding of the history of narrative. If we are to construct workable models it is necessary to prove that among the vast number of characteristics of written narrative certain specific ones are common and, further, that the flow of historical change will yield perspectives which can be correlated to the formal aspects. It is not easy to go beyond the commonsense notion of the novel as an extended narration, for to do so requires either encyclopedic knowledge of narrative or a thoroughgoing theory for the construction of hypothetical models. My choice is for the latter course, and the major concern is, therefore, how to present these models in an acceptable form.

From a strictly logical point of view it is possible to define literature as an essential set of characteristic forms which are accepted universally as a distinct category of writing. A synchronic approach to the narrative offers the most promising means for the distinction and study of basic characteristics. For example, among a number of distinctive characteristics in narrative texts we can enumerate four: voice, persona or character, temporality, and referentiality.

There is good reason to be sceptical of a postulate that is based on considerations independent of the phenomena under examination. I shall now turn to some rather basic observations about narrative and its structure. The aim is to establish the basis for a synchronic examination of texts in the search for basic characteristics.

The development of formalist systems to describe the literary text has dominated an important part of literary theory in Europe and North America for the last fifty years. In the face of the obvious limitations of strict formalist enquiry and the failure to develop a universal methodology, critics like Greimas and Genette have persisted because they profess a faith in method which in the last analysis can only be understood as a platonic nostalgia of eternity and a denial of time. My position is quite different, for I do not seek to escape time; on the contrary, my project is to record the history of formal change.

The American anthropologist Franz Boas, writing in 1911, observed that 'the three personal pronouns – I, thou, and he – occur in all human languages' and that 'the underlying idea of these pronouns is the clear distinction between the self as speaker, the person or object spoken to, and that spoken of.'[5] Wolfgang Kayser, Emile Staiger, and before them the German Romantics have based the generic divisions of lyric, dramatic, and epic on these fundamental linguistic universals of the self-other reality.[6] There can be no doubt that the linguistic dimension expressed in pronominal systems is related to the classical generic divisions, but it is another matter to demonstrate the fixed points of narrative structure. The essence of the narrative is the voice that serves as source for the story. The point of view of the narrative voice is but one aspect of its various properties, such as authority, privilege, attitude, and dramatization. Thus we can say that although the story-teller is usually narrating from the third person point of view, the first and second are also used. The essential point about narrative voice is that whatever the pronominal form used, the ultimate posture is that of a source addressing a general public, the reader. The narration is consequently rooted in a linguistic attitude: 'he (the character) is because I (the narrator) know or you (the alter-ego of the narrator) think he knows.' A first characteristic of narrative structure is therefore the voice(s) of the source.

A second basic characteristic is the referential object of the narration. This means that if the source is to say something he must refer linguistically to another. Whether this other is the narrator himself in his past life or a completely independent person, a self-other relationship is an essential development of fictive narrative form.[7]

A third characteristic of narrative is the passage of time. All narrative language, indeed all writing is time-bound. We distinguish, however, between the interior and exterior dimensions of time. The narrative has been written in time and is read in time. Activity of any kind can only happen within a spatio-temporal frame of reference. The narrative itself is just as inexorably chained to time. What is time in the novel? To be more exact, what entities are in a temporal relation within the purported reality of a narrative? The answer is made complex because the narrative has a purported reality which is realized imaginatively within the reading experience. We can begin by distinguishing events as the basic manifestations of temporal relations from physical objects which are only indirectly in time; they are in time only insofar as they constitute part of the conglomerate of events which we refer to as state of affairs, situations, circumstances, and so on. A more important question, however, is to ask whose perspective of action determines the temporal relationship. It is this question and its response that brings us to the specific consideration of narrative time. Three perspectives of time are available to us in the narrative: event as perceived and described by a narrator, event as witnessed by a character, and the interjection of the author's and the reader's time into the narrative.

A fourth characteristic of the narrative is the orientation of the self to a phenomenological world of objects that are discriminated, classified, and conceptualized with respect to attributes which are culturally constituted and symbolically mediated through language. It is this concretizing function of narrative language that makes possible the connection between the world of human experience and the narrative world. Without this relationship the written language would not be meaningful beyond the level of graphic imagery. In short, there would not be a narration. The most common mistake made in considering the narrative world is to attempt a simple univocal one-to-one correspondence between designata in any two of these worlds. All narrative worlds are derived from a fundamental ground (observable broad similarities) in the nature of man, his environment, his social life, and his culture including his language. Thus it is accurate to refer to narrative worlds as fragmentary simulations instead of implying equivalents.

Most narrative worlds are based on the three-dimensional space of human perception and probably this basis will continue to be dominant. However, we must also recognize that a number of contemporary writers have attempted to structure their worlds on a fourth dimension of relativity.[8] The technique of creating simultaneity between events that are spatially separate has been one of the major formal innovations of the modern narrative.

An argument has been made that there are universals of the narrative and that their pristine form defines the narrative. Without minimizing the importance of the hypothesis or its validity I wish to emphasize that I am not prepared to follow it. My position is that a synchronic analysis of the structure of the narrative yields a hypothetical set of factors with which we can begin to classify narrative form, but we become victims of our own method if we do not recognize that form is a product of the text and not the other way around.

If the classification of the narrative is to work, it becomes crucially important to show how all narratives resemble one another as well as how they differ. Logically, the concept of variation assumes knowledge of the base from which phenomena vary. To my way of thinking the likeness of narratives is to be found in the formal structures – hence, the four characteristics of form I have touched upon – and the variations are due to the historically determined evolution of aesthetic direction – hence, the diachronic analysis I shall take up in the third part of this chapter.

It may well turn out that what we recognize as a constant formal characteristic in narrative functions much more powerfully and in a more fundamental way to shape the specific text than what is different. There is growing evidence that contemporary synchronic analysis will have in the long run given us a marked gain in critical method.

The problem I have taken up is to reconcile diachronic and synchronic considerations into a functional logic of classification. If we are to achieve a usable system, it is essential ro remove all vestiges of absolute claims to categories from our method by explaining as fully as possible the process by which we arrive at the heuristic categories of classification.

I have identified the constant elements of narrative structure as narrative voice, character, time, and world. Narrative voice differs from the other three by virtue of its being exclusive to the narrative form. Whatever the manner of presentation in a literary work, the use of a narrative voice establishes a relationship between the story-teller and his audience. Thus, when we consider the narrative structure, we are studying the story-telling relationship as the fundamental elaboration of the other basic elements of character, time, and world.

Let us begin with a simple and elementary formal arrangement. First we can consider the kind of narrative that has a story-teller who is recalling the great events of the past, based on what his audience considers unimpeachable traditional sources. Let us further assume that the protagonist of this kind of story is of heroic stature but flawed like lesser men, that the narrative world is identifiable by his audience and, finally, let us also assume that the story is being narrated in chronological order from the earlier to the later and climactic events. At certain points in the composition of the narrative the author will have to decide which narrative elements he wishes to stress and which he can keep in the background. If the author decides that the major thrust of his story will be to retell the past and the great events that led up to the major and decisive event, he will tend to regulate the narrative world into an ancillary position of background and the protagonist into a role of participant in the series of events. This is a narrative model which stresses causality and significance of events. Thus, for purposes of our scheme I shall henceforth refer to it as a model of action.[9]

There is need to take care not to confuse narrative world and plot. Narrative world is the sum total of phenomena between which there is an established relationship of continuity and distance. The plot is a specific system of spatial relationships within the narrative world. Plot serves as a structural plan or organization and for the disposition of the personae within the textual continuum. In this description of narrative models, I am trying to distinguish between separate organizing principles. It is also important to stress that narrative voice or voices are the source and the operational and controlling focus by which the specific emphasis is realized.

This model has been used in numberless texts from the episodic plot of the mediaeval epic and, of course, beyond that the Homeric model of *The Iliad*, which establishes action as the basis for plot as distinct from the vicissitudes of individual lives to the modern tragic tale of *La barraca*, and in a long line of historical reconstructions as well as in tales of terror and the modern detective story. In all of this enormous diversity of subjects, languages, and traditions, the keystone of the model is the dominance of order over chaos. This is a victory for the relentless logic of a temporal sequence of cause and effect over the unknown.

Quite rightly, it can be objected that the narrative model of action is not a generic classification. Undoubtedly the large number of texts which develop out of a structure of action must be classified more specifically, and diachronic as well as synchronic factors must be considered. We have therefore taken only a tentative first step in the direction of our system of classification.

A second formal model emerges when we consider the kind of narrative which stresses the development of the fictional character as a complex, multifaceted projected persona with a singular personality. It is the study of the personality of the character which separates this model from the others.

In many modern texts there is an intricate pattern of reflection between the character and his world. At times we receive the character's point of view about his world while at others the independent assessment of the world by the narrator. In this common situation we need only to determine where the centre of focus lies. A character whose perspective has been so deeply unfolded as to be in a distant position separate from a general perspective of the world is obviously the central focus of the text. The point I am making is that in the narrative model of character, an individual fictive persona is favoured over either the sequence of events or the totality of a narrative world. The key to this model is therefore the stress on depth and singularity of the fictive persona over breadth and quantity.

Jurij Lotman has used the analogy of the map to illustrate the relationship of fictional character to the narrative text. A map, he writes, establishes a basis for the designation of distance, relative size, and possible movement. When we draw a line across a map to indicate an air route (eg, Toronto to Paris) we will have indicated a possibility of travel from one place to another; this is a geographical plot which surmounts the structure, but when we indicate the movement on a map of a specific flight from one place to the other, we have introduced the concretization of what was before only a potential for movement and we therefore introduce a new set of co-ordinates. With this addition of the concrete we become concerned with questions of time, duration, deviation, and completion. Now let us move from the model of the map to the narrative text. We can establish the fictional character in place of the concrete flight and thus focus on the relational place of character as the concretization of what were before potential events. Thus it will be understood that the initial point of plot movement is the establishment of a relation of distinction and mutual independence between the character and the semantic field surrounding him. If the character is indistinguishable from his environment, if he does not have the capacity which allows us to distinguish his separateness from the environment, the development of plot does not take place. On the other hand it is quite possible to proceed with non-plot and to disclose further the dimensions of narrative world. The narrative model of character arises when the character's own development surmounts the narrative world.[10]

The range in this case is just as overwhelming as in the previous discussion of the model of action. Consider the ground covered from Don Quixote to Leopold Bloom or from Richardson's heroines to Michel Butor's *Modification*. Novels of the most diverse origins with quite varied techniques relate to the same formal model which places the character at the centre of the narrative universe.

Using an elementary model similar to the one drawn up for the discussion of the structure of action, we can demonstrate the structure of character in its basic formulation.

Let us consider a stable narrative voice depicting the personality of the protagonist without any limitation on privilege or authority. At this point a crucial decision must be made by our hypothetical author. Whose time and whose space will be featured in the novel? If time and space are external to the character and imposed as the world he lives in, we are not dealing with the formal model of character. On the other hand, if chronological time is exchanged for experienced time and if vision substitutes for world, we have the narrative form of character. It goes without undue explanation that the most frequent form of creating this structure is through the first person narrator or the epistolary technique.

However, let us return to the third person omniscient narrator conjured up before and follow the argument. If the narrator presents a spatio-temporal order other than – and ultimately imposed on and superior to – that of the character, the structure must necessarily subordinate the individual to the totality in which he lives. A paradox thus develops which makes the presentation of a fictive mind's independent vision of reality incompatible with a world view. This paradox occurs when the same narrative attempts to attain both sides of the 'individual-world' opposition. The resolution of the paradox goes like this: whenever the duality of character and world is presented it must be through separate conflicting narrative voices of limited authority. The clearest examples are *Don Quixote* and the novels of Galdós, notably the works of the *serie contemporánea* between *Fortunata y Jacinta* and *Misericordia*, with the clear distinction that whereas in *Don Quixote* the character is dominant, in Galdós it is the world which controls.

Perhaps the most distinguishing characteristic of twentieth-century literature has been the way in which novelists have responded to the ageless imperative of imagining the totality of life. Because of this direction historians have seen the narrative form as an orderly progression from the epic to the novel. Although only some epics sought the world view and only some novels have attempted to follow suit, it must be acknowledged that the narrative, in general, is markedly elastic and can accommodate a diversity of materials, thus making it particularly adaptable to presenting a world view. We need only remember that a narrator has no limitation apart from the patience of his readers on the inclusion of detail and the expansion of dimensions. We can further recognize that the broader the canvas on which the world is drawn the more authors have been motivated to create a well-ordered and coherent world view. The narrative model of world is based on the premise that the organization of the totality can cope with a myriad of detail and produce an ordered universe in place of immediate diversity.

The structure of the narrative model I have called world is in fact a structure of purported 'total narrative space,' for the ultimate aim in this kind of text is to establish the dimensions of space. It is important that I clearly emphasize the complete dependence which this kind of structure has on the narrative voice's range and capacity. The dimensions of a narrative cosmology are usually presented by a fully privileged, authoritative voice who in most cases is undramatized, but there are also often variations within the same text as, for example, the use of voice by Galdós.

A second clarification needed is the reiteration of the narrative totality as a cosmos in appearance only, since the narrative voice is giving a singular, albeit one without particular identity, organizational structure to the world. The master architects are able to diffuse the singularity of their presentation by a multiplicity of characters who dwell in a self-contained world and elaborate the purported dimensions of the narrative world through a variety of narrative techniques.

Let us consider some examples of the narrative forms developed in this basic structure. Quevedo's *Buscón* utilizes a subtle interplay between the narrating character's commentary and the world he is describing. The 'conceptista' language constantly foregrounds the ironic presence of Pablos. In the view of A.A. Parker narrative strategy 'reaches through the pressure of external circumstances into the heart of the conflict between the individual and society.'[1] On the other hand the world of *La Regenta* is a structure of refraction. The characters are built up through the play of multiple perspectives through which the narration moves. The array of techniques which were to become part of the avant-garde's repertoire in the twentieth century, such as dream sequences, stream of consciousness, and the inner voice of remembrance, all serve to bring about the complex relationship of the fictional personae and society. Camilo Jose Cela's *La colmena*, written some sixty-seven years later, allowing for important differences in the use of fragments and simultaneity, develops the same mode of world-making as Clarin wherein the individual's identity is created through the social forces he contends with.

The dominant attitude of this type of narrative structure can be summarized thus: the structure of a novel which purports to present world in such a way that it is a substitute world and is a self-contained relational whole.

The basic concept on which we have been working can be summed up as the hypothesis that amid infinite diversity all narratives are cut from three basic patterns of action, character, and space. Further, we can recognize that uniformities are implicit in any classification. Consequently, we have been working on the texts traditionally called novels as a collection of variations on one mode of writing – the narrative – and three distinct models of narrative form. We shall return to reconsider narrative and its implications.

Experienced reality concerns change and replacement of elements in time in a process we call history (a process that is only discernible from a considerable distance of generations if not of centuries because it is also hypothetical order). Consequently, we seek to find rules of change concomitant with the assumption that there are constant elements involved. What kind of hypothesis can account for change in literature? Must it be a hypothesis which can link the structural dimensions of the literary work to the external distances which lay between the writer and his readers or an examination of the historicity of discourse?

The system I propose consists of correlates of synchronic formal aspects and historically-bound interpretations directed at the massive body of the written narrative. Theses correlates are to be understood as being fundamentally interrelated. The broadest definition of change is that of a shift in focus within a system of possibilities. The relationship between permanence and change in the text is that no constant character- istic can exist which is not the outcome of a perspective of historical interpretation, and no interpretative proposition can be hypothesized which contradicts a formal characteristic. A class distinction derived from non-linguistic factors, for example, the Mexican Revolution, cannot be of use to us in this endeavour since it ignores the formal aspects of the texts in question. The validity of such a purported classification would have to be proven entirely on historical grounds and not on the logic of classification since it begins outside of expression, which is the basis of all formal considerations. The opposite pole, which excludes historical considerations, is also not functional for our purposes since it removes the texts in question from their cultural context. Thus, all purported class distinctions based on formal characteristics such as stream of conscious- ness or first person narrative voice are of little use unless they are at the same time tied to history.

The system of classification which I am proposing establishes each class on the basis of specific diachronic changes in perspective within a network of synchronic relations. I have insisted above on the interrelation of the synchronic and the diachronic aspects of the narrative. I have discussed the basis for the synchronic aspect as an internal structural organization based on the distances between narrative voice and narrative world within narrative spatio-temporal dimensions. Let us now turn our attention to the diachronic perspectives of interpretation. We are here concerned with the changing distances between the text and its readers.

The historical relationship of narrator to reader (listener) has been changing from the earliest times of a story-teller's adopting a role vis-à-vis his audience. The historical manifestations of these changing relation- ships, however, can be viewed as perspectives. I would like briefly to describe these heuristic perspectives. Let us assume for the time that the reader is a willing and responsive recipient of the narration. First, the narrator may choose to take the reader along a development which is largely in agreement with his own sense of reality. Second, the narrator can try to transform the reader's sense of reality. Third, the narrator can be primarily concerned with an expansion of awareness on the part of his reader. Fourth, the narrator may choose to integrate the reader into the story-telling process itself. Henceforth I shall refer to these perspectives as: parallel realities, moral order, expansion of reality, and integration of reality, and I shall use them as my frame of reference for the study of the narrative reading experience.

Parallel realities: The aim here is for the general reader to find himself in a recognizable replica of his own situation. The external world is assumed as a vital support for the reality of the work of literature since it is owing to this similitude that the reader can rapidly penetrate into the writing with confidence and expect to find identifiable human characteristics in the text. Of course, identification is high in this category, and the sense of reliving a past experience vicariously is very pronounced. The essence of this parallel aesthetic is to simulate external reality through a fabricated symbolic representation. As in the case of the other aesthetic perspectives I shall discuss, it is not limited to any structure, but rather transcends all of the forms of literary expression.

At various times in the history of literature this aesthetic position has become dominant. It has been given many names, ranging from realism to neo-realism to mimesis. In the nineteenth century it became a major force in narrative literature and has in popular criticism merged with the name novel. Thus, we are likely to find in popular criticism a contemporary text downgraded for not being 'realistic.' The history of the parallel aesthetic is a history of man's attempts to capture reality by way of his language. The reader's and the narrator's realities thus co-exist on separate but parallel planes, from which soundings are constantly made, and in the works of great writers transcend both the realities of reader and narrator as symbols of humanity.

The most notable trait of this aesthetic position is that its temporal design is always one which features the past retold by narrative voice or voices from a vantage point of where it has been united in memory.

Among the numerous narratives whose aesthetic and temporal process reflect this position there are a few privileged texts which can serve as models because of the clarity of exposition. *Misericordia*, written by Pérez Galdós in 1897, is such a text. The dialogue and interior monologue of the characters create an autonomous world within the world of the narrative voice, a world to which they can escape in order to mitigate the suffering of their beggars' reality. The reader is also participating in this duality, for his own imaginative fabrication has removed him from his everyday reality. Another excellent example can be found in Unamuno's *San Manuel Bueno, mártir*. In this text there is an inner metaphorical world as symbols of change and duration serve to create the reality of the priest's crisis of faith. Yet this narrative world of San Manuel is contained within a larger text which is the gospel-like confession of Angela Carballino and this in turn is contained within the frame of Unamuno's existential narrator, who openly reminds the reader that all of this is a parallel world of his own making.

Moral order: The aesthetic objective is to establish a transformation of reality, positively or negatively, with which the reader will be confronted. The reader cannot remain uninvolved morally, since his own standard of values is in question as he is called upon to judge the literary situation before him. In its negative form, the aesthetic objective is satire, where the literary situation is presented in such a way that the reader will join in the implicit condemnation. This is not a world which could have been, as in the case of the aesthetic of parallel realities; it is the world that the reader is told should be or should never be. We can appreciate this literary tendency best if we remember that the artistic aim is a moral order, not the assembling of an analogous reality.

Historically, the high point of the aesthetics of moral order has come at periods when writers are openly seeking renewal and change. The low points come when chaos threatens and writers seek to understand the cosmos by creating one. On many occasions the aesthetic positions of parallels and transformations have been seen as contradictory opposi-tions. The temporal dimensions of this aesthetic position is a projection either to the past or to the future but always inexorably linked to an implicit commentary on the present.

It has often been observed that the moral imperative dominates mediaeval literature, but we must not lose sight of the fact that this aesthetic position asserts itself throughout literary history as a refraction on the present. Thus, for example, Quevedo's satire of the *picaro*'s sorry plight is above all an indictment of seventeenth-century society. If there be further need of examples from later literary periods, consider the novel *Cinco horas con Mario* by Miguel Delibes published in 1966. The contemporary situation is used as the starting point for the remembrance of the immediate cataclysmic past of Spain's civil war and the moral imperative, as in the case of Quevedo's *Buscón*, emerges obliquely. With Quevedo it was satirical humour, in Delibes' novel it is the transformation of ordinary gesture into symbolic representation of tolerant political co-existence.

Expansion of reality: The principle involved here is the almost limitless capacity of man to conceptualize and abstract himself from his external situation into an inner world of his own dimensions. The aesthetic of expansion creates an inner cosmos where the established norms of empirical reality are transcended by singular norms of the imagination. The imaginative construction of the literary situation does not in this case correspond to an existing model, either empirical or moral. The organizing principle is an interior form which establishes the farthest reaches of human creativity. Additionally, the inner dimensions of the work must attain their own coherence and limits. The apparent freedom from established order is in fact a demanding aesthetic goal, since the primary aim becomes the creation of a new order of the intellect.

While I was able to describe the first two aesthetic relationships geometrically in a rather simple manner, the third aesthetic is more complex. It resembles the radiation of waves emanating from a disturbance much like a rock tossed on still water. Writers who attempt this form of mind expansion are writing on the assumption that their readers will do the same or close the book.

The temporality of this aesthetic position is one of expanded present. The time of the metaphorical creativity is the only possible dimension for the inner cosmos. The verb tenses may all be past, but the past of the discourse has never been, therefore it is becoming and only becoming which is its time band. Bécquer's *Leyendas* offer us a good example of this aesthetic position. The Middle Ages treated as a remote landscape of gothic architecture serve as the background for tales of the supernatural. The point I am making is that the aesthetic position itself in its temporal manifestation is always moving away from the reader's reality into a hypothetical time which gains its position in a kind of imaginative counterpoint to the immediate palpable real of the reader.

Integration of reality: The key to this aesthetic is the active participation and collaboration of the reader in the realization of the work. All literature depends on the imaginative capacity of the reader to enact and transform the written symbols into an experience; however in this case this general characteristic is expanded to the point where there is no ready-made model for the reader to accept passively. In this aesthetic direction the reader finds himself confronted with an unfinished model and directions on how to build his own poem, novel, drama, and so on. Clearly the objective is active and willing collaboration in the creation of the literary experience. The negative aspect of this aesthetic is almost as important as the positive one, for the reader is not given any interpretation of the model. The aesthetics of integration are based entirely on the premise that the highest achievement in literature is the creation of a rich experience by the reader and that writing is dedicated to that end. Therefore, instead of offering the reader a past to be relived, a proposed moral order, or an ideal to be elaborated, it offers only and exclusively the potentiality of an imaginative experience – a potentiality that can only be realized by the active participation of the reader, for in a literal sense there is nothing concrete without his activity. The text in this aesthetic becomes a complex net of symbols that provoke associations in the reader without the restraints of established form.

The writers of this group have usually been the creators of texts which cause much consternation to the literary public. Writers like James Joyce or Unamuno have been radical figures in their own time, but in contemporary writing their aesthetic position appears to have come into its own.

The temporal dimension of this aesthetic position is simultaneity, for its basic premise is the establishment of a tension of concurrence between the time of the reading and the purported time of the text. The play between reader and text is essentially a temporal game of wits.

We have no difficulty in finding contemporary and modern examples such as *Fragmentos de Apocalipsis* by Torrente Ballester and Unamuno's *Niebla*, but should be reminded that the roots run deep in Spanish literature, going back at least to the second part of *Don Quixote* when the reader becomes openly implicated in the purported reality of Cide Hamete Benengeli. There are also a number of extraordinary seventeenth- and eighteenth-century texts which have been overlooked as aspects of this facet of the history of narrative form because of their break with the established conventions of genre or worse yet because they did not conform with the precepts of genre which would develop in Spain in the late nineteenth century. For example, Diego de Torres y Villarroel published an extraordinary text in 1725 with the title of *Correo del otro mundo al gran piscator de Salamanca: Cartas respondidas a los muertos por el mismo piscator*. The book consists of the correspondence purportedly exchanged between the author and representatives of the various professions. The wit and satire which characterized this follower of Quevedo is in evidence in this text as well as his moral zeal for condemning society's ills. There is, however, another aspect which must not go unnoticed and that is the skilful involvement of the reader in affairs of the narrative.

In this diachronic study of narrative I have approached the documents armed with two assumptions: that modes of expression change because man's perspective on reality changes, and that changes in narrative form can become the basis for clarification on the relation between the author and his reader. Changes have been frequent in the history of narrative, but the kinds of changes have been quite limited. I have outlined the four positions which have been adopted or rejected by writers across time. Each position was either sufficient or insufficient to manage the problems of author and readers. However, the recurrence of these positions has established traditions which are powerful determinants today. My conclusion, that of four aesthetic positions, is hypothetical and has been verified only to the limited extent that one reader can study the phenomena of change throughout literary history.

I have been arguing in favour of a system of classification which works without exception – a way through which we can organize the vast array of fictional narrative. The criteria upon which I have based this system are the synchronic characteristics and diachronic perspectives necessary to the narrative.

I have reached a critical point in my argument, for once I have examined the formal aspects of narrative and subsequently have considered the narrative from the vantage point of the sociocultural reflection of history, I am in danger of allowing these two perspectives to split our enterprise into two parts. But I would like to recall the initial methodological outline I gave whereupon I identified a third level of the text, that is the level of actualization by the reader. It is at this third level that the two poles of formal synchronic aspects and diachronic sociocultural factors come together in the reading experience. How does our logic of classification work? It works by re-establishing the three levels of the texts for the person using this book; this is accomplished by working out the sociocultural status of the text in relation to its formal aspects so that the tension of opposition between these two can echo the reading experience which is the actualization for the reader and for the potential reader who is consulting a study such as a history of narrative form.

The narrative text has been my central focus in this book; I have sought to establish a system of classification which will be compatible, indeed fundamental, to literary history. At the core of this consideration of narrative, whatever its form, has been discourse which constitutes reality by means of a stream of heuristic fictions. Discourse thus redescribes the known, but what it has made is both *discovery* and *invention*. This power in discourse resides in the referential aspect which is common to all texts, but in narrative it is organized into a temporal arrangement of cumulative growth and progression. Thus the creation of fictions in the discourse of narrative is tied both to the form of expression and to the organizing principles of textual referentiality which literary tradition has elaborated.

If the aim of classification be that of establishing a taxonomy, the forms of writing which have been given an aesthetic function do indeed defy classification. An effective taxonomy presupposes that the subject matter be fixed within a logical perimeter of enquiry. I have argued for a theory of literary classification that accepts phenomenological literary theory and the necessity of classification. In such a theory any concept of form must be considered as a heuristic device established for purposes of understanding the nature of literary expression.

The idea of literary history cited at the beginning of this book which rules out classification of texts can now be fully challenged as illusory. The idea that an historical period of composition effectively isolates the literary work is clearly not true, for if we were to hold to this position with any consistency we would not only be deprived of classification, but also of any possibility of understanding the past. The awareness of differences between the past and the present for purposes of interpretation is an essential requirement. The hermeneutic position recognizes that the present is knowable only insofar as it stands as the culmination of tradition that includes the past.

Notes

CHAPTER ONE: UNAMUNO: THE POINT OF DEPARTURE

1 All translations are mine unless otherwise indicated.
2 Cf. Jorge Guillén on Gabriel Miró in *Lenguaje y poesía* 183–232, and A. de Albornoz, *La presencia de Unamuno en Machado*.
3 Cf. James Ward, *Psychological Principles*; also *Essays in Philosophy*.
4 The commentator cited by Unamuno, Henry Jones of the University of Glasgow who distinguished himself as an authority on Lotze – cf. *A Critical Account of the Philosophy of Lotze: The Doctrine of Thought* – was an appropriate critic for James Ward's writings owing to the strong influence exercised by Lotze on Ward's thinking.
5 Ludwig Wittgenstein, *Zettel*, ed. G.E.M. Anscombe and G.H. von Wright, trans. G.E.M. Anscombe 12, 12e

CHAPTER TWO: PHENOMENOLOGICAL PREMISES FOR LITERARY CRITICISM

1 The study of the literary work of art in terms of the distinction between form and content has been one of the major obstacles in the way of a development of a theory encompassing the whole of the work. In this book I address the issues of this distinction rather than dismiss it as arbitrary because the distinction is prevalent among many literary critics today and it is useful. My position is that the distinction between form and content is arbitrary but useful and of course it is not part of the reading experience; it is based on an examination of the text as a formal cause. These are points I shall develop further in the course of this book, but suffice it to state here that the tripartite plan – formal cause, historical reflection, and reading

experience – is based on the conjunction of several writers to whom I am indebted. The major debt is to Ricoeur's *Rule of Metaphor*, chapter 7, 'Metaphor and Reference,' where he examines the 'realistic' intention that belongs to the redescriptive power of poetic language in terms of (a) tension within the statement, (b) tension between two interpretations, and (c) tension in the relational function of the copula. Standing behind Ricoeur's theoretical organization I have placed two further texts: Benedetto Croce's *La Poesia: Introduzione alla critica e storia della poesia e della letteratura* and Martin Heidegger's *Der Ursprung des Kunstwerkes*, ed. Hans-Georg Gadamer. I am in agreement with Croce that what appears to be a distinction, say between prose and poetry, is inherited from historical convention and usage. Turning to Heidegger's essay on the origin of the work of art I accept his distinction between *world* as human projection and *earth* as the mute physical mass. Croce's concept reinforces the level I have called the text as historical reflection, and Heidegger's distinction has helped to establish the validity of the text as reading experience which as a form of world-making cannot be confused with the actual earth.

CHAPTER THREE: THE NARRATIVE TEXT

1 It is generally agreed that reading consists of cognitive constructions, not mechanical decoding of a fixed message. If, therefore, there are cognitive constructions they must be realized through a capacity to apprehend cognitively and they must be related to other cognitive activities. The reading of a sentence is most naturally defined as a group of cognitive constructions having the following three properties: any member of the group is individually meaningful in a restricted sense of the linguistic lexicon to which it belongs; each member of the group partially limits and defines the other members; and all members of the group operate together to form a unique semantic combination. The cognitive construction is in all cases an immediate experience of appropriation of these properties by the reader, and it is in the appropriation that the reader participates and creates meaning.

2 If I understand Gadamer correctly this is what he means when he states that the 'text speaks to me.' His view of hermeneutics developed in *Wahrheit und Methode* is a way of describing what actually happens in the reading experience. He does not attempt to stipulate what understanding ought to be, for his premise is that we cannot alter the experience; we can only seek to explain what happened. Further, he clearly recognizes that the most powerful forces at work in our experience are the presuppositions we hold rather than our stated motives.

3 The response of the reader to the shifts in point of view by the narrative voice is a subject of very great importance not only in literary criticism, but also in psycholinguistics. This chapter develops the concept of reading experience, introduced in the preceding chapters, from the viewpoint of textual probabilities. This change in perspective can be made clear by referring to Paul Ricoeur, 'Metaphor and the Main Problem of Hermeneutics' (unpublished lecture, University of Toronto 1972). In his discussion on the referential aspect of language he distinguishes between linguistic and extralinguistic poles of reference. The history of this approach is long and particularly rich on both sides of the Atlantic (eg, C.S. Peirce, 'On Signs and the Categories,' in *Collected Papers* VIII; C.K. Ogden and I.A. Richards, *The Meaning of Meaning*; R. Wells, 'Meaning and Use,' in *Psycholinguistics*, ed. S. Saporta 269–83). For my purposes Ricoeur is the starting point. Ricoeur finds the basis of meaning in the linguistic user, in this case the reader, and what goes on in the reader is a meaning relationship which is established with the linguistic elements on the one hand and with the objects which lie beyond the language on the other. In my adaptation of Ricoeur's theory I establish three constituencies of experience: first, the linguistic (in the case of the novel, the narrative voice's expression); second, the objects of referents of the language (narration); and third, the realm of the reader himself. In this chapter the focus shall be on the first two constituencies and the third will be treated in full in the fifth chapter.

4 The philosophical basis for this concept has been worked out with thoroughness by a number of philosophers. For example, José Ferrater Mora (1969) in his article, 'Reality as Meaning,' explains that 'intentional acts are, in sum, real acts of intentions, capable of actualizing what is intentional or intentionable, in the realities.' But Ferrater Mora cautions against the mirror concept of realizing intentionality: 'Actualization is not a passive reflection of realities; it is a seeing, understanding, meaning, or conceiving of them.' He further develops the concept of value which I shall discuss in chapter 6 when he states: 'The process just described may lead to an "enrichment" of reality of which the best (perhaps the only) example is the human cultural process ... To be sure, the knowledge of a reality does not add anything to the being of the latter; the reality remains the same in its being, whether it is known or not. However, the knowledge does add something to the reality in its meaning; at any rate, it makes explicit an implicit meaning and by so doing enlarges it. Meanings are given neither in nor outside of reality once and for all. They result from a relation to the reality which makes it increasingly better known and, in consequence, increasingly significant' (pp 133–4).

A direct application to aesthetics of the principle of actualized intentionality is worked out by Mikel Dufrenne in his *Phénoménologie de l'expérience esthétique*. Dufrenne rejects the view that there are objective significations in art and holds that the only meaning that is available is the effective realization in the work itself, which if probed can yield the intentional structuring for the realization.

5 Our realization of a fictional text is largely composed of beliefs and of what we usually call facts. However, we do not experience facts themselves; rather, we construct present images based on our knowledge of things in the past. Consequently, the personal past becomes an active part of the present which we take as the facts described in the narrative. It is thus obvious that it is due to memory that we experience the world of the novel. The memory which extends our personality backwards in time is the memory of ourselves experiencing and not merely of the objects experienced. Thus we are led to conclude that all so-called facts in the literary reading experience are the personal constructions of one's own past. Then, is it possible to distinguish between beliefs and 'facts' in the reading experience if they are both products of my personal capacity to construct images based on previous knowledge? The principal distinction is that beliefs operate in the literary reading experience as explicit personal value systems while images of facts are based on different kinds of objects about which we hold beliefs. My main point is that literary reading experience can be examined on the basis of these two directions, beliefs and external referents, or, in other words, self-reference and extralinguistic reference. I shall develop this concept in this chapter and in chapter 5. My sources for these remarks are Ricoeur ('Herméneutique et structuralisme,' in *Le Conflit des interprétations: essais des interprétations* 31–97); Merleau-Ponty ('On the Phenomenology of Language,' in *Signs* 84–97); and Aron Gurwitsch (*Studies in Phenomenology and Psychology* 124–40).

6 'Intentionality' is a central characteristic of phenomenological philosophy introduced by Brentano and revised by Husserl. It is today the general concept that denotes the guidelines by which an object is presented to a subject. Gurwitsch comments on intentionality of consciousness: 'To be aware of an object means that in the present experience, one is aware of the object as being the same as that which one was aware of in the past experience, as the same as that which, generally speaking, one may be aware of in an indefinite number of presentative acts' (1966, p 12). Also see A. de Waelhens, *Husserl et la pensée moderne*; and Stephen Strasser, *The Idea of Dialogal Phenomenology* 12–14. It is particularly from the earlier writings of Husserl that I have adapted the concept of the intentionality of a literary text; see *Ideas: General Introduction to Pure Phenomenology* 170ff.

7 It is essential throughout my commentary on the narrative world to insist on

its perspectivist character. Reality is subject to an indefinite change of perspectives and is still unexhausted after we have done our best to know it. Insofar as a literary text is the human construction of the reader, it is limited to the particular reader's range of viewpoints. But insofar as the literary text represents real things in an intentional framework it is as virtually inexhaustible as reality itself. At all times we distinguish between our interpretation of the world and the world as intentionality. And so it is also with the narrative world, which becomes available to me only through limitations of my viewpoint, but will also become available to a succession of other readers with other viewpoints. The aspect which I have been concerned about isolating in this chapter is the basic unity of the narrative world which underlies the limitless viewpoints in which it is known. The unity is the deep-rooted basis of organizing the referents of language which I have described as the *Lebenswelt*. This unity develops as the inner distance between the narrative voice and his narration. For the philosophical basis for this commentary see John Wild, 'Man and His Life-World,' in *For Roman Ingarden: Nine Essays in Phenomenology* 90–109.

CHAPTER FOUR: THE AUTHOR

1 We come now to the question left on one side during the presentation of the argument in the preceding three chapters; namely, what is the relation of the author and his *Lebenswelt* to the literary text which he has written? In a brilliant apologetic for the consideration of the author and his perspective, D.E. Hirsch has presented the hypothesis that the validity of an interpretation ultimately rests on what the author meant at the time he wrote it. Hirsch's argument places the burden of historical reconstruction on a systematic hermeneutics. My criticism of his hypothesis rests on the general principle that the reconstruction of the author's situation is only partially attainable and always through the value system of the scholar critic. Consequently, it is a most unstable ground upon which to base an interpretation. See D.E. Hirsch, *Validity in Interpretation*.

There is another position which holds that the only truth in literary interpretation is to be found in internal consistency. This hypothesis has generally been known as extreme formalism and in North America as the 'new criticism' of the last quarter century. Throughout this book and in ealier articles on Unamuno I have argued that the basis for interpretation is to be found in correspondence rather than in internal consistency or unattainable reconstructions of the author's *Lebenswelt*. Cf. 'Archetype and Recreation,' *University of Toronto Quarterly*.

I have thus far examined the correspondence which emanates from a text, but we must take note that there are two directions: one which leads to the reader and the other which points toward the author. The former will be examined in the next chapter and the latter is the objective of this chapter.

2 The general nature of the correspondence between author and text can be seen from the simplest case: an author uses language to go beyond language into the whole of the human context. He writes words which have specific and concrete limitations based on the daily commerce of life, but he is writing about the experience of living itself. The major part of my argument in this chapter is the complement to the next chapter ('The Reader') and the two together are the direct application of the theory proposed in the previous chapters to the central question of the relations between expression and experience.

Cyril Welch in his article 'Speaking and Bespeaking' presents an argument on language similar to my own albeit from a philosopher's point of view: 'Language is grounded in being – if by being we mean the emergence and submergence of man and the things with which he has to do. But, if so, we will search in vain for a language which can speak about the being of man and the being of things. A language will always serve to speak about junctures and movements within a contextual whole. If philosophy and poetry convey something of this whole and what might issue from the whole, it is not so much because they speak about it as because they bespeak it. In any event, though, we cannot rightly expect to find in these realms any glaring and self-sufficient evidence to the effect that there is anything distinctly bespoken or to be bespoken. Potently speaking, a context of experience evidences nothing but various forms of reference within itself. But not all evidence need be potent and self-evident. There might be evidence which manifests itself only if we are prepared to witness it' (p 82).

In terms of my argument the literary text emanates a context of experience which has a number of referential directions within, which I have identified as self-reference and extralinguistic reference. These references become manifest in the reader who is prepared to witness them and they reveal the partially hidden creative experience of the author.

3 A study of the textual changes in *San Manuel bueno, mártir*, has been published by Ediciones Cátedra (Madrid 1979); it had been partially anticipated in my article 'Archetype and Recreation.'

4 Hirsch's *Validity in Interpretation* is an eloquent and well-reasoned defence of the author's meaning as a basis for interpretation. He begins his study with a direct attack on the banishment of the author: 'It is a task for the historian of culture to explain why there has been in the past four decades a heavy and largely victorious assault on the sensible belief that a text means

what its author meant' (p 1). Far from being a simple call for a return to historical source-searching, Hirsch lays the foundation for a rigorous methodology of interpretation. He presents his case forcefully: 'Of course, the reader must realize verbal meaning by his own subjective acts (no one can do that for him), but if he remembers that his job is to construe the author's meaning, he will attempt to exclude his own predispositions and to impose those of the author. However, no one can establish another's meaning with certainty. The interpreter's goal is simply this – to show that a given reading is more probable than others. In hermeneutics, verification is a process of establishing relative probabilities' (p 236).

It is evident from this summation of his position that Hirsch is fully aware of the reader's process of actualization of a text as we have been discussing; the major difference between our positions lies in his idealistic premise of truth. In my view the reader's (critic's) job is to understand the basis of the meaning he has construed to the text. Reading, being a fundamentally subjective act, can never exclude the reader's predispositions, and when he attempts to impose those of another (let us say, the implied author), he is imposing the predispositions he thinks the other has had. Consequently, the interpreter's goal is to explain the directions and foundations of a given reading. For review articles of Hirsch's book, see the special issue of *Genre* 1 (July 1968) devoted to his book. Especially significant are the contributions by Morse Peckham (pp 190–4) and Monroe C. Beardsley (pp 169–89).

5 Literary history is vital to literary study in general and it is in need of much rethinking in regard to its assumptions, premises, and aims. Literary historians have been drawn in two opposite directions since the first major scholars of the nineteenth century. On the one hand, the concept of a universal literature of man (usually reduced to Western Europe with some acknowledgment of America) has tended to blur all local, regional, and even national characteristics in favour of the humanistic ideal that art, including literature, 'is a language by which the human mind gives utterance to its own integrity.' See Albert Hofstadter, 'On the Consciousness and Language of Art.' On the other hand, we have seen numerous histories of writers within the narrow confines of nation and even city. Reflection on this opposition will show that the reduction of the literary tradition to either universals or local peculiarities is a falsification of the literary reality of authors and their readers.

I will attempt to cope with this seeming impasse in chapter 10 of this book and I shall not repeat my arguments here, but in general my view is that authentic literary history is only possible by co-ordinating the synchronic

with the diachronic aspects of our literary heritage. I agree with Geoffrey
Hartman's appraisal of the possibility of literary history which respects
'the precarious marriage between genius and *genius loci*' (p 232). See 'Toward
Literary History,' in *In Search of Literary Theory*, ed. Morton W. Bloomfield.

6 The concept of background in my hypothesis is logically demanded by the
central concept of intentionality. The textual reality which emerges as
intentionality is fulfilled, and the very idea of textual intention that is to be
actualized presupposes a horizon upon which it is founded. The term
'background' with its essential relationship to foreground serves our purposes of literary theory as the expression of the horizon from which intentionality rises and against which the literary reality comes to be. The philosophical bases for these ideas are to be found in Edmund Husserl's
Cartesianische Meditationen und Pariser Vorträge, especially 81–3.

7 The philosophical orientation of this chapter has been derived primarily
from the works of Maurice Merleau-Ponty. The radical rethinking which
Merleau-Ponty thrust at complacent art critics in his 1961 article, 'L'Œil et
l'esprit,' can be considered a theoretical point of departure for this chapter. More specifically, the dialectic of foreground and background has been
suggested to me by reading Merleau-Ponty's unfinished *The Visible and the
Invisible: Philosophical Interrogation*, especially chapter 4, 'The intertwining –
The Chiasm,' where Merleau-Ponty comments on Proust: 'We touch here
the most difficult point, that is, the bond between the flesh and the idea,
between the visible and the interior armature which it manifests and
which it conceals. No one has gone further than Proust in fixing the
relations between the visible and the invisible, in describing an idea that is not
the contrary of the sensible, that is its living and its depth' (p 149).

8 In *Life-World and Consciousness*, ed. Lester E. Embree.

CHAPTER FIVE: THE READER

1 There have been many recent and significant studies of the reader as the
source of literary reality. Beginning with the fundamental studies of
Roman Ingarden, *Vom Erkennen des literarischen Kunstwerkes* and *Das literarische Kunstwerk*, a phenomenological approach to literature has turned its
focus on the reader. The arguments presented in this chapter are in principle very near to the views of Wolfgang Iser; cf. 'The Reading Process: A
Phenomenological Approach,' *New Literary History*. His opening statement
will attest the common cause which I am pleading 'The phenomenological
theory of art lays full stress on the idea that, in considering a literary work,
one must take into account not only the actual test but also, and in equal

measure, the actions involved in responding to that text. Thus Roman
Ingarden confronts the structure of the literary text with the ways in which it
can be *konkretisiert* (realized). The text as such offers different "schema-
tised views" through which the subject matter of the work can come to light,
but the actual bringing to light is an action of *Konkretisation*. If this is so,
then the literary work has two poles, which we might call the artistic and the
aesthetic: the artistic refers to the text created by the author, and the
aesthetic to the realization accomplished by the reader. From this polarity it
follows that the literary work cannot be completely identical with the text,
or with the realization of the text but in fact must lie halfway between the
two. The work is more than the text, for the text only takes on life when it
is realized, and furthermore the realization is by no means independent of
the individual disposition of the reader – though this in turn is acted upon
by the different patterns of the text. The convergence of text and reader
brings the literary work into existence, and this convergence can never be
precisely pinpointed, but must always remain virtual as it is not to be identified either with the reality of the text or with the individual disposition of
the reader' (p 279).

2 I am well aware that any significant discussion of the reading process
entails specialized study which is beyond the scope of this book and of my
training; consequently in this section I acknowledge a great indebtedness
to the research of colleagues in psychology and philosophy of mind. Cf. Eugene T. Gendlin, *Experiencing and the Creation of Meaning*, especially 100–6
on 'Recognition': 'Recognition refers to the case where symbols adequately
conceptualize ... As we read it [the page], the symbols call forth in us the
felt meanings that constitute our having of the meanings of the symbols, that
is our understanding of what is printed on the page. Hearing, reading, or
thinking familiar symbols includes – for us – not only the symbols, but also
the felt meaning they call forth in us.' Also, pp 111–37 on 'Creative Functional Relationships': 'Symbols that already have parallel felt meaning are
put together in such a way that a new felt meaning is created and symbolized by them. This occurs to some extent in all creative thought, problem
solving, therapy and literature.'

3 Although we acknowledge individual differences in the degree of self-
awareness, it must be maintained that the structure is the same in all cases.
The concept of background against which foreground becomes identifiable (cf. chapter 4) is based in part on Aron Gurwitsch's commentary on
consciousness. See 'Phenomenology of Thematics,' in *Studies in Phenomenology and Psychology* 175–286, especially 196ff.: 'Every mental state has its
environment in the sense that what is experienced through it, its noema,

has surroundings, a noematic environment, also given in experience. When I apprehend a thing in the mode of the cogito, I grasp it as emerging from a background. Turning to the thing so grasped, and busying myself with it, I am conscious of the components of this background which, in spite of being set off from my theme, are conjoined with it in a peculiar way. The thing, of which I am conscious in the mode of cogito, is given as part of my "natural surrounding world," as a thing among things; other things are "contiguous," juxtaposed, forming together with it a "perceptual field" – precisely that part of the "natural surrounding world" which falls directly into my perception' (p 196). Further, he establishes the basis for the structure of the thematic field: 'We never deal with a theme *simpliciter*; instead, we confront a theme standing in a field. Our attitude is determined by the thematic field, and we deal with the theme as pertaining to this field. The thematic field itself is a context of objects intrinsically related as materially belonging together ... The thematic field is not a conglomeration of any contents whatever, not like a box in which sundry things can be put and from which they can be taken out, a conception which is at the basis of problems of the range of consciousness and the narrowness of consciousness and which necessarily leads to these pseudoproblems' (p 203). Finally, what has come to be a key concept in our theory of interpretation: 'For a theme "to be taken into grasp" and for "thought to come into order" is one and the same thing. Correlative with becoming-figure and being-figure of the theme is becoming-oriented and being-oriented of the thematic field; both are brought about by one and the same process. Consequently, a theme is always a theme in a thematic field. It is erroneous to speak of the "theme *simpliciter*" without mentioning its relation to, and its insertion into, the thematic field, just as it is also inappropriate to speak of the thematic field without taking into consideration its organization and orientation with reference to the theme' (p 205).

4 The conquest of subjectivity by philosophy is the hallmark of phenomenology from Husserl to Ricoeur. The concern with methodology throughout reveals the basic aim of developing a systematic method which can cope with the endless possibilities of human experience. Following Humboldt, Ricoeur sees language as an intermediary between human will-to-order and human experience, and it is in the analysis of this condition of mediation that philosophy can discover the structure of subjectivity. See Paul Ricoeur, 'Husserl and Wittgenstein on Language,' in *Phenomenology and Existentialism*, ed. E.N. Lee and M. Mandelbaum 207–17, and also 'Structure, Word, Event,' *Philosophy Today*.

5 Paul Ricoeur has the most explicit theory of a dialectic which encompasses

structure and experience in the reality of interpretation. It will be readily seen that this theory is the very keystone for the present book. See Paul Ricoeur, 'The Model of the Text: Meaningful Action Considered as a Text,' *Social Research*, especially 556–7: 'I want now to show in what way "explanation" (erklären) requires "understanding" (verstehen) and brings forth in a new way the inner dialectic which constitutes "interpretation" as a whole ... Could we not say that the function of structural analysis is to lead from surface semantics, that of narrated myth, to a deep-semantics, that of the boundary situations which constitute the ultimate "referent" of the myth?'

6 It is not my purpose in this book to present a method of discourse analysis beyond a basic orientation of how it is to be linked to the full study of the text in its actualization as reading experience. Recent critical articles show the interest of other critics in such a theory of interpretation. I am particularly interested in the work of Seymour Chatman, 'The Semantics of Style,' in *Essays in Semiotics*, who makes an attempt to devise a system based on the distinctions between cognitive, emotive, and general purport. The article by Stanley Fish, 'Literature in the Reader: Affective Stylistics,' *New Literary History*, begins with the vigour of a man pleading a cause but unfortunately fails to provide his reader with any resolution to the problems and questions he opened. As mentioned before, significant work in this field has been done by the French, for example Tzvetan Todorov, 'Les Transformations narratives,' *Poétique*. The most complete presentation of the history, methods, and logic of discourse analysis is in J.L. Kinneavy's *A Theory of Discourse*; see especially ch. 5, 'Literary Discourse' 307–92.

7 The enrichment of the reader as a goal of criticism is discussed in the next chapter. I do not believe that the implicit reader is ever an ideal reader, for the concept of ideal reader is in fact only a limit concept. We are here referring to the human potentialities of reading.

8 Richard Kuhns in his important contribution to criticism, *Structures of Experience: Essays on the Affinity between Philosophy and Literature*, makes my point admirably: 'Art can be successful only when it leads the reader to join himself, in an aspiration of anamnesis, to the reality of imagination. Art fails when it demands that attention be centered on its separated, momentary, essentially private manifestations as the poetry of this or that one poet.' Kuhns then gives what can serve as a definition of the aims of this book: 'A phenomenology of the imagination, like the phenomenology of mind in the Hegelian sense, is an account of how the awareness moves to fullest self-consciousness in the merging of the one recollection with the anamnesis available to all finite memories' (p 125).

9 The paradox confronting us when we examine the wanton ritual sacrifice of hundreds of hapless victims is that the Aztec religion had a very profound moral purpose. The paradox is only on the surface, for the Aztecs were the crude inheritors of a culture and civilization far beyond their intellectual capacities. These nomadic warriors inherited a subtle philosophy of stoic-like religion while they were still in a primitive stage of witchcraft religion. After their conquest of the Toltec peoples they adapted the symbols of the latter to their hunter mentality. See Laurette Séjourné, *Pensamiento y religión en el México antiguo* 35–52.

10 See Séjourné, pp 74–5, 112–24, and Miguel León-Portilla, *Quetzalcóatl* (Mexico: Fondo de cultura económica 1968) 8–15, and for more extensive studies see Miguel León-Portilla, *La filosofía nahuatl estudiada en sus fuentes*, and Laurette Séjourné, *El universo de Quetzalcoatl.*

11 See Fray Bernardino de Sahagún, *Historia general de las cosas de Nueva España* II, 12–14. See especially p 12: 'El buboso que se llamaba Nanauatzin, en lugar de ramos ofrecia cañas verdes atadas de tres en tres, todas ellas llegaban a nueve.'

12 Séjourné, *Pensamiento y religión en el México antiguo*, comments on the myth with clarity: 'Se ha visto que el elegido de los dioses es el buboso aquel cuyo cuerpo se desintegra, es decir, del hombre que habiendo cumplido la tarea de la reconciliación de los contrarios ha empezado a desprenderse de su yo fragmentado' (p 87).

13 Alfonso Caso in *Los calendarios pre-hispánicos* has established the full correlation of the Christian calendar with the Toltec-Aztec calendar – see pp 41–65; the interpretation of the Tonalpohualli is on pp 4–41. The dates of Artemio Cruz's third person presentations are interpreted in terms of the sign of Tecpatl for one born on 9 April 1889.

14 Pieter Geyl, *Debates with Historians* 9

15 See C.G. Jung, *The Archetypes and the Collective Unconscious* 293.

16 F. García Calderón, *Latin America: Its Rise and Progress* 202

17 See Germán Guzmán Campos, *La violencia en Colombia.*

18 Cf. the hero myth of the Yakuts of Siberia: 'The goddess offered her milk to the youth from a sumptuous breast, and after partaking of it he felt his strength increase a hundred-fold. At the same time the goddess promised the youth every happiness and blessed him in such a way that neither water, nor fire, iron, nor anything else should ever do him harm.' See Joseph Campbell, *Hero with a Thousand Faces* 336.

19 Cf. Campbell, *ibid.* 335, and Mircea Eliade, *Cosmos and History* 12–21.

20 The female archetypes are the subject of extensive research. Cf. 'Psychological Aspects of the Mother Archetype,' in Jung's *The Archetypes and the*

Collective Unconscious 75–110, and C. Kerényi, *Eleusis: Archetypal Image of Mother and Daughter.*

21 Campbell's commentary on the duality of light and dark sides of the eternal female are most appropriate for this discussion: 'She encompasses the encompassing, nourishes the nourishing, and is the life of everything that lives. She is also the death of everything that dies. The whole round of existence is accomplished within her sway, from birth, through adolescence, maturity, and senescence, to the grave. She is the womb and the tomb: the sow that eats her farrow' (p 114).

22 One of the most interesting archetypes which prevails in all myths is that of the 'wise old man.' The basic source for study on this archetype is Jung's *The Archetypes and the Collective Unconscious* 35–7, 217–30. See p 35: 'The wise old man, the superior master and teacher, the archetype of the spirit, who symbolizes the pre-existent meaning hidden in the chaos of life.' And on p 222: 'The old man thus represents knowledge, reflection, insight, wisdom, cleverness, and intuition on the one hand, and on the other moral qualities such as goodwill and readiness to help which make his spiritual character sufficiently plain.' Cf. with the Menqueteba myth from Colombia reported by Jesús Arango Cano, *Mitos, leyendas y dioses chibchas* 55–62: 'Llegó a la alti-planicie, por el oriente, un venerable anciano, cabalgando un extraño jumen-to. El vetusto personaje llevaba largos cabellos y luenga y nivea barba que le caía majestuosamente hasta la cintura ... Traía el anciano gran misión que cumplir. El pueblo chibcha cuando apareció esta patriarcal figura estaba sumido en la más completa ignorancia.' The particular characteristics of the archetype change from one culture to another, but he is always a mysteri-ous figure of wisdom who has the answers to the enigmas of life. Another principal source for this archetype is the biblical figure of Melquisedec – see Genesis 14:18, Psalms 109:4, and Hebrews 7:1–3 – where he is described as the wise king, priest for all time, a figure without antecedents whose function as intermediary can be likened to the son of God.

23 Cf. Campbell, *Hero with a Thousand Faces*, on the hero of wisdom: 'The su-preme hero, however, is not the one who merely continues the dynamics of the cosmogonic round, but he who reopens the eye – so that through all the comings and goings, delights and agonies of the world panorama, the one presence will be seen again. This requires a deeper wisdom than the other, and results in a pattern not of action but of significant representation' (p 345).

24 One of the most significant aspects of this novel is the assimilation of the vast array of mythical symbols of the self in what is the ageless search for the meaning of life. See Jung's study of the basic symbols of this quest in his *Aion*, especially 'The Sign of the Fishes,' pp 72–94; 'The Prophecies of Nostra-

damus' 95–102; 'The Fish in Alchemy' 126–53; and 'The Structure and Dynamics of the Self' 184–221. The anonymous author of the scholia to the 'Tractatus aureus' writes about the search for the philosopher's stone: 'Reduce your stone to the four elements, rectify and combine them into one, and you will have the whole magistery. This One, to which the elements must be reduced, is that little circle in the centre of this squared circle. It is the mediator, making meaning between the elements.'

25 This Buddhist scripture of the Lokabyuhas is translated by Henry Clarke Warren in his *Buddhism in Translations* 38–9 and is cited by Campbell, *Hero with a Thousand Faces* 374.

26 My study of the Voluspá is based on two books: E.O.G. Turville-Petre, *Myth and Religion of the North*, see especially chapter 16, 'The Beginning of the World and Its End' 275–85. I used the translation of the Voluspá by Lee M. Hollander, *The Poetic Edda*.

CHAPTER SIX: THE CRITIC

1 Few have defined the critic's role with more care than Leo Spitzer when he answered Karl Shapiro's negation of criticism. Shapiro had argued in 'A Farewell to Criticism,' *Poetry* (1948) that poetry had a sense beyond sense which made criticism impossible and Spitzer answered him with this statement of purpose: 'Poetry consists of words with their meaning preserved, which, through the magic of a poet who works within a prosodic whole, arrive at a sense beyond sense; and ... it is the task of the philologist to point out the manner in which the transfiguration just mentioned has been achieved. The irrationality of the poem need not lose anything at the hands of a discreet linguistic critic; on the contrary, he will work in accord with the poet (although with no regard to his approval), insofar as he will patiently and analytically retrace the way from the rational to the irrational: a distance which the poet may have covered in one bold leap' (*Essays on English and American Literature* 141–2). Murray Krieger comments on Spitzer's definitions in *The Play and the Place of Criticism* (pp 4–8), and is at pains to explain the use of the terms rational and irrational: 'Clearly what Spitzer must mean is that the multiple and simultaneous ways in which words – their sounds, their meanings, their extension into metaphor, archetype, character, and action – interact within the poetic context defy rational operations of our critical discourse, which after all owes the same obligations to the semantic, syntactic, and logical operations of language as all other non-poetic discourse does.' There is a basic difference in the purpose which guides Spitzer and

that followed by Krieger and contextualism in general. Spitzer is oriented by the how-was-the-poem-written question while Krieger is concerned with the what-does-it-mean question. The presupposition behind Spitzer's enquiry is that it is important to know how man creates poetry while the presupposition behind Krieger's is that the text is in need of mediation. I fully subscribe to the concept of criticism which these distinguished scholars profess; I would, however, add a third dimension to the creative and explicative pre-suppositions and that is that as a reader's reader the critic can help to in-crease the reader's capacity for self-fulfilment. The Brazilian critic Massaud Moisés has expressed these ideals admirably in *A criação literária* 301: 'Portanto, o crítico litérario busca, em última instância, analisar, compreender e julgar essa totalidade da obra literária, em que se completa ema visão multiforme do mundo e do pensamento humano.'

2 The number of brilliant studies on the novel is large on both sides of the Atlantic. See, for example, the anthology *The Theory of the Novel*, ed. Philip Stevick, and its excellent bibliography on the subject. I have read extensively among critics of the novel in English and in the Romance languages, but I have made no attempt at an inventory of these readings since I do not believe it would serve any useful purpose. I wish to acknowledge here only those critics who have had a formative influence in the development of my thinking. In the 1950s these critics were fundamental to me: René Wellek and Austin Warren (*Theory of Literature*), Wolfgang Kayser (*Das sprachliche Kunstwerk*), Northrop Frye (*Anatomy of Criticism*), Monroe Beardsley (*Aesthetics: Problems in the Philosophy of Criticism*), Erich Auerbach (*Mimesis: The Representation of Reality in Western Literature*), R.S. Crane ('The Concept of Plot and the Plot of Tom Jones,' in *Critics and Criticism*). In the 1960s the major forces in my reading on the novel were Wayne C. Booth (*The Rhetoric of Fiction*), *A Prague School Reader on Esthetics, Literary Structure, and Style*, ed. Paul Garvin, Murray Krieger (*The Tragic Vision*), Georges Poulet (*Studies in Human Time*), and Wayne Shumaker (*Literature and the Irrational*). More recently there are the works of my colleagues in France and Germany as well as North America which have already been mentioned in the text and notes.

3 See G.S. Kirk, *Heraclitus: The Cosmic Fragments*, fragments A10, B1, 2, 8, 10, 30.

4 See John Burnet, *Early Greek Philosophy*, Parmenides' fragment B3, 8, 34.

5 See Burnet, *Early Greek Philosophy*, Leucippus, B, 2.

6 See Kirk, *Heraclitus*, fragments B91, 103ff. I have taken the unusual move to seek out sources in ancient Greek philosophy because of the conviction that basic principles such as these are inherited and elaborated across time and are

not the product of any period or nation. My basic source for this orientation has been the excellent study of scientific principles by Eduardo Nicol of the University of Mexico; see *Los principios de la ciencia*.

7 This interview with George Steiner was conducted by Elizabeth Hall and published in *Psychology Today*.

8 This point has been made by a number of critics. A recent strong argument against critical self-promotion was made by Murray Krieger, *The Play and Place of Criticism* 9ff.

CHAPTER SEVEN: A STRUCTURE OF ENQUIRY

1 The basic argument of this chapter was first presented in the Comparative Literature Seminar on Hermeneutics held at the University of Toronto in October 1970, and was published in *New Literary History* 3 (1972) 263–78.

2 D.W. Gotschalk finds a prevalence of values in all human activity (*Patterns of Good and Evil* [Urbana, IL: University of Illinois Press 1963] chap. 6). This convincing argument must not, however, be taken to mean that methodology cannot be constructionally independent of the researcher's value system. The phenomenological method does not deny the prevalent values; it only postpones their discussion.

3 K.R. Popper in *The Logic of Scientific Discovery*, chap. 1, finds that the inductive process of thought is beyond logic and has only psychological significance. However, Gotschalk, *The Structure of Awareness* 34, adds this commentary: 'All this, the logical inconclusiveness and insecurity of induction, may be granted. Yet one may feel that something has been left out. Induction may logically be a leap into the dark. But does this reduce its cognitive importance to only psychological value? Epistemologically, it remains an effort to tie in our accumulated observations and knowledge with the unknown, and widen the horizons of awareness.'

4 Cf. E.D. Hirsch, *Validity in Interpretation*. Underlying Hirsch's procedure is the belief in the necessity of historical reconstruction of the literary text and subsequently of mediation between our historical context and that of the literary work. My disagreement with this theory is that it hides the true concern of interpretation, which is to expand the awareness of the reader or, in other words, the understanding of the work cannot be separated from the attempt to understand oneself.

5 Analysis here is a phenomenological examination. The basic steps of the method are four: (1) a direct study of the text is made and for the moment excludes all indirect considerations; (2) the components of the text are

described and identified; (3) the structure of the work is formulated on the basis of the accumulated data of the first two steps; and (4) the structure is demonstrated not only as possible but as the necessary structure for this work. Cf. Paul Ricoeur, *Husserl: An Analysis of His Phenomenology*.

The systematic study of literature has at times been called the science of literature by its practitioners in order to emphasize the need for analytical observation. Cf. Wolfgang Kayser, *Das sprachliche Kunstwerk. Eine Einführung in die Literaturwissenschaft* 17–25.

6 L.S. Vygotsky, *Thought and Language* 153, quoted by Gotschalk in *The Structure of Awareness* 67. It should be noted that the phenomenological analysis of literature begins with the most essential elementary part: the word in context.

7 This is of course a problem that has received the closest attention by philosophers and critics. My own usage here is elementary since I am developing the broader question of the place of analysis within criticism. Cf. Monroe C. Beardsley, *Aesthetics* 220–37, 254–6.

8 As Merleau-Ponty states, the word 'image' is in bad repute among philosophers because it has come to mean a copy of the original which is the private possession of the perceiver. Cf. Maurice Merleau-Ponty, *The Primacy of Perception* 164.

Cassirer's views on imagery are basic to this discussion. 'The image itself has no form of truth; truth and reality are imputed only to the substantial elements from which it is pieced together like a mosaic. But this insight gained by the psychological critic need not hamper or restrict the use we make of this image in actual physical life. Even though the image may be recognized and, as it were, epistemologically exposed as a fiction, it has reality as a fiction – that is, it arises according to definite and necessary laws of the imagination and that suffices. A necessary and uniform mechanism of consciousness produces it from sensory experiences and their associative combination. Thus the image acquires no logical independence and no specific meaning different from mere sensation.' In the next paragraph he goes on to write: 'Consciousness cannot devote itself in every moment with equal intensity to all the various sense impressions that fill it; it cannot represent them all with equal sharpness, concretion, and individuality. Thus it creates a schemata, total images into which enter a number of particular contents, and in which they flow together without distinction. But these schemata can be no more than mere abbreviations, compendious condensations of the impressions.' Ernst Cassirer, *The Phenomenology of Knowledge: The Philosophy of Symbolic Forms* III 191–2.

The literary image is an imaginative re-enactment achieved through the language which is analogous to the externally perceived image only in its essential characteristics: (1) a synthesis of the given; and (2) the (reader's) intentionality of significance. It is the task of interpretation to examine the relationship (distance of these two).

9 Beardsley's definition of metaphor (*Aesthetics* 134) serves as a basis for my discussion. 'A metaphor is an indirectly self-contradictory or else an obviously false attribution in which "the modifier has connotations that could be attributed to the subject." He adds that "the connotations of words are never fully known, or knowable, beforehand ... The metaphor does not create the connotations, but it brings them to life".' Commented upon and quoted by F.E. Sparshott, *The Structure of Aesthetics* 262.

The problems, philosophical and literary, that a full discussion of metaphor entails must await another occasion. In the present context I am interested in establishing fundamental categories. Therefore, my intent is to simplify and not exhaust the problems. Metaphor is, in the first instance, an identification of usually incompatible subjects, for example, 'the river of life.' It is the identification that causes the imaginative response in the reader; however, semantically we are all aware that this is an identity of relation and not of substance, since no speaker of English would understand 'the river of life' to mean that river and life were the same substance. There is implicit in the identity of relation contained in metaphor a semantic unity of all things as named through language.

10 The word 'symbol,' like 'image,' has applications which lie outside of the literary concern. Sparshott enters into the problem with accustomed lucidity and rigour: 'Symbols stand for or refer to the things of which they are signs. These things may be near or distant, it makes no matter. Language, which is among other things a way of dealing with things by proxy, is a system of symbols.' Further in his exposition Sparshott reproduces the 'triangle of meaning' in order to clarify the double significance of the words 'standing for.' Thus we have

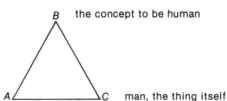

where A expresses the concept B which has been abstracted from the thing C, and in ordinary discourse we say A (word 'man') stands for C man. Sparshott quotes from Susanne Langer with approval in order to reach a summary: 'We form concepts in order to make experience manageable; concepts are embodied in symbols, symbols, then, may be defined as "any device whereby we are enabled to make an abstraction" (Langer, 1953, xi), that is to say, to make something intelligible; a work of art in some sense makes something intelligible if only itself' (p 369).

11 The eidetic study of 'symbol' by Paul Ricoeur is methodologically a model of phenomenological analysis which I have applied to the study of literature. Cf. *The Symbolism of Evil* 3–24.

12 The first level of analysis is critical to the entire process, for it establishes the direction and pace of development of the entire imaginative production.

13 The second analytical order is based in part on Beardsley's 'Principles of Congruence and Plenitude.' Cf. *Aesthetics* 144–7.

14 These terms are used in order to avoid the endless debate about 'meaning.' I am here concerned with the recognition of awareness of the symbol and its assimilation by the reader to the growing context. Cf. Ricœur, *Husserl* 45–9.

15 The second step in this methodology is the utilization of the descriptive information in phenomenological hermeneutics. The change from the descriptive analysis to the intersubjective experience is obviously crucial to my argument. The plurality implicit in the term *reader* enters into the make-up of the literary work (which until this point has been treated as a thing) because literature has its fulfilment only in the reading. The point here is that in this system of criticism, the intersubjectivity of the work is founded on the objective achievement of analytical description. Interpretation in practice is the explication of the intersubjective signification of the literary work.

CHAPTER TEN: HEURISTIC MODELS OF ENQUIRY

1 The case against systematic classification has been increasingly pressed. Cf. George Watson, *The Study of Literature* 90: 'I have argued that any system of classification demands a static property, and that the historical sense has rendered it difficult or impossible for modern man to see literature as a given object in the sense that must have seemed natural to Aristotle and Horace.'

2 See H.J. Pos, 'Phénoménologie et linguistique,' *Revue Internationale de Philosophie*. My basic sources on the phenomenology of language are Maurice Merleau-Ponty, 'On the Phenomenology of Language,' in *Signs* (1964), and Paul Ricoeur, *Le Conflit des interprétations* (1969), especially 'Structure et herméneutique' and 'La Question du sujet: le défi de la sémiologie.' Ricoeur's *Husserl: An Analysis of His Phenomenology* (1967) provided my research with the broader background on the general question of the relation of positivistic analysis and phenomenological interpretation. Subsequently I examined the unpublished Husserl manuscripts which deal with this problem, especially 'Aesthetik und Phänomenologie' (A-VI-1 1906-IX-31).

In brief, the position Husserl presents and which I have taken quite independently as my starting point is the following: the realization of language through expression is the actualization (*Verleiblichung*) of what would otherwise be mere potentiality implicit in the intersubjective structure of language. Thus there are two aspects of language, the universal intersubjective structure which is demanded if there is to be communication and the expression itself. A simplified adaptation to literary criticism places the literary text in its encounter with the reader as a confrontation of linguistic potentiality and the reading experience and considers expression (the written language) as the medium which links the two.

3 The heuristic nature of historical classification has been first expounded by Karl Popper in *The Open Society and Its Enemies* 269, 278, and has been variously defended and attacked by historians and philosophers of history. In this book, the view that historical categories are heuristic in function whatever the intentions of the historian may be is derived from the phenomenological theory of language and literature I share with Ricoeur, Iser, and many others.

4 For a full discussion of Darwin's theories and their application to history see Stephen Toulmin, *Human Understanding*. See especially 'Interlude: Evolution and the Human Sciences' 319–56. On pp 324–5 Toulmin observes: 'Looking back at Darwin's *Origin of Species* from a century later, we can see that his theories were built – from the very beginning – around the novel conception of organic species as modifiable populations, possessing not a specific essence, but a statistical distribution of properties; and of the "peak" or "mean" of these populations as shifting in the face of ecological changes, or in response to the colonization of new environments.'

5 Franz Boas, *Handbook of American Indian Languages*

6 Wolfgang Kayser, *Das sprachliche Kunstwerk: Eine Einführung in die Literaturwissenschaft* (pp 536ff.). Kayser bases his own interpretation of genre on the work of Emil Staiger, *Grundbegriffe der Poetik*; Ernst Cassirer, *Idee und Gestalt*; and, especially, Heinrich Junker, *Festschrift für Streitberg*, whose basic concepts of philosophy of language are quoted with approval:

Leistung	Richtung	Person	Erlebnissphäre	Gruppen
Kindgabe	expressiv	ich	emotional	Stimmung, Gefuhl
Auslosung	impressiv	du	intentional	Befehl
				Wunsch, Frage, Zweifel, Streben
Darstellung	factiv	er, sie es	rational	Vorstellung
	demonstrativ			Denken

It is quite significant that Ernst Cassirer in *The Philosophy of Symbolic Forms* takes the same position as Kayser, with the acknowledged shadow of Wilhelm von Humboldt's work cast over his theory. Cassirer writes (p 302): 'Thus, the principle of classification, once arrived at, not only governs the formation of nouns, but thence spreads to the whole syntactical structure of the language, becoming the actual expression of its organization, its spiritual "articulation." Hence the work of the *linguistic imagination* seems throughout to be closely bound up with a specific methodology of linguistic thinking. Once again language, with all its involvement in the sensuous, imaginative world, reveals a tendency towards the logical and universal, through which it progressively liberates itself and attains to a purer and more independent spirituality of form.'

7 The root experience of reading a narrative is the encounter with an ongoing relationship between the speaker and his referent. However, we must note that the word 'experience,' which is so important to this concept, has a technical usage but is obviously taken from the language of everyday life and retains some ambiguity in spite of efforts at definition herein. In seeking to examine the 'I-other' experience of the narrative we are at the same time looking into a linguistic strategy and to a state of consciousness in the reader. Common sense leads us to divide experience in the narrative into the implicit reality of the narrative voice making reference to the other and the actual reality of the reader who realizes this relationship by creating another reality between himself and the reading. This division is so familiar that it has become habitual. We read *about* another's view on the other about which he has chosen to speak. The reading experience is what we know from within – our thoughts, feelings, and attitudes in process – while the 'I-other' experience in the text is fixed and outside of our mind awaiting our meeting with it. This dualism is based, as I have said, on a common sense of habit, but it is imperative for us to delve beyond the habit and into the realities themselves. Three positions seem to be clearly distinguishable with regard to the 'I-other' experience. We can concentrate solely on the textual relationship and avoid the reader's experience, or we can take up the reader's relationship to the text but not go into the inter-textual relationship's essential aspects, or we may adopt a dualistic position and examine both relationships as separate positions.

All three are insufficient to cope with all of the implications of the 'I-other' experience. My argument is that if we are to gain knowledge over the subject matter we must begin with the verifiable and proceed to the lesser known without granting an independent status to any of these. The basic meaning of experience indicates an activity of encounter I call 'experiencing.' This phenomenon is expressed linguistically as a two-term relation between *subject* and *object*. Thus, grammatically, *subject* is anything which has acquaintance with other-than-itself and this other-than-itself is object. Consequently, we can sum up the argument. The voice in the narrative is always the speaker who has acquaintance with the objects of his narration and on occasion can make himself the other, that is, objectify himself. Now then, this two-term relation of narrative voice experience is based directly and exclusively on the two-term relation we call our own experience of life. By way of example, I – the reader – have an acquaintance with a man who writes; this acquaintance is a part of my life experience. When I take up the narrative and begin to read about a writer's experiences, two relationships emerge at once. My acquaintance with the writer is activated through my memory. This activated 'experience' becomes part of the new relationship I am enjoying with the text. Finally, a third relationship comes to be in the text where there is an emergent relationship between the narrator and his object, which I understand and can vitalize only because of my experience in living.

8 Eg, Michel Butor, *La Modification*; Mario Vargas Llosa, *La casa verde*; Carlos Fuentes, *Cambio de piel*.
9 I have adopted this part of my theory of classification from Kayser's study of genre; see *Das sprachliche Kunstwerk* 479ff.
10 See Jurij Lotman, *The Structure of the Artistic Text*, trans. R. Vroon 217–39.
11 See Alexander A. Parker, *Literature and the Delinquent* 62.

Bibliography

Abrams, Meyer H. *The Mirror and the Lamp* Oxford: Oxford University Press 1958

Adorno, Theodor W. 'Der Essay als Form' *Noten zur Literatur* I. Berlin: Suhrkamp 1958

Albornoz, Aurora de *La presencia de Unamuno en Machado* Madrid: Gredos 1970

Arango Cano, Jesús *Mitos, leyendas y dioses chibchas* Manizales (Colombia): Tercera época 1967

Asemissen, H.U. *Strukturanalytische Probleme der Wahrnehmung in der Phänomenologie Husserls Kantstudien* Erganzungshefte 73. Bonn: Bouvier 1957

Auerbach, Erich *Mimesis: The Representation of Reality in the Philosophy of Criticism* Princeton: Princeton University Press 1953

Ballard, E.G. *Art and Analysis* The Hague: Martinus Nijhoff 1957

Barthes, Roland *Le Degré zéro de l'écriture* Paris: Seuil 1953

– *Sur Racine* Paris: Seuil 1963

– *Essais critiques* Paris: Seuil 1964

– *Critique et vérité* Paris: Seuil 1966

Beardsley, Monroe C. *Aesthetics: Problems in the Philosophy of Criticism* New York: Harcourt, Brace and World 1958

– 'Textual Meaning and Authorial Meaning' *Genre* I, 3 (1968) 169–81

Binswanger, Ludwig 'Über Sprache und Denken' *Studia Philosophica* 6 (1949) 30–50

Boas, Franz *Handbook of American Indian Languages.* Washington, DC: US Government Printing Office 1911–21

Booth, Wayne C. *The Rhetoric of Fiction* Chicago: University of Chicago Press 1961

- 'Distance et point de vue' *Poétique* 4 (1970) 511–24
Burke, Kenneth *The Philosophy of Literary Form* New York: Random House 1957
Burnet, John *Early Greek Philosophy* London: A. and C. Black 1892
Butor, Michel *La Modification* Paris: Editions de Minuit 1957
Campbell, Joseph *Hero with a Thousand Faces* New York: Meridian Books 1970
Caso, Alfonso *Los calendarios pre-hispánicos* Mexico: Instituto de Investigaciones Históricas 1967
Cassirer, Ernst *Idee und Gestalt* Berlin: B. Cassirer 1924
- *The Philosophy of Symbolic Forms* 3 vols. New Haven: Yale University Press 1953
- *An Essay on Man* New Haven: Yale University Press 1944
Cervantes, Miguel de *Don Quijote de la Mancha* Ed. Martín de Riquer. Barcelona: Juventud 1969
Chatman, Seymour 'The Semantics of Style,' in *Essays in Semiotics* The Hague: Mouton 1971, pp 399–422
Cohen, Jean *Structure du langue poétique* Paris: Flammarion 1966
Communications Nos 4, 8. Paris 1964, 1966
Cortázar, Julio *Rayuela* Buenos Aires: Sudamericana 1959
Crane, R.S. *The Language of Criticism and the Structure of Poetry* Toronto: University of Toronto Press 1953
- 'The Concept of Plot and the Plot of Tom Jones' *Critics and Criticism* Chicago: University of Chicago Press 1957, pp 62–93
- *Critical and Historical Principles of Literary History* Chicago: University of Chicago Press 1971
Croce, Benedetto *Problemi di estetica* Bari: Laterza 1910
- *La Poesia: Introduzione alla critica e storia della poesia e della letteratura* Naples 1935
Derrida, Jacques *L'Ecriture et la différence* Paris: Seuil 1967
- *De la grammatologie* Paris: Editions de Minuit 1967
- 'La Mythologie blanche' *Poétique* 5 (1971) 1–52
Dewey, John *Logic, the Theory of Inquiry* New York: Henry Holt 1949
- and A.F. Bentley *Knowing and the Known* Boston: Beacon Press 1949
Doubrovsky, Serge *Pourquoi la nouvelle critique?: Critique et objectivité* Paris: Mercure de France 1966
Ducrot, O., et al., eds *Qu'est-ce que le structuralisme?* Paris: Seuil 1968
Dufrenne, M. *Phénoménologie de l'expérience esthétique* Paris: Presses Universitaires de France 1953
- 'Wittgenstein et la philosophie' *Etudes Philosophiques* xx, 3 (1965) 281–306
Eco, Umberto *Opera aperta* Milan: Bompiani 1962

Edie, James M., ed. *New Essays in Phenomenology* Chicago: Quadrangle Books 1969
– F.H. Parker, and C.O. Schrag, eds *Patterns of the Life-World: Essays in Honor of John Wild* Evanston, IL: Northwestern University Press 1970
Eliade, Mircea *Cosmos and History* New York: Harper and Row 1959
Farber, Marvin *The Foundations of Phenomenology* Rev. 3rd ed. Albany: State University of New York Press 1967
Ferrater Mora, José 'Reality as Meaning' *New Essays in Phenomenology* Ed. James M. Edie. Chicago: Quadrangle Books 1969, pp 131–47
Fish, Stanley 'Literature in the Reader: Affective Stylistics' *New Literary History* II, 1 (Autumn 1970) 123–62
Flew, Antony G.N., ed. *Essays on Logic and Language* Oxford: Oxford University Press 1951
Foucault, Michel, et al. *Théorie d'ensemble* Paris: Seuil 1968
Friedman, Melvin *Stream of Consciousness* New Haven: Yale University Press 1955
Friedman, Norman 'Point of View in Fictions' *Publications of the Modern Language Association* 70 (1955) 1160–89
Frondizi, Risieri *The Nature of the Self* New Haven: Yale University Press 1953
Frye, Northrop *Anatomy of Criticism* Princeton: Princeton University Press 1957
Fuentes, Carlos *Cambio de piel* Mexico: Joaquin Mortiz 1967
– *La muerte de Artemio Cruz* Mexico: Fondo de Cultura Económica 1962
Gabriel, Leo 'Integrale Logik' *Zeitschrift für philosophische Forschung* 10 (1956) 44–62
Gadamer, H.G. 'Zur Systemidee in der Philosophie' *Festschrift für Paul Natorp* Berlin 1924, pp 55–75
– *Wahrheit und Methode* Tübingen: Mohr 1960
García Calderón, F. *Latin America, Its Rise and Progress* London: Unwin 1913
García Lorca, Federico *Obras completas* Madrid: Aguilar 1954
García Márquez, Gabriel *Cien años de soledad* Buenos Aires: Sudamericana 1967
Garvin, Paul L., ed. and trans. *A Prague School Reader on Esthetics, Literary Structure, and Style* Washington, DC: Georgetown University Press 1964
Gendlin, Eugene T. *Experience and the Creation of Meaning* Glenco IL: Free Press of Glencoe 1962
Genette, Gérard 'La Rhétorique et l'espace du langage' *Tel Quel* 19 (1964) 44–54
– 'Structuralisme et critique littéraire' *L'Arc* 26 (1965) 30–44
– *Figures, Essais* Paris: Seuil, 1966
– 'Métonymie chez Proust ou la naissance du Récit' *Poétique* 2 (1970) 156–73

Genre I, 3 (1968)

Geyl, Peter *Debates with Historians* New York: Meridian Books 1958

Gide, André *Les Faux-monnayeurs* Paris: Gallimard 1925

Goodman, Nelson *Languages of Art: An Approach to a Theory of Symbols* Indianapolis: Bobbs Merrill 1968

Gotschalk, D.W. *Patterns of Good and Evil* Urbana: University of Illinois Press 1963

– *The Structure of Awareness* Urbana: University of Illinois Press 1969

Graham, A.C. 'Being in Linguistics and Philosophy: A Preliminary Inquiry' *Foundations of Language* I, 3 (1965) 223–30

Greimas, Algirdas Julien *Du sens: essais sémiotiques* Paris: Seuil 1970

Guillén, Claudio 'Poetics a System' *Comparative Literature* 22 (1970) 193–222

Guillén, Jorge *Lenguaje y poesía* Madrid: Revista de Occidente 1962

Gurwitsch, Aron *Studies in Phenomenology and Psychology* Evanston: Northwestern University Press 1966

Gusdorf, Georges *Speaking (La Parole)* Trans., introd. Paul T. Brockelman. Evanston: Northwestern University Press 1965

Guzmán Campos, Germán *La violencia en Colombia* Bogotá: Ediciones Tercer Mundo 1962

Hall, Elizabeth 'Interview with George Steiner' *Psychology Today* (February 1973) 57–69

Hartman, Geoffrey 'Toward Literary History' *In Search of Literary Theory* Ed. Morton W. Bloomfield. Ithaca: Cornell University Press 1972, pp 197–235

Hegel, Georg Wilhelm Friedrich *Ästhetik* Berlin: Aufbau-Verlag 1955

Heidegger, Martin *Der Ursprung des Kunstwerkes* Ed. H.-G. Gadamer. Stuttgart: Reclam 1960

Hernadi, Paul *Beyond Genre* Ithaca: Cornell University Press 1972

Hester, Marcus B. *The Meaning of Poetic Metaphor* The Hague: Mouton 1967

Hirsch, D.E. *Validity in Interpretation* New Haven: Yale University Press 1967

Hofstadter, Albert 'On the Consciousness and Language of Art' *New Essays in Phenomenology* Ed. James M. Edie. Chicago: Quadrangle Books 1969, pp 83–99

Hollander, Lee M. *The Poetic Edda* Austin: University of Texas Press 1962

Humboldt, Wilhelm von *Studienausgabe* I: *Ästhetik und Literatur*. Ed. Kurt Muller-Vollmer. Frankfurt: Fischer-Bücherei 1970

Humphrey, Robert *Stream of Consciousness in the Modern Novel* Berkeley: University of California Press 1954

Husserl, Edmund 'Aesthetik und Phänomenologie' (unpublished manuscript) A-VI-1, 1906. ix–31

- *Ideas: General Introduction to Pure Phenomenology* Trans. W.R. Boyce Gibson. London: Allen and Unwin 1931
- *Cartesianische Meditationen und Pariser Vortrage* The Hague: Martinus Nijhoff 1950
- *The Phenomenology of Internal Time-Consciousness* Ed. Martin Heidegger. Trans. J.S. Churchill. Bloomington: Indiana University Press 1964

Ingarden, Roman 'Aesthetic Experience and Aesthetic Object' *Philosophy and Phenomenological Research* 21 (1960–1) 289–313
- *Das literarische Kunstwerk* Tübingen: Niemeyer 1960
- *Von Erkennen des literarischen Kunstwerkes* Tübingen: Niemeyer 1968

Iser, Wolfgang 'The Reading Process: A Phenomenological Approach' *New Literary History* III, 2 (1972) 279–99
- *The Implied Reader* Baltimore: Johns Hopkins University Press 1974
- 'The Reality of Fiction: A Functionalist Approach to Literature.' *New Literary History* VII, 1 (1975) 7–38

James, Henry *The Art of the Novel* Ed. R.P. Blackmur. New York: Scribner's 1934

Jones, Henry *A Critical Account of the Philosophy of Lotze: The Doctrine of Thought* Glasgow: Maclehose 1895

Jung, C.G. *Aion* Princeton: Princeton University Press 1968
- *The Archetypes and the Collective Unconscious* Princeton: Princeton University Press 1968

Junker, Heinrich *Festschrift für Steitberg* Berlin: Springer 1924

Kaufmann, Felix *Methodology of the Social Sciences* Oxford: Oxford University Press 1944
- 'John Dewey's Theory of Inquiry' *Journal of Philosophy* LVI, 21 (1959) 826–36

Kayser, Wolfgang *Das sprachliche Kunstwerk: Eine Einführung in die Literaturwissenschaft* Bern: Francke 1948
- *Kleines literarisches Lexicon* Bern: Francke 1953
- 'Qui raconte le roman?' *Poétique* 4 (1970) 498–510

Kerényi, C. *Eleusis: Archetypal Image of Mother and Daughter* New York: Bollingen 1967

Kinneavy, James L. *A Theory of Discourse: The Aims of Discourse* Englewood Cliffs, NJ: Prentice-Hall 1968

Kirk, G.S. *Heraclitus: The Cosmic Fragments* Cambridge: Cambridge University Press 1954

Krieger, Murray *The Tragic Vision* Chicago: University of Chicago Press 1960
- *The Play and Place of Criticism* Baltimore: Johns Hopkins University Press 1967

Kuhns, Richard *Structures of Experience: Essays on the Affinity between Philosophy and Literature* New York: Basic Books 1970

Kwant, Remy C. *From Phenomenology to Metaphysics: An Inquiry into the Last Period of Merleau-Ponty's Philosophical Life* Pittsburgh: Duquesne University Press 1963

– *Phenomenology of Language* Pittsburgh: Duquesne University Press 1965

Langer, S.K. *Feeling and Form* New York: Scribner's 1953

Lee, E.N. and M. Mandelbaum, eds *Phenomenology and Existentialism* Baltimore: John Hopkins University Press 1967

Léon-Portilla, Miguel *Quetzalcóatl* (Mexico: Instituto de Investigaciones Históricas 1965)

Linguistic Analysis and Phenomenology. The Monist 49, 1 (1965)

Lotman, Jurij *The Structure of the Artistic Text* Trans. R. Vroon. Ann Arbor: University of Michigan Slavic Texts 1977

Lukács, Georg *The Theory of the Novel: A Historico-philosophical Essay on the Forms of Great Epic Literature* Trans. Anna Bostock. London: Hill and Wang 1971

Mackay, D.S. 'Philosophical Interpretation' *Meaning and Interpretation* University of California Publications in Philosophy 25. Berkeley 1950, pp 25–53

Marrou, Henri *De la connaissance historique* Paris: Seuil 1959

Merleau-Ponty, Maurice 'L'Oeil et l'esprit' *Art de France* I, 1 (January 1961)

– *Phenomenology of Perception* London: Routledge and Kegan Paul 1962

– *The Primacy of Perception* Ed. J.M. Edie. Evanston, IL: Northwestern University Press 1964

– *Signs* Evanston: Northwestern University Press 1964

– *Sense and Non-Sense* Evanston: Northwestern University Press 1964

– *The Visible and the Invisible* Ed. C. Lefort. Evanston: Northwestern University Press 1968

– *The Prose of the World* Evanston: Northwestern University Press 1973

Métraux, Alexandre, 'Vision and Being in the Last Lectures of Maurice Merleau-Ponty,' in *Life-World and Consciousness*, ed. Lester E. Embree (Evanston: Northwestern University Press 1972) 323–36

Metz, C. 'Une Etape dans la réflexion sur la cinéma' *Critique* XI, 214 (1965) 227–48

Moisés, Massaud *A criação literária* São Paulo: Edições Melhoramentos 1971

Morris, Charles *Signification and Significance: A Study of the Relations of Signs and Values* Cambridge, MA: Harvard University Press 1965

Muller-Vollmer, Kurt *Towards a Phenomenological Theory of Literature: A Study of Wilhelm Dilthey's Poetik* The Hague: Mouton 1963

Neruda, Pablo *Libro de las odas* Buenos Aires: Losada 1972

Nicol, Eduardo *Los principios de la ciencia* Mexico: Fondo de Cultura Económica 1965

Ogden, C.K. and I.A. Richards *The Meaning of Meaning* London: Kegan Paul 1936

Parker, Alexander A. *Literature and the Delinquent* Edinburgh: Edinburgh University Press 1967

Paz, Octavio *Libertad bajo palabra* Mexico: Fondo de Cultura Económica 1960

– *Discos visuales* Mexico: Era 1968

– *Ladera este* Mexico: Joaquín Mortiz 1969

Peckham, Morse 'Semantic Autonomy and Immanent Meaning' *Genre* I, 3 (1968) 190–4

Peirce, Charles Sanders 'On Signs and the Categories' *Collected Papers* VIII. Ed. A.W. Burks. Cambridge, MA: Harvard University Press 1958, pp 220–31

La Pensée sauvage et le structuralisme Esprit XIX, 322 (1963) 545–751

Pepper, Stephen *The Basis of Criticism in the Arts* Cambridge, MA: Harvard University Press 1956

Pérez Galdós, Benito *Obras completas* Vols IV and V. Madrid: Aguilar 1950

Piquet, Jean Claude 'Analyse réflexive et langue' *Studia Philosophica* 19 (1959) 193–213

– *De l'esthétique à la métaphysique* The Hague: Martinus Nijhoff 1959

Popper, Karl R. *The Open Society and Its Enemies* 2 vols. 5th rev. ed. Princeton: Princeton University Press 1966

– *The Logic of Scientific Discovery* London: Hutchinson 1968

Pos, H.H. 'Phénoménologie et linguistique' *Revue Internationale de Philosophie* 2 (Bruxelles 1939) 354–65

– 'Remarques sur les catégories du devenir et de l'être' *Tenth International Congress of Philosophy* II. Amsterdam 1949, 61–9

Poulet, Georges *Studies in Human Time* Baltimore: Johns Hopkins University Press 1956

Ricœur, Paul 'Le Symbolisme et l'explication structurale' *Cahiers Internationales de Symbolisme* 4 (1964) 81–96

– *The Symbolism of Evil* New York: Harper and Row 1967

– 'Husserl and Wittgenstein on Language' *Phenomenology and Existentialism* Ed. E.N. Lee and M. Mandelbaum. Baltimore: Johns Hopkins University Press 1967, pp 207–17

– *Husserl: An Analysis of His Phenomenology* Evanston: Northwestern University Press 1967

– 'Structure, Word, Event' *Philosophy Today* XII, 204 (Summer 1968) 114–29

– *Le Conflit des interprétations: essais des interprétations* Paris: Seuil 1969

- 'The Model of the Text: Meaningful Action Considered as a Text' *Social Research* XXXVIII, 3 (Fall 1971) 529–62
- 'Metaphor and the Main Problem of Hermeneutics' *New Literary History* VI, 1 (1974) 95–110
- *La Métaphore vive* Paris: Seuil 1975

Russell, B. 'On Denoting' *Mind*, n.s. 14 (1905) 479–93

Sahagún, Fray Bernardino de *Historia general de las cosas de Nueva España* Mexico: Editorial Nueva España 1946

Saussure, Ferdinand de *Cours de linguistique générale* Ed. Tullio de Mauro. Paris: Payot 1972

Schlegel, Friedrich *Literary Notebooks* Ed. H. Eichner. Toronto: University of Toronto Press 1957

Schrecker, Paul 'Phenomenological Considerations on Style' *Philosophical Phenomenological Research* 8 (1947–8) 372–90

Séjourné, Laurette *Pensamiento y religión en el México antiguo* Mexico: Fondo de Cultura Económica 1957

- *El universo de Quetzalcóatl* Mexico: Fondo de Cultura Económica 1962

Shapiro, Karl 'A Farewell to Criticism' *Poetry* 71 (1948) 197–217

- 'What is Anti-Criticism?' *Poetry* 75 (1950) 339–51

Shumaker, Wayne *Elements of Critical Theory* Berkeley: University of California Press 1952

- *Literature and the Irrational: A Study in Anthropological Backgrounds* Englewood Cliffs, NJ: Prentice-Hall 1960

Sparshott, F.E. *The Structure of Aesthetics* Toronto: University of Toronto Press 1963

Spiegelborg, H. *The Phenomenological Movement* 2 vols. The Hague: Martinus Nijhoff 1960

Spitzer, Leo *Essays on English and American Literature* Princeton: Princeton University Press 1962

Staiger, Emil *Grundbegriffe de Poetik* Zurich: Atlantis Verlag 1946

- *Die Kunst der Interpretation* Zurich 1955

Steenburgh, E.W. van 'Metaphor' *Journal of Philosophy* LXII, 22 (1965) 678–88

Stevenson, Charles 'Interpretation and Evaluation in Aesthetics' *Philosophical Analysis* Ed. Max Black. New York 1950, pp 341–83

- 'On "What is a Poem?"' *Philosophical Review* 66 (1957) 329–62

Stevick, Philip, ed. *The Theory of the Novel* New York: Free Press 1967

Strasser, Stephen *The Idea of Dialogal Phenomenology* Pittsburgh: Duquesne University Press 1969

Strawson, P.F. *Individuals: An Essay in Descriptive Metaphysics* London: Methuen 1959

Tablada, José Juan *Obras. Poesía* México: Universidad Autónoma de México 1971

Todorov, Tzvetan *Littérature et signification* Paris: Librairie Larousse 1967
- *Introduction à la littérature fantastique* Paris: Seuil 1970
- 'Les Etudes du style' *Poétique* 2 (1970) 224–32
- 'Les Transformations narratives' *Poétique* 3 (1970) 322–33

Toulmin, Stephen E. *The Uses of Argument* Cambridge, Eng.: Cambridge University Press 1958
- *Human Understanding* Princeton: Princeton University Press 1972

Turville-Petre, E.O.G. *Myth and Religion of the North* London: Weidenfeld and Nicolson 1971

Unamuno, Miguel de *Niebla. Obras completas* II. Barcelona: Vergara 1958, pp 783–1000
- 'Prólogo a la versión castellana de *La estética* de B. Croce' *Obras completas* VIII. Barcelona: Vergara 1958, pp 242–68
- *San Manuel Bueno, mártir* Ed. Mario J. Valdés. Madrid: Ediciones Cátedra 1979

Vachek, J., ed. *A Prague School Reader in Linguistics* Bloomington: Indiana University Press 1964

Valdés, M.J. 'Archetype and Recreation' *University of Toronto Quarterly* 14 (1970) 58–72
- and Maria Elena Valdés *An Unamuno Source Book: A Catalogue of Readings and Acquisitions with an Introductory Essay on Unamuno's Dialectic Enquiry* Toronto: University of Toronto Press 1973
- and Owen J. Miller, eds *Interpretation of Narrative* Toronto: University of Toronto Press 1978

Valéry, Paul *Tel Quel. Œuvres* II. Paris: Gallimard 1960, pp 473–784

Vargas Llosa, Mario *La casa verde* Barcelona: Seix Barral 1966

Vivas, Eliseo *The Artistic Transaction* Columbus: Ohio State University Press 1963

Vygotsky, L.S. *Thought and Language* Cambridge, MA: Massachusetts Institute of Technology Press 1962

Waelhens, Alphonse de *Existence et signification* Louvain: Publications Universitaires 1958
- *Husserl et la pensée moderne* The Hague: Martinus Nijhoff 1959

Ward, James *Psychological Principles* Cambridge, Eng.: Cambridge University Press 1920
- *Essays in Philosophy* Cambridge, Eng.: Cambridge University Press 1927

Warren, Henry Clarke *Buddhism in Translations* Cambridge, MA: Harvard University Press 1915

Watson, George *The Study of Literature* London: Penguin Books 1969

Welch, Cyril 'Speaking and Bespeaking' *New Essays in Phenomenology* Ed. J.M.
  Edie. Chicago: Quadrangle Books 1969, pp 72–82
Wellek, René *Discriminations* New Haven: Yale University Press 1970
– and Austin Warren *Theory of Literature* New York: Harcourt, Brace and
  World 1956
Wells, R. 'Meaning and Use' *Psycholinguistics* Ed. S. Saporta. New York: Holt
  Rinehart 1961, pp 269–83
Wild, John 'Man and His Life-World' *For Roman Ingarden: Nine Essays in
  Phenomenology* The Hague: Martinus Nijhoff 1959, pp 90–109
Wimsatt, jr, W.K. *The Verbal Icon: Studies in the Meaning of Poetry* Lexington, KY:
  University of Kentucky Press 1954
Wittgenstein, Ludwig *Zettel* Ed. G.E.M. Anscombe and G.H. von Wright.
  Berkeley: University of California Press 1970

Index of authors

UNIVERSITY OF TORONTO
ROMANCE SERIES